HOS

"READS LIKE A NOVEL ... VOLTING, FUNNY ... FASCINATING"

—*Psychology Today*

"ATTENDING PHYSICIANS, RESIDENTS, NURSES, TECHNICIANS, AND OTHER EMPLOYEES ... THE OBLIGATORY NURSE WHO CHEERFULLY PROCEEDS TO HAVE SEX WITH EVERY INTERN SHE CAN GET HER HANDS ON ... A COLD NEUROSURGEON WITH A PENCHANT FOR WAGNER ... WHAT THEY SAY ABOUT EACH OTHER AND ABOUT SUCH ISSUES AS DEATH, HOSPITAL HUMOR AND THE 'PATIENT AS ENEMY' IS AT LEAST AS REVEALING AS WHAT THEY SAY ABOUT THEMSELVES ... MOVING AND ABSORBING."

—*Philadelphia Inquirer*

"A BONANZA ... A TELLING COMMENT ON THE PEOPLE WHO DO THIS KIND OF WORK, AND WHAT IT DOES TO THEM."

—*Kirkus Reviews*

"EXTRAORDINARY ... a rare achievement of intriguing insight—wise, witty and indispensable."

—*Mike Douglas*

"COMPELLING TO READ, HARD TO PUT DOWN, SATISFYING TO FINISH."

—*San Francisco Examiner*

MICHAEL MEDVED

HOSPITAL

The Hidden Lives of a Medical Center Staff

PUBLISHED BY POCKET BOOKS NEW YORK

POCKET BOOKS, a division of Simon & Schuster, Inc.
1230 Avenue of the Americas, New York, N.Y. 10020

For Nancy

CONTENTS

VITAL SIGNS

In the spring of 1980, one of my close friends suffered an apparent nervous breakdown. I sat with him through a long night of tears, hallucinations, and suicidal fantasies. By the time the sun came up he had become thoroughly incoherent and attempted to run naked through the streets. At seven A.M. I managed to coax him into a bathrobe and we drove together to a nearby hospital. At my urging, the officials in the psychiatric ward agreed to place him on "seventy-two-hour hold"—detaining him against his will because he represented an imminent danger to himself and to others. During this period of hospitalization, the patient received heavy doses of Thorazine, a powerful antipsychotic medication that helped him regain at least a semblance of normal behavior. The law required that he be released after three days, regardless of his emotional state, and my friend took advantage of the earliest opportunity to walk out of the hospital and back into his job. In subsequent conversations, he could make no sense of his experience, and he refused to rule out the possibility of a similar break in the future. "I can't waste time worrying about it," he shrugged. "I guess it's in the nature of an occupational hazard."

My friend is a physician—a brilliant young obstetrician-gynecologist with a thriving practice centered at one of California's most prestigious hospitals. Within four hours of his release from the psychiatric ward, he had returned to the demanding business of seeing patients, delivering babies, and performing abortions. The women he treated were unaware of his recent crisis, and those few professional colleagues who knew what had happened seemed to accept it as a matter of course.

There is a mounting body of evidence to suggest that the problems which my friend experienced are becoming alarmingly common among today's physicians. Several recent studies indicate that the practice of medicine extracts a high price in return for the tangible and intangible benefits it bestows. . . .

—In a long-term project at Harvard, psychiatry professor George E. Vaillant analyzed a representative group of New England physicians. He discovered that 36 percent regularly used tranquilizers or other mood-altering drugs, 34 percent had made ten or more visits to psychiatrists, and an astounding 17 percent had been *hospitalized* for psychiatric reasons.

—The rate of drug addiction among American doctors has been estimated at thirty to one hundred times that of the population at large. Reports from abroad display a similar pattern, with studies in England, Germany, Holland, and France showing that 15 percent of all known drug addicts are physicians, while an additional 15 percent are members of the nursing and pharmaceutical professions. In 1973 the American Medical Association reported that based upon data from state licensure boards, an estimated 6 percent of all American physicians—or some 20,000 doctors nationwide— are "significantly impaired" by drug addiction or alcoholism.

—A 1972 study in the *New England Journal of Medicine* reported that 47 percent of physician respondents rated their marriages as "unsatisfactory." In addition, the *American Journal of Psychiatry* reported that 13 percent of all male physicians in a 1973 survey engaged in "erotic behavior" with their patients, despite ethical standards strictly forbidding such conduct. Dr. Robert E. Taubman of the University of Oregon, who has studied 1,200 physician marriages in ten cities, has found that the moderate divorce rate among doctors is no indication of healthy family relationships. "One of the occupational hazards of physicians is marital misery," he observes, "but it is hidden by the mask of marital conformity."

—All of these problems help to produce a suicide rate among physicians four times higher than the national average. At least a hundred U.S. doctors take their own lives each year, a group that is equal in size to the average medical school graduating class. Among male physicians under thirty-nine, 28 percent of all deaths are suicides. Statistics from England, Canada, and Denmark show the same bleak trend. A 1974 article in the *Medical Journal of Australia* entitled "The Disease of Being a Physician" reported that in that country "at least one doctor in fifty kills himself, and quite likely the proportion is twice as great."

These statistics reflect only the most visible aspects of a complex problem. Even those physicians who cope successfully with their responsibilities—who manage to avoid drug addiction, psychiatric breakdown, and marital disaster—will at times feel overwhelmed by the demands of their profession. In a society which isolates most people from death and suffering, physicians are continually exposed to every sort of human misery. And in no other field are the expectations of the public so high, or the consequences of failure so disastrous.

In this book, I am less concerned with what occurs in examining rooms or on operating tables than I am with what happens to the person who delivers the care. Behind the impregnable facade afforded by their white coats, what do physicians think and feel? How do the demands of their job shape a distinctive personality or change their emotional makeup? How does the practice of medicine affect the human soul?

To answer these questions, I have focused on a group of twenty-eight individuals—attempting to take their emotional pulse, to monitor their vital signs. They describe their experiences in their own words, and the resulting revelations tell more about the suffering and joys of hospital life than any amount of generalization or analysis by an outsider. They all work at the same institution—Memorial Medical Center outside San Francisco. It is a real hospital, though Memorial Medical Center is not its real name. The names of nearly all the characters have also been changed in order to protect their privacy, but their stories—aside from minor editing for the sake of clarity—are presented exactly as they told them.

In addition to the physicians who provide the primary focus here, the book also introduces a supporting cast of nurses, technicians, and administrative personnel to provide a varied view of medical reality. These people illustrate the wide range of responses to hospital work, but no attempt has been made to select a statistically representative sample.

Midway through the interview process, one of my subjects expressed concern over my response to this investigation. I had spent more than a year interviewing "crazy docs," and she assumed that I would be terrified at the prospect of ever entering a hospital myself. I assured her, however, that my research had produced exactly the opposite effect. After exploring the private dimension of the people who operate a major medical center from the delivery room to the morgue, I felt less intimidated and more comfortable with the hospital world than I had ever felt before. By the end of this project, I could walk down the halls without the floating anxiety that laymen usually feel in that environment. Part of it, no doubt, was my increased familiarity with the physical surroundings, but by far the larger part was a new sense of kinship with the people who worked there. They were neither the noble Dr. Kildares of medical mythology nor the pompous, money-mad monsters of popular caricature. They were flawed and complex human beings, doing their best for a succession of strangers. Struggling against the implacable facts of disease and death, facing the impossible demands of an increasingly hostile public, these hospital people turned out to be at once less glamorous and more heroic than I had previously believed.

This book is intended as neither an exposé nor a critique of the medical profession, but rather as a small contribution toward that balanced understanding that will benefit everyone, on both ends of the stethoscope. The extreme and one-sided images of medical practitioners—as either healing saints or hopeless incompetents—have become obstacles to optimal health care. What is needed above all is a more realistic and humane approach from the public to its physicians, and that approach requires the fundamental recognition that it is not the patients alone who suffer within hospital walls.

THE WALKING WOUNDED

Memorial Medical Center is one of the finest teaching hospitals in the United States. Patients come to Northern California from across the country and around the world to benefit from the facilities of this distinguished institution. The people who work there, however, are no different, in terms of the pressures they feel and the problems they face, from those who toil at any large medical center. Like their hospital colleagues in other cities and situations, they are seldom prepared for the private cost of their professional commitments.

DR. ARNOLD BRODY, *Director of Medical Oncology*

When I selected oncology as my specialty, I never thought about the psychological significance of this kind of practice. I knew that all my patients would have cancer, but I had no idea how that would affect me. As a matter of fact, I don't think I became aware of the ominous aspect of this practice—ominous with respect to me personally—until perhaps three or four years ago. Perhaps it is part of that crisis that is supposed to be part of midlife. I'm not sure. There was no single event, but I have begun to have an increased sense of my own vulnerability.

When you begin to take care of people and they last over some period of time, you develop relationships. When you work as hard as I do, when you see as many people as I do, you collect quite a stable of sick friends. Then they start knocking off. It's like losing a friend every month. Every goddamn month! Year after year after year. That's a bad thing to be exposed to. These young kids who are going into medical oncology, they don't know their ass about what they're doing.

Today, everybody uses expressions like "support systems." Well, Jesus, in this field you need a support system like the Empire State Building. At the end of the day I go home feeling like a sow with twelve sore tits. And then somebody wants to chew on one of them at home. And it hurts. Maybe I'd like to chew on somebody's tit for once.

DR. BEN BRODY, Psychiatric Resident

My dad spends a great deal of time at the hospital, and it's because he wants to. He'll tell you that people are demanding, sucking on him every which way. That's the life he chose for himself. It's a vicious cycle. You get most of your goodies, most of your rewards from medicine, so you pursue medicine and ignore the outside world. Before you know it, medicine is the only thing you've got going in your life.

DR. HARRISON O'NEILL, Gastroenterologist

As I've gotten older I feel more and more that these horrendous life-and-death situations are only another part of life. Are they really that much more important than coming home and fixing dinner for the kids? I feel I've exaggerated the importance of these dramatic events in the hospital. Right now we've got a guy who's dying of advanced liver disease. A good guy, a former cop, with a great sense of humor. I'd like to keep him going as long as I can. But does it really make any difference whether he hangs on for another two weeks or if he slips into a coma tomorrow? By blowing up the importance of those two weeks, I'm blowing up my own ego. That feeling of power in the hospital can be addictive, and you've got to fight it.

DR. STANLEY RUCKERT, Intern

Medicine attracts a lot of people of unstable personalities to begin with. But it's medicine itself that pushes them over into real problems.

Aside from the hours, there's the unpredictability. You just never know when things are going to go wrong. When we feel sick or feel down, we can't just call up and say, "I don't feel like coming in today." You've got to come in. The patients depend on you. It's like giving away your life.

Everybody has to deal with it, but different people handle it in different ways. One morning in the garage I saw a surgeon, an orthopedist who's a well-known guy. He was standing by his car, a big Lincoln Continental, and he took a bottle of Bacardi 151 rum out of the back seat, and took four big slugs. Then he put it back and walked up to work. I just said, "Wow, this can't be happening!"

MARIAN DONAHUE, Social Worker, Cystic Fibrosis Unit

A lot of physicians are just emotional cripples. They are not accustomed to sharing with the dying patients in a way that I have been used to doing. They leave when a patient gets to a certain point, and usually it's just when I think a patient needs the most support. So that's when I will be there around the clock, twenty-four hours, three and four days in a row, until the child finally dies. Even when they're semicomatose, the kids know whether you're there or not.

Some doctors don't seem to understand that. They talk about the patients like they're not even there. Well, I don't care if a kid's two or he's sixteen, he can hear what you're saying and can understand it.

The physicians who work here may be dedicated to their careers and to the profession of medicine, but they're not very sensitive. There have been some that have really hurt my patients emotionally, really been cruel to them.

Most of the doctors here don't have much personal life. They give up so much in terms of getting themselves educated, and they limit themselves in order to stand the grind of medical school. They relate to a human being as a bunch of physical parts, as opposed to a total person. In a way, all of their running around and giving orders is just to cover up for their shallowness and their limitations. As far as I'm concerned, the hospital is a shelter for doctors.

DR. GARLAND LOCKWOOD, Obstetrician-Gynecologist

I know I use the fact that I'm a really busy doctor as an excuse for not doing the most menial chores of life. Well, see, my basic response to taking the garbage out is, "Why should I do this, I'm a doctor, I'm just too busy." In fact for six months, after I separated from my wife, I didn't even manage to go to the market once. No food in the refrigerator. No sort of normal life.

Yesterday I missed my son's birthday party because I was doing an operation. It was his fifth birthday party, and my ex-wife made a big deal out of it. I could have gotten someone to take my calls. But see, I didn't do it, and I'd never do it, and that's getting down to my basic personality.

DR. EDWARD FERRARO, Medical Oncologist

My main enemy is a sense of failure, a sense of frustration, when I've done something wrong. I have lots of failures, hundreds of them. Almost always they have to do with the interpersonal relationships rather than medical decisions. The experience of facing death is awful for a person and a family. And a doctor can seldom be neutral. He either helps the situation or makes it worse. Lots of times I think that by not helping enough, I made it worse. I didn't recognize what the people needed or wanted, or was unwilling to give it, or couldn't give it emotionally.

It is particularly difficult for me to get away from it all when I go on vacation. I spend a lot of time preparing notes for whomever I'm going to turn the practice over to. I'll go away, and I'll be depressed for two or three days. Sometimes the whole time I'm gone.

I just feel shitty about myself. It takes me a long time before I get enough distance to even think about enjoying myself.

Then I come home, and there's more guilt, and it just goes on and on. I always bring it home. There are times when I have gotten into my car and driven home and said, this is killing me. I feel like I'm dying. But you have to get up the next morning, and you face it all over again.

PEGGY HAGERTY, Head Nurse, Delivery Room

I was talking to a guy the other day, an anesthesiologist. He said, "Is this what it's all about? It's like I've made it now. I've arrived where I wanted to be. And this is what I've knocked myself out for? Is this what it's all about? Some paradise!"

Something happens to people who become doctors. I have my own little theory. Erik Erikson talks about the various stages one person needs to go through to become a complete human being. Doctors really don't have the chance to go through those stages. So much time is spent in those really crucial years from eighteen to thirty just competing furiously. And once they're all through, and they're out in private practice, what then? More hustling, more running around. It's inhuman what we do to people when we expect them to become doctors. For a lot of these people, it never slows down.

THE WELCOMING
COMMITTEE

PEGGY HAGERTY
Head Nurse, Delivery Room

DR. LARRY BUCKMAN, Pediatric Resident

Peggy Hagerty is always wide-awake, full of energy, right on top of things. She runs that delivery room with an iron hand. She's very protective of the patients and the newborns, but her attitude towards the doctors is kind of suspicious—she assumes we're all guilty until proven innocent.

DR. DAVID ANZAK, Obstetrician-Gynecologist

She is definitely a women's libber. At times, I think she's working on a Bella Abzug imitation. She has the same loud voice, same obnoxious personality. She has a tough time with me in particular because I'm more in the traditional doctor's image, and I don't like her calling me by my first name.

Peggy Hagerty is top of the heap. There are some people who just have an ability to cut through all the bullshit, and she's one of them. She's very liberal in her politics, see, and she also has her family life really together. A lot of people here are bothered and down and sometimes they use medicine to escape. Peggy's solid. When I get down or upset, she can really bring me back. She's one of my all-time favorites.

———————

I interviewed Peggy Hagerty on a mild summer evening on the patio of her suburban tract home. She apologized immediately for the undistinguished, middle-class surroundings, but explained that her husband's salary as a social worker and hers as a nurse amounted to very little. The small swimming pool which occupied every available inch of their backyard seemed an incongruous touch of luxury in this setting, but she insisted that it constituted a necessity rather than an indulgence. "I need the water. I go swimming every day. Even when I come home in the middle of the night, I have to go swimming before I get to sleep. There's just something about it that keeps me going." She explained that water has always been associated with the life force. "At the very beginning, the first tiny organisms got started in water. Even the Bible says that God made creatures in water before He made them on land. And human embryos get started by swimming in the amniotic fluid."

She is a vigorous, stocky, square-jawed woman of thirty-seven with a bushy head of tightly curled red hair. During our time together she smoked one cigarette after another, going through three of them before I even turned on the tape recorder. I expressed surprise at her chain-smoking in view of her personal emphasis on life and health. She laughed aloud at her own inconsistency, lit another, and launched into an explanation.

I'VE QUIT SMOKING a lot of times. I quit for four years at one point, but then I started again when I went to work at Memorial. I have to keep a calm exterior at work. I'm doing too many things at one time. I'm being a wife and a mother, with three teenagers at home. Trying to stay intellectually alive. Trying to be a good nurse and human being, maybe stay a little politically active. And smoking just seems to take the steam off.

I started off in nursing relatively late in life. I got married when I was eighteen and had my first child when I was twenty. We moved a lot in those first years of our marriage. I was always taking university classes based on my kid's nap schedule and, if I was real pregnant, based on what classes were on the first floor.

Then the civil-rights movement and the peace movement became very much part of my life. I decided, why should I go back to school and get a degree if there might not be a world for us to live in? My dad was an electrical worker back in Philadelphia and very union-oriented, very left-wing, so politics came naturally to me. I got very active when we moved back to Philadelphia in '64 and I became the head of the Woman's Strike for Peace. I'd go to meetings at night and my husband would watch the kids or I'd go on demonstrations during the day where I could take the kids along.

I met a lot of interesting people, and I got exposed to a lot of new ideas. There was one woman who was really excited about the Lamaze method of childbirth, and when I was going to have my last kid, she taught it to me. I told the doctor I didn't want any medication this time, and I was going to use Lamaze. His attitude initially was, you don't get in my way and I won't get in your way. To make a long story short, he let my husband in the delivery room and when the doctor saw how it worked he got converted to the whole method. It was a wonderful experience. And it came at the time I was struggling with what I was going to be when I grew up. The war was over, and I had become involved in doing counseling for an illegal abortion group in Philadelphia. I did the medical intakes and we did abortions right in my apartment. My doctor called me up one day and said, "I've figured out what you should be.

12

You're already teaching this Lamaze method to a lot of my patients. So why don't you become a midwife?''

This clicked with me right away. It was a commitment to women. It was a commitment to family, to a mother and father participating together in a delivery. It was probably going to be a commitment to poor people, because I didn't think middle-class people were going to go for midwives initially. My childbirth experiences had been so neat that I sometimes thought, well, you're special. But I knew I wasn't, that anybody could really enjoy it. So it clicked.

To become a midwife you had to go back and get a Bachelor of Science in nursing. I had never wanted to be a nurse. But before I could be a midwife I had to get this degree, so I went to the nursing program at St. Joseph's College. And I loved it! I wasn't sure my brain still worked after all those years, so I started slow and then I did great.

Then my husband got this job offer out here in California. I had finished my nursing degree and I was right in the middle of my midwife training. If we moved I knew I'd have to give up midwifery and concentrate on nursing, but at that point I didn't mind. I'd always wanted to move to California. So we came. And we got this great apartment and I made sure each kid had a friend and the apartment was fixed up, and then I started applying for a job. I called Memorial, because everybody said that was the best hospital around. The secretary said, "Do you have a year's experience in labor and delivery?" I said no, and then she said, "We don't even interview people unless they have a year's experience."

I knew if they met me they'd want me, so I had to get past that secretary. And I called up one time and said, "I'm considering applying for a job in labor and delivery. I recently moved here from Philadelphia and before I apply I'd like to have a tour of your facilities to see if they meet my standards." She was so surprised that she forgot to ask about experience. So they gave me a tour and we talked and I said to the head nurse, "Do you want to know how many enemas I've given? Or vaginas I've shaved? I haven't done that, but if that's where your priorities are, I question what you're all about."

Anyway, they gave me the job. Right away, I was in over my head, but I hung in there and I made it. I thought I had strange, avant-garde ideas, and I was going to have to fight for what I believed. But the other nurses' heads were just where I was. So I liked them and they liked me and three years later they put me in charge of labor and delivery.

It's a great job, but the tension is high. The delivery room is really like an emergency room. You're talking about life-and-death stuff. Talking about mothers and babies, and making an experience good for them, and a lot of hustle and bustle. In that unit, it's really a team. A doctor, when he's delivering a baby, can't do anything really without the nurse giving him what he needs or helping him monitor the situation. So after a real tough case or a real emergency, or something really nice, we'll all step back and kind of relax together. A lot of people on that unit smoke, so that's how I started up with cigarettes again. That was one of the big changes after I went to work at Memorial.

Another change was my whole attitude toward medicine and toward the hospital. Before when somebody was sick and I had to visit a hospital I'd start perspiring, get very nervous. I couldn't stand the noise of a hospital. The crowds coming in and out, the sick people getting wheeled onto elevators. I felt like I was not in control and was real afraid. Now nursing has given me a strength to deal with death and dying and people in pain that I never had.

Working in labor and delivery is a pretty protected area. It's not like working in an oncology unit with cancer patients and that whole thing. We rarely lose a mother. We had one lady who blew an aneurysm while in labor and subsequently died. And the staff was so shook up they had to call a psychiatrist to deal with some of the doctors and nurses, that's how rare it is. Of course, Dr. Lockwood lost two patients last year. He's a young black guy who is somewhat unconventional, and he's made a lot of enemies. Some people are saying he's incompetent. Otherwise, we don't lose mothers anymore. We get some pretty sick ones who will tax every energy, but most of the time we save them.

That's why this part of the hospital is kind of a happy place. To see life coming into the world, it's just incredible. You don't get quite as profoundly moved at every delivery, but every once in a while there'll be a couple that you take care of, and the relationship will really click. A couple who really wanted a baby for a long time, or a couple who was really scared, but you helped them and it turned out okay. And we stay in the delivery rooms longer now.

Sometimes the lights are dimmed and it's warm, and the mother will breast-feed the baby and it's just really lovely.

When I'm helping with a delivery, I'm just glad to be alive, glad to be participating in something that's so significant to somebody else. I try to make it a little more human and a little less sterile, a little more personal, a little bit more where the mother and father feel like they're in control. I always go in when I'm admitting a patient, and I say, "Well, tell me what your fantasy of your labor is. Tell me how you want it to be so I can try to make it as close to that as possible."

Sometimes you've got to break the rules to do a good job. Once we had this lovely couple who came in for their second baby, and it was a repeat cesarean section. They were both very intelligent, very gracious people. They were both artists, teaching painting at the university. She really wanted her husband to be there when they did the C-section, even though we had pretty strict rules against that. I thought those rules were really stupid, so I told them I would try to help. I asked their doctor if it would be all right with him if the father came into the operating room. The doctor had no objection, as long as I took responsibility for doing it. So I went back to the father and I said, "I'm going to get you in greens right now. If anyone asks, we'll say you're a medical student. And you can go into the operating room." He was a really outstanding and sensitive guy who wanted to be part of this baby's birth, because he felt especially hurt when they had been separated with their first kid.

He went in and they were both really great. He got to help me dry the baby off. His baby. And it was the first time at Memorial, as far as I know, that the father had gone in for cesarean section.

Now, it's fairly common to sneak people in, and nobody seems to mind. Before long they'll change that whole rule about fathers and cesareans. That makes me feel good. To help patients the way you want to, you've got to be willing to make waves. To stand up when you see something that's wrong.

Once I refused to hand forceps to a resident who I knew had never used a pair of forceps. And he went to the head of the department, who came to me and told me I should have handed him the forceps. Then when he screwed up the kid I could have busted him! And I said, "No way, there's no way I'm going to take that risk. How can you do that when you're talking about a kid? Or a mother?"

15

So they know where I'm at. And they haven't fired me. Even though a lot of people think of me as sort of a troublemaker.

Some of it comes from symbolic kinds of issues. When you talk about nurses as a group, you're talking about the least feminist group in the world. They are very much in the classic female image in terms of helping, and caring, and being willing to do all the scutwork.

When I first came to Memorial, all the doctors called the nurses by their first names. But the nurses were calling the doctors by "Dr. So-and-So." It was a superficial issue but it bothered me. So I started calling the doctors by their first names and I was reported to the head of the department. Some doctor didn't like it—I don't know who it was. So we had a big meeting about it. What I said, essentially, was if they want to call us by our last names, we'll call them by their last names. Otherwise, forget it.

And the final result is that now everybody is on a first-name basis. There's a lot more camaraderie between doctors and nurses. Even the patients are on a first-name basis with a lot of the doctors now.

I work a minimum of forty hours every week, but sometimes a lot more. I have stayed around the clock a couple of times. We have a minimum staff of nine. That's what we feel we need to get through a shift. We have eleven beds for labor patients, and five delivery rooms. We have had as many as seventeen patients going into labor at the same time. You've got to call people in from home and say, *"Help!"* The nurses are usually pretty good about it, and they'll even come in on their day off.

Sometimes, when you get done working, you just feel like a rag. I have to drive for forty minutes to get home, and it's almost therapeutic. That ride really helps me, so when I come home I'm sort of recharged. Of course the kids always ask me, "Well, what did you have today? Did you have boys, did you have girls? Were there any interesting cases?"

They know the people that I work with. My friends from work come over and use the pool and swim on a day off. And we'll have parties here. One of the nurses just turned thirty, and we had a slumber party for her birthday. My kids were away on a camping trip with my husband, so we had just the women here. And the woman whose birthday it was, the doctor she's living with had given her one of those Polaroid cameras. It was during that real heat wave. We were all going to sleep out around the pool, because the house isn't air-conditioned. We were all swimming in the pool and we said, come on, we'll just take off our suits. And the next thing I knew, we were using that camera, and everybody was posing for Penthouse Pet pictures. So we were taking these totally illicit shots, having a ball, just feeling very ripped. We wound up cooking a tremendous meal. And of course the word got out that we had a wild party, and the head of the department came up kiddingly and said, "I'll pay you a thousand dollars for those pictures." Well, we never sold.

You get to know people pretty well when you work together the way we do, and I'd say a lot of the doctors are pretty strange. They always surprise me. I had a friend who had a traffic accident. There were a lot of complications and she needed some blood, so they put out a call for O positive blood for her. I ran around labor and delivery saying, "Who is O positive?" But these doctors have the attitude like, nobody's going to stick me with a needle. And here they are, sticking other people right and left!

And you know, there's the old rumor that obstetricians and gynecologists either love women or hate women, and I've definitely seen some of them who fall into the category of hating their patients. A woman will be in a lot of pain, and they'll say, "It's for her own good. We're not going to give her anything for the pain because we're not sure she's going to make it from below." That's outrageous, because all the other doctors in the same position would allow this woman to have some significant pain relief. I can only see it as an incredibly hostile act.

They have a lot of hostilities, but I can understand why. They're just overloaded. You see these guys and what they go through, and I don't know how they do it. Night after night after night. They can be there for deliveries until five in the morning, then catching two hours' sleep and then running full offices. Running full schedules in the operating room. I don't know how they do it, and I don't know why. It's not the money, because most of them have plenty of money. It's more like a personal motivation that pushes them and keeps on pushing.

Take Garland Lockwood. I don't know how he keeps it up. He's got lawsuits, and they're trying to throw him out of the hospital, his wife broke up with him, his life is a mess. But he comes in every night and the patients love him. That's his big joy in life, doing deliveries and getting the positive feedback and all the warm feelings.

So he's not even the one I feel sorry for the most. At least he's part of the delivery room, where things turn out okay for the most part.

The guys I really worry about are the ones on oncology. Just down the hall they get a lot of patients with ovarian cancer, cervical cancer, terrible situations. We frequently go back and forth and see what's going on. I'm still afraid of death and dying, of losing my dignity and that whole process. And I see these people who are dying, and I'm really glad I work where I do. But right on this same floor there are people who deal with cancer day after day. People like Eddie Ferraro, like Arnold Brody . . . and I can't even imagine how they do it.

BIG DADDY

DR. ARNOLD BRODY
Director of Medical Oncology

DR. HARRISON O'NEILL, Gastroenterologist

He's a big human being. The things he does, he does in a big way. If the breaks had come a little differently, he would be dean of the medical school at the university. If he had that job, I think he would do extremely well with it.

I think many people are intimidated by him, but unnecessarily so. Below the surface, he's very generous, very loving, and very decent. He's an excellent doc, but I don't think he enjoys the practice of medicine anymore.

He has had a lot of problems with his family. As a father and husband, he's domineering and intolerant. He is more tolerant of his friends than he is of his wife and family, I think. His expectations are just too high, and his wife, Marty, wasn't able to deliver.

DR. EDWARD FERRARO, Medical Oncologist

I've known him since medical school, and I think you'll find him quite a contrast to me. Being a doctor and being successful and recognized, accumulating money and power, are all very, very important to him. But he's also a thoughtful guy. He's a dynamite raconteur, and he'd be a good guy to go drinking with, except he doesn't drink. That's another thing about Arnold—he's always got to be in control. He'll entertain you, he'll talk your head off, but don't forget he's in charge. He's the doctor.

DR. BARNETT GOLDSTEIN, Plastic Surgeon

I like him. He takes care of sick people and he still maintains a good sense of humor. He's a very honest doctor.

I got to know his wife when I did her eyes. She met someone at a beauty shop who recommended me. She's a very aggressive lady, but she's also into herself a lot. A few months ago I saw her at a play. I almost didn't recognize her. She had her nose done since I saw her last and it was a terrible job. I was disappointed she hadn't come back to me. She lied to me, she told me she had an accident, it's such a bunch of bullshit. But she's a nice lady, and that's her choice.

DR. BEN BRODY, Psychiatric Resident

When we were kids, we used to call him Big Daddy. That was a specific reference to the way we used to wear his T-shirts. We'd wear his big white T-shirts and they'd hang down to our ankles and we'd call them Big Daddy T-shirts. The name really fits him, but when I call him that today he usually gets mad.

I would say he's kind of a warm guy who likes to be very much in control. In some ways he's like a kid. He wants what he wants, right there and then. He's not good at distancing himself from the people he loves.

But the further I go into medicine, the more I realize what a good doc he is. I would definitely want him to take care of me if he weren't my father. But as it is, he's too subjective; he doesn't treat me like his other patients.

There's one example that kind of gets me mad. As a kid I played ball and I used to get stubbed toes and sprained fingers and that kind of thing. My right index finger got mashed a lot and was probably fractured several times. I would show it to him and he'd say something like, "Well, it's not malignant, you know." It never got X-rayed or splinted or anything like that. As a result, the finger is permanently damaged and sort of deformed. Now I'd need surgery to make it right.

Of course, he sees such gross pathology every day in his practice that my finger looked like nothing. It was black and blue, so what? He naturally figured it would take care of itself.

Arnold Brody is a shambling walrus of a man, nearly six feet, four inches tall, with broad shoulders and a swelling paunch. His bushy gray eyebrows follow the same downward tilt as his drooping mustache. He never smiles, but occasionally registers amusement or pleasure by opening his blue eyes wider than usual.

I met him on a Sunday morning at one of the medical office buildings adjoining Memorial Hospital. I had suggested that we get together at his home, but Dr. Brody dismissed that idea. He worried that his wife, Marty, would be "underfoot" during our conversation and might become nervous and upset over the interview process. His private office, on the other hand, was always deserted on the weekend and provided a reliable sanctuary whenever he needed to be alone.

In his inner office, Brody tilted back in the brown leather chair, threw his enormous feet onto the desk, and carefully lit his meerschaum pipe. He spoke in slow, dramatic cadences, punctuating his remarks by waving his arms or pounding the desk.

To survive in medicine you've got to learn to be an iron man. If you have deep personal weaknesses, you may not make it.

Suicide is a common problem. You've probably heard about one guy who killed himself right here in this hospital. That came as a complete surprise, because if a physician is going to kill himself, you can usually see it coming.

There was another guy—an oncologist—who shot himself two years ago. He followed more of the classic pattern. He was a very smart guy, but, man, he was always nuts! He cheated his patients; he overprescribed drugs and got a lot of them addicted. He probably was a drug addict himself. I inherited a lot of his practice and I am privy to his notes on the patients. You can see the steady erosion of capacity. The writing jiggled and the words didn't make any sense. Incredible, the way the guy was able to pull it off and keep the patients coming back for more.

That's an extreme case, but a lot of guys have trouble, particularly in this specialty. Oncology takes all the bad things that go into medicine and kind of amplifies them.

When I started private practice in 1956, I was just an internist with a special interest in hematology and metabolic diseases. Then in the sixties, some etymologically inclined physician came across the Greek word *oncos,* meaning tumor. All of a sudden, people started using the term "oncology." I was already concentrating on cancer cases, on solid tumors, so more or less overnight I became an "oncologist." Actually, I kind of backed into it.

It was the same way I decided to go into medicine in the first place. I never wanted to be a doctor when I was growing up. But I happened to be a very unathletic, pudgy, studious kid, so naturally my mom thought I should be a doctor. We lived in Oklahoma City and we were generally considered to be a family of hopeless oddballs. For one thing, we were Jewish in a place that is not exactly a center of Hebraic civilization. Sure, there were some other Jews in town, but they were all involved in business, while my dad struggled to make a living as a musician. A piano teacher. We were very poor. My two older brothers went to work right out of high

22

school, but I was supposed to be the genius of the family. And when the time came for college, my brothers put up the money to pay my way.

I enrolled at the University of California, Berkeley, and planned on becoming a chemical engineer. Then I met Marty, my future wife. She was a pretty, very petite girl who came from a wealthy and deeply troubled family. She was half Jewish and I think she found herself attracted to a similar sort of half-breed quality in this rawboned Jewish Okie.

Of course, she soon became a major influence on my life. I remember one afternoon, I walked out of inorganic chem lab to meet her for dinner. I had been working with hydrogen sulfide gas, which smells just horrible, and she sniffed my sweater, wrinkled up her nose, and said, "I'm not so sure you should be a chemical engineer. Why don't you become a doctor?"

That's the way the story has been handed down in our family, but of course it wasn't that simple. Her father wanted me to be a doctor and he offered to pay my way through medical school. The idea of medicine also addressed a personality defect which I've carried with me all my life, the same defect that most of my colleagues have. It's a basic question of insecurity—the need to be in a place where you are wanted and respected, where you try to get rewards that you can't have if you're in business or even if you're an engineer. I don't apologize for the fact that I like taking care of people.

Naturally, there is a considerable distance between this sort of idealistic motivation and the realities of day-to-day practice. It gets pretty wild in this office, and I'm like a short-order cook. I keep track of several things at once and make a lot of rapid-fire decisions about what has to be done.

I don't like to examine people. It takes a lot of time to do a full examination and it's usually not necessary. But there are times when I say, "Man! I'm sure glad I took a look at that one!" Like on Friday, a lady came in with a lot of pain in her ear. Four years ago she had a tumor removed from her neck and since then everything had been fine. But I hadn't seen her for about nine months, so I looked her over. It turns out she had a carcinoma of the breast. I could have easily passed up the examination, but I had some kind of instinct that told me to do it.

I've got my technique honed down to the point where I can go through the patients a lot faster than most guys. It may sound immodest, but I also don't think that I miss anything—or at least no more than anybody else. It's a heavy load, every day. There are twenty-five to thirty patients here in the office, then another twelve to fifteen when I make rounds in the hospital.

The fact that I see these patients for only a few minutes at a time doesn't mean that we don't develop a relationship. I can't help feeling a deep emotional attachment for these people who are desperately ill and come back year after year, counting on me to keep them alive.

There's one kid named Joey Guttman, who's come to me for eight years now. His father is a very prominent businessman in Phoenix, Arizona. This guy is about my age, a Jewish papa, and he called me long-distance with a voice just choked and full of emotion, and told me this god-awful story about his sixteen-year-old son. They were at the Mayo Clinic, and this kid had just been diagnosed as having osteogenic sarcoma of the left wrist. The kid was left-handed and the doctors wanted to disarticulate his arm at the shoulder, and even then they thought the likelihood of his survival was very small. So having received this devastating news, the father started calling all around the country to see if he could find anybody who could do something for his son.

I told him I didn't think it made any sense to lop the arm off. We could try something else, but he'd have to understand that I wasn't sure whether it would work or not.

And this Joey was one hell of a kid. There were aspects to this youngster that put me on my ear more than once. His courage, his generosity, the bond of love between the father and the son. I arranged a treatment for him that sort of broke new ground. I did chemotherapy, radiation therapy, and immunotherapy. Just about everybody from the scientific standpoint thought that it was a real good idea, but they didn't have the guts to do it. And I give a lot of credit to Irv Guttman, the father, who turned out to be an intelligent man capable of making tough decisions. In fact, I find it a lot easier to explain things to intelligent lay people than putting them across to doctors, because the docs are usually so locked into their one narrow way of doing things.

It was rough going. There was one time when Joey was vomiting his head off, the way they do in the first or second course of chemotherapy. And the father was standing right there and he was really suffering with the boy. Poor Joey was just wagging his head back and forth, sort of doubled over, and saying, "I can't take it anymore. I just can't take it." And I am alleged to have put my arm around him and said, "Hang in there, Joey. You're going to make it, and someday I'm going to dance at your wedding."

Well, Joey did make it, and last year, he got married. It was a remarkable wedding, at the biggest hotel in Phoenix—five hundred people from New York and Israel and New Zealand and all over the world. It was all a tribute to Irv and Joey Guttman, the papa and the son. Naturally Joey's bride was the prettiest and sweetest girl in town. It was the best wedding I ever attended.

And then right in the middle of the celebration the papa gets up and tells the band to stop playing. He takes the microphone and gets everyone to quiet down and then he starts talking about me. And then he called me up and said, "Okay, Brody. Now keep your promise and *dance* at this wedding." Well, I couldn't even talk. I just came up and hugged both of them and started weeping.

I wish to hell the story ended there. But life doesn't work out like a doctor show on TV. What happened was that two months after the wedding, Joey flew out to see me. He was complaining of pain in his left wrist. And I examined it and I sent him to two other guys to have a look. The X-rays showed only the residue of the previous treatment. But finally in January he came back with persistent pain, and I felt we had to biopsy the area, even though there was nothing that suggested any recurrent malignancy. Of course, this was all a question of medicine plowing through uncharted seas. There are no long-term survivors of osteogenic sarcoma. So this kid was out seven years, and here's something strange happening to him, and what does it all mean?

And the biopsy was positive for recurrent osteogenic sarcoma. Well, when I looked down the microscope and saw that slide, I felt like I'd been kicked in the balls. I couldn't even look at it, I started crying like a baby.

So three months ago he lost the arm. They amputated just below the elbow, and he seems to be free of disease. And Joey, as usual, has been just terrific. He's playing tennis already. He's learned to use his other arm very well. He's working in his father's business and he's very optimistic.

But the whole thing just scared the shit out of me. Of course I felt terrible for Joey and his family, but I also felt sorry for myself. I had a terrific jar to my confidence.

And I tried to explain it to any number of people, but nobody wanted to believe it. That's one of the things I've helped to create, the myth of my personal omnipotence and resilience and endurance. I am regarded by everybody as the Rock of Gibraltar. Nothing ever happens to me. And I say, bullshit, man, I feel lousy! I hurt. But I'm not permitted that. I'm supposed to go around John Wayne-ing it all the time.

I'm increasingly of the opinion that our greatest role should be taking care of people within the limits of what we've got, instead of trying to act like we should figure it all out. There's nothing to figure out. Everybody's going to die.

But doctors can't admit that, and they can't admit they're human beings. So we pay the consequences—stupid little things, like patients saying, "Gee, doc. You've got a cold. I didn't think doctors were supposed to get colds." I mean, I've actually heard that from people. It's an unfunny joke. The classic stupid remark from patients, but we bring it on ourselves.

The public plays along because they have to. For most patients, lay people, it's too devastating an experience to go into a doctor's office unless you assume some kind of superhuman ability on the part of the person who's taking care of you.

So we are forced into this role of being high priests, sorcerers, and witch doctors and nobody bothers to question us. Some of the toughest, most hard-nosed guys, smart as hell in everything else they do, come into a doctor's office and they've got their thumbs in their mouths. These guys that run big corporations and do all kinds of things just act like babes in the woods. "Whatever you say, doc." It's a rare one that wants to know what I'm doing and why I'm doing it.

Doctors really do fancy themselves a cut above the crowd. We don't have titles or noble orders in this country, but we do have an M.D. to put after our names. Doctors are assumed to have a certain level of money, of social prestige, of accomplishment. But it's an empty aristocracy really. The money is a huge part of it, because everybody knows that physicians bring home the bucks. I know one guy named Barnett Goldstein, a plastic surgeon who earns more than a million dollars a year. That's a million dollars *net*. And he brags about it, he tells everybody.

I never cared much about money until recently. For years, I brought in about a hundred thousand dollars, before taxes, which isn't considered very much for a guy who works as hard as I do. My net worth five years ago was, honest to God, no more than two hundred and fifty thousand. Man, that is pathetic! Now I think it's up around a million. I'm paying attention to it now. It's part of the same sense of increasing vulnerability. I know I can't keep grinding it out forever, pouring the bucks out like a cornucopia, so I'm trying to stockpile my resources. But it's been a struggle with my wife every step of the way.

Marty's the only daughter of a very rich daddy who just spoiled her silly. Then I took over and kept the cash flowing until five years ago, when I decided to get things under control. We had some very violent arguments over her outrageous expenditures on clothes, redecorating, vacations, you name it. I told her that if she wanted to preserve the marriage she had to stop wasting her life and my money. It was shock therapy, but it seemed to work and things got better. But no doubt that issue and the emotions it generated contributed to the problems—the very serious problems—she developed later on.

For all her weaknesses, Marty is a classic as far as she goes. If you bow on her badly she makes terrible sounds. But if you bow on her nicely, she makes the greatest sounds. She's a real touchy violin.

We've been married now for thirty-one years. And as dissatisfied as I have been at times with Marty, I've never met anybody else who I felt I would want to be married to. She is absolutely devoted to the family. She keeps herself looking like a million dollars, which I particularly appreciate, and she is available to go with me whenever, wherever I want to go. I defer to her on a lot of unimportant stuff—where do you want to go out to eat, what movie do you want to see, stuff like that. But anything important, I get to call the shots. And that's because I'm smarter than she is. She knows it. I know it. So she just leaves it up to me.

We never had arguments of a really serious nature until the early seventies, when Marty turned forty. Two things precipitated a change for the worse. First, the kids were growing up and needed her less and less. She had always played this role of supermomma, and now the kids were gone, and it began to offer less and less.

Then her brother, a frustrated painter, thirty-five years old, com-

27

mitted suicide in 1972. She blamed herself, because she had always been sort of a surrogate mother to him. His death really knocked the wind out of her for years. She went into a depression that just wouldn't go away. Here she was, this very healthy, very good-looking lady in her early forties who just couldn't stop feeling sorry for herself.

At first, it came out as an irascibility and a difficulty in getting along with her husband. That led most people—including the three kids—to conclude it was my fault. I know I'm not the easiest guy in the world to get along with. I work hard and I play hard and I sleep well at night. I've always had a lot of energy, and I think that's a blessing. But as her depression deepened, Marty wanted me to slow down, to give more time and energy to working on our relationship. That was impossible, given the rigors of my practice. So the situation got progressively worse for the better part of ten years.

That was a very difficult time for me. I tried a couple of affairs, but on balance it wasn't worth it. Yet at the time it was like aspirin for a headache. It helped me weather the storm. I enjoyed the adoration of these very willing females, but I didn't feel good about it afterwards.

I really do believe in the family. And maintaining the integrity of a family in our world can be tough with all the outside attractions. But I really do not envy the guys my age who go around with tight pants and shirts open to their navels and gold chains and are making out with the young chickies. I feel sorry for those guys. I'm really proud of my family, and my role in the family. I have really done the best I could, and my best, in this day and age, is pretty damn good. I stuck it out with Marty even though she got to be pretty near impossible. The worst part was when she got pregnant. She was forty-six years old, and I just couldn't believe it. She was always kind of a slob about contraception. Now, it takes two to tango, but I still think it was more her responsibility than mine. To this day, she still doesn't know when she's going to get her period. Plus the fact that I think she just loved the idea of being pregnant again. She's kind of a fertility symbol. But I knew we couldn't have the baby. Our kids were finally out of the house and we were free and independent and I did not want to be encumbered by another little one. Plus the fact that I felt we had been damn lucky, with three healthy kids, and I did not want to roll the dice.

So I leaned on her very heavily to get an abortion, and she gave in without much protest. But as it turned out, it was just that last, extra kick downward for somebody who was already sliding, already falling.

After the abortion, she couldn't sleep, she couldn't eat. She went from one hundred and twenty pounds to below ninety-five. She spent hours locked in the bathroom, crying her eyes out. God, I remember one night getting a genuine sense of terror. In the years that I've been taking care of patients with advanced malignancies, there usually comes a time when they'll look up and say, "I'm tired of this. And I want to go." Marty gave me that same kind of signal. When she finally went into the hospital, I had kind of a feeling of relief.

It was her psychiatrist's decision for the most part. She had been seeing this same guy for twenty years, and I never thought he was any damn good, but she had a lot of confidence in him. He called me one afternoon two years ago—it was a Thursday, I remember—and took me away from my patients. He told me my wife needed to be admitted to the hospital right away. I said that was okay with me, but I didn't want her coming to Memorial. We had enough gossip already, without putting her there under everybody's nose. And this comment, as he apparently passed it on to my son, Benny, is supposed to show my heartlessness and selfishness. Actually, I think it says more about this psychiatrist and his lack of discretion than it says about me.

So that same day Marty went into the hospital. She wanted me to take her in but I had a full schedule and I couldn't leave the patients high and dry. My daughter Mickey helped her pack up and brought her in. I ran over to see her the minute I got done with work, but her psychiatrist had left strict orders that I was not allowed to see her. I was absolutely furious that he hadn't discussed this with me in advance. I started shouting and telling the house staff they couldn't keep me out of her room. I was a doctor, and I knew a damn lot more about my wife than some quack psychiatrist. But they wouldn't give in, so when I threatened to push past them, they said they were calling security to have me thrown out.

Finally, I just gave up. I wasn't permitted to see my wife for an entire week. She was allowed to see the kids, but she couldn't see me. I went home that night and the house was big and dark and lonely. And I felt as lousy as I could possibly feel. But the next day was Friday, and it was a working day, and I had patients expecting me. Did I feel sorry for myself? Sure I did. Did I feel like going to the office and seeing these twenty-five patients? Hell no. But I did it. I continued to practice, and that afternoon I went to the hospital and made rounds. I just got up and went in there with my head down, like a battering ram.

That was a hell of a week. The kids weren't much help. Benny in particular, who was an intern at the time, could have done a lot for me, but he just stood aside. His behavior throughout his mother's illness was not great; he was too reserved and too withdrawn. I think he was reading all the psychiatry books where, you know, it says not to get involved.

Then three weeks later Marty came home from the hospital. I was really optimistic, but right away I saw she was worse than ever. The month after she came out she was terrible. She was stuttering and all kinds of stuff. They were keeping her on routine antidepressants and I could see they didn't do a damn thing, really. We were on the verge of separating. And I kept suggesting to her psychiatrist that maybe lithium was worth a try, but it took him three months before he listened to me.

Then four days after she started taking lithium, this jammed-switchboard phenomenon just subsided. She stopped stuttering, she stopped the hysteria, she quieted down. She became a *mensch*.

I'm a bit leery of what might happen when Marty is taken off lithium. But I sure as hell don't think that I'm going to sit back and let the damn psychiatrists make all the decisions. I'm not going to be just the patient husband, letting these jerks ruin my wife's head. I can tell those guys to stick it up their ass, man, because I don't trust 'em.

It's been two years now, and—knock wood—she has been much, much better. I actually enjoy living with her again. She's still disorganized. She doesn't do nearly as much as she should. She still devotes an inordinate amount of time to her personal appearance, which is, however, extraordinarily good. She's in good spirits, and in a way we're closer than we were before. We spend a lot of time talking about the kids.

I'll tell you how screwy our family is. Marty and I and the three kids went to the Far East together. About three months ago there we were, the five of us, marching around Japan and Hong Kong and Bangkok and Singapore. We like to be together.

Those kids are good kids. I've been damn lucky. The relationships aren't all lovey-dovey, because I've set tough standards for them. They all strive to win praise from me. With their mother, if they took a crap in the living room she'd say it matched the draperies!

Benny, the oldest, is a resident in psychiatry here at Memorial. He's spent years working in my office, earning some extra money. And he's going to be a real standout in that psychiatry crowd because he's not nuts!

I think about him a lot these days. Maybe that's all part of the same thing, part of getting older. The trouble with Marty and all the other things I told you about, it's had sort of a cumulative effect. I kind of feel smaller, sort of cut down to size. I haven't slowed down on the outside at all, but on the inside it's just different.

Last weekend it was really hot and Mickey and Benny and I drove down together to Santa Cruz and we all went swimming in the ocean. I love the ocean, and I always used to go swimming out there in waves way out over my head and not give a thought about it. But this time it occurred to me, suppose I have a coronary out there? So I slowed down and came in and dried off. And I never would have done that before.

So I think about Benny a lot because he's the one who's more or less carrying on the family tradition. I always thought psychiatry was a bunch of bullshit, and I always hated psychiatrists, but at least he's an M.D. And he's very good, my son. He's not going to be one of the stupid peasants out there following the dumb regulations. He's going to be one of the big shots who's making all the new rules. He's already better than most psychiatrists. And he's going to be the best.

THE HEIR
APPARENT

DR. BEN BRODY
Psychiatric Resident

DR. REUBEN PESKIN, Director, Hospice Project

I met Benny when he was a second-year med student and I was teaching a seminar. And he was a sweet boy who's become a sweet man. It's hard for me to be objective about him because of our friendship. I like to think I contributed to Benny's final decision to go into psychiatry. He'll be an excellent psychiatrist, but at this point he thinks he knows more than he really does. He'll learn about his limitations later and he'll grow out of his cockiness.

MARIAN DONAHUE, Social Worker, Cystic Fibrosis Unit

As a psychiatric resident, he spent some time on our unit. He's pleasant enough, but he's a lightweight, really. He's not the kind of man you want if you've got a desperate situation. And like most of the young doctors, he thinks he's God's gift to women.

DR. HARRISON O'NEILL, Gastroenterologist

Having watched him grow up, and seen all the conflicts he had with his father, it's funny to think he ended up as a doctor. Arnie had a tough time with that boy. Benny is very perceptive, and just brilliant. In that sense he reminds me of his father. But beyond that there are huge differences. He's not aggressive, he's more easygoing; his awareness of what's going on may be greater than Arnie's. Benny has more awareness of the patient as an individual, as a complete person, than anybody I've ever met at his stage of training.

DR. ALLEN BARSAMIAN, Staff Psychiatrist

Benny Brody is a perfect example of the famous-father syndrome. In the context of this hospital, he's never really emerged from his father's shadow. As a result, he comes across as somewhat insecure with almost a smart-aleck attitude. I don't think he's that deeply committed to psychiatry or to medicine.

———————

Ben Brody, like his father, stands nearly six and a half feet tall, but in place of Arnold Brody's hefty, lumbering frame, Benny displays the slender grace of a basketball player. Dressed in sandals, jeans, and a Grateful Dead T-shirt, he managed to live up to the prevailing California standard of slow-moving indifference described by the terms "mellow" and "laid back."

At the beginning of our interview he expressed scant enthusiasm for a discussion of his hospital responsibilities. "A residency is always a drag," he insisted, "even a psychiatric residency." He much preferred his parents as a subject for conversation. "To me, my folks are the most interesting topic in the world. Naturally, I love to talk about them. I guess that's part of the Freudian tradition."

WHEN I WAS growing up, we lived on a street that was closed in, a dead end. There were a bunch of kids all around the same age, and my dad was like the block father. He would buy baseball mitts for everybody, and he'd take us to play baseball. In basketball season we'd play basketball and in football season we'd play football. He would provide everything and do all the organizing. He had more time for us than any other father on the block. When I look back and realize what he was going through in his career at that time, it's amazing to me.

If he ever got depressed, he did a pretty good job of hiding it. Sometimes he'd be upset and I'd be aware of it, but that was usually situational, related to my mom. Sometimes he'd be embarrassed. Sometimes he'd have to go to work with a scratch on his face from my mom. He would tell people he got it playing basketball.

My father is very rational. Feelings, in and of themselves, really don't hold water for him. My mother is just the opposite. She'll express a feeling and won't back it up with a reason. And she acts kind of flaky and off the wall. I think they assumed those roles—my dad would do the thinking for both of them and my mom would do the feeling, the emoting, for both of them.

My mother has been identified as the one with psychiatric problems, but I don't think she's any worse off than my dad. He's more of an obsessive-compulsive personality. In western culture that's very acceptable and well respected, but I think he's just as sick as she is. My mother may have some kind of affective disorder—it's a mood disorder. But she does not have manic-depressive illness the way my father thinks she does.

They were always fighting, and, being the oldest kid, I was put in the role of mediator a lot. To me, that's one obvious place where I can see the seeds being planted for me wanting to be a psychiatrist. I was always trying to arbitrate between them, helping them explain things to each other, because they weren't communicating well.

Money was always an issue and started to become more of an issue a few years ago. My mother is just wild in some of her expenditures, particularly what she spends on clothes. And my dad is a poor boy in rich man's clothing, but he doesn't fool me. He'll still put his hand in his pocket and rattle his change. He can be real generous—like he was with the kids on our block—but it's got to be under his conditions.

People in my family are very open with their emotions. There was none of this "Johnny, you've been a bad boy. We're going to ground you next week." When I was a teenager, my friends had parents like that. What bothered me about it was the very controlled, cold way that they did it. In my family, if I came home late or got in trouble, they would yell and holler and antagonize me to the point where I would just say, "Go fuck yourself!" Which is exactly what my dad would be waiting for, and then he would come after me and try to hit me. Then the chase would be on. At first, I wasn't big enough to fight back physically, but when I got older it got more serious.

The last real fight we had was when I was eighteen. Our relationship was really bad because I was basically telling him and the rest of the establishment to go fuck themselves. Somehow I let him talk me into going down to Santa Cruz one weekend that summer. We used to go down there when I was a kid and rent a boat and swim and go fishing. He always let me bring my friends along and he paid for everything. This time I didn't want to go, because I thought I was too old for it, but he kept pushing me, so I dragged some friends along and it wasn't real great.

We drove back in two cars, and I was driving separate because I didn't want to ride with him. And I got a speeding ticket on the way back. He was behind me, and when he saw the cop give me the ticket he pulled up and really let me have it. He said, "You asshole! You insolent, lousy kid!" So of course I said something back like, "You can go fuck yourself, it's none of your business!" He wanted to get out and fight right there, but somehow we were both held back.

We drove the rest of the way home and I think we were both furious. When we got back home, we were still fuming. And he kept after me, and said, "You're never going to drive again." And I said, "Bullshit, I'm going to do whatever I want." We knew just how to get at each other, and pretty soon we came to blows. He chased me outside—this was another routine that we did, sort of putting on a display for the neighbors. By this time he had been buying Cadillacs, big cars, and the trunk was still open because we had been unpacking the suitcases. We tussled, and he took me and threw me into the open trunk. Then I jumped out and went at him like a bull at a matador. I burrowed my head into his belly and pushed him back about ten feet, which I had never been able to do before, because he is big and strong and he weighs considerably more than I do. But I pushed him back into a brick wall, and then his back hit the wall and I heard a thud. When that happened I kind of stood up and I was scared. All this stuff started occurring to me all at once. It's hard to describe: that he was mortal, that he was flesh and blood, that the thud I heard was him. My father. And that I had the power to hurt him. I think he had the wind knocked out of him, nothing serious, but the bottom line was that we were too big to be doing that. And I just said, "Oh my God, forget it. We just can't do this anymore."

So we stopped fighting after that, but we kept on arguing for another couple of years. One of the big arguments was school. I wanted to go away to college, but my parents wanted me to stick around. And I sort of gave in and applied to the university right here. I actually lived at home the first year, which pisses me, and I'm sort of embarrassed about it too. I was eighteen and really starting to rebel. I was smoking dope. My hair was long. I was getting stoned every day, but I never did heavy-duty drugs.

My parents pretty much knew what was going on. They saw I wasn't studying. The fact is I should not have been in school at all. But it was expected that I should go to school, and I was still very much connected to the family and their expectations. So I sort of escaped from all of that by forming this very tight relationship with my girlfriend, Katie, who later became my wife.

She was still a senior in high school when I was in college. She was feisty and independent and cute. She was considered attractive and desirable, and I was always affected by what other people thought.

We started having sex about a week after we met, but it took a while before we got emotionally involved. Katie has never been superbright, but she always liked hanging around with the intellectuals and academic achievers. She worshiped me and looked up to my family, because her dad was a construction worker. Before I met her, I never had anybody put me in a power position like that, and I found out that I liked it. So that relationship helped give me the guts to leave home and to leave school for six months.

We went to Europe with backpacks and kept traveling the whole time. We were really roughing it. We got stoned a lot. I had some money saved up from all the summers I'd been working in my dad's office. When that ran out we came home and I camped out at my folks' house. And came face to face with the decision of what I really wanted to do with my life. My parents pretty much let me alone. They figured I was so well programmed to go into medicine from the time I was a little kid that there was nowhere else I could go.

So I finally decided at the age of twenty to settle down and earn good grades to get into medical school. My parents were real happy about that, so I had to do something to keep them mad at me, just to show my independence. I decided to get married, and that did the trick. They hated the idea. They hated Katie.

My mom did one of her crazy freakout numbers because my wife-to-be wasn't Jewish. Which was ridiculous became my mom was only half Jewish herself. But that didn't stop her from acting like a lunatic for a while and trying to get everybody to listen.

We got married in November of '73 and by that time I was already concentrating on school. I finished up my B.A. in two and a half years by taking extra courses every quarter. I got into med school, but I continued to have my doubts about medicine. Maybe that's one of the reasons I chose psychiatry. There's this feeling among a lot of doctors that it's not real medicine, it's sort of a soft, bullshitty area. And the fantasy that I have is that it gives you a chance to be a lot more of a Renaissance person. It allows you to read James Joyce or Shakespeare and still have it relevant to what you're doing. It's not too difficult to stretch psychiatry like that, whereas regular medicine is a lot more focused.

My biggest problem with med school was that Katie felt totally excluded from what I was doing. When we were both flower children, everything was okay, but when we started to grow up we found out we were totally different people. Katie got heavily involved in politics, left-wing politics, and then she became a radical feminist. Everything I did was evil, it was part of class oppression and sexism and male supremacism. Meanwhile, the only people I associated with were med students and doctors, and that didn't include a lot of Marxists and feminists. By the time we finally broke up I felt that I had to choose between hating myself or hating Katie. It felt a lot more healthy to turn the hostility on her.

The divorce was final about four years ago and since then I've dated a lot of different people, women I know from medical school. Nothing serious has worked out so far, but that's okay with me because in internship and psychiatric residency you don't have much time for social life. And even when you do have free time, you don't have much energy. In psychiatry, you don't have to put in as many hours as a surgeon, or somebody in internal medicine, but the intensity is there . . . the emotional experience in hearing the pain and suffering that goes on, the inevitable empathic connection that you make with some of the patients.

Working the wards here, you find most of the patients are in very bad shape. Schizophrenia, manic-depressive illness. I tend to identify more with the patients that are not as sick. We have a couple of what we call ''high-functioning'' patients who are depressed and bring up a lot of issues I can relate to. Almost existential issues about life and how shitty it can be, and how things aren't fair and that stuff. I find myself thinking about being depressed and hoping I don't get depressed.

We've had some doctors who have come through here as patients. We have an M.D. on the ward right now, this very good-looking woman who was doing a residency in anesthesiology. She's about thirty. Admitted with depression, personality disorder. And she regularly tells her psychiatrist, who is a resident, that he is full of shit. She's just waiting to catch him on some medical mistake, and she's very sharp.

That's why everybody in the psychiatric ward hates having doctors as patients. They usually give you a rough time, and they get worse treatment than your average patient. People are sort of vengeful toward them, like they're a disgrace to the profession.

See, in medicine there's very little cooperation. Everybody's working against each other. So when a guy comes in here, it's a good way for everybody to kick ass. Even the nurses can get on him. It's a way for the nurses to get back for all the frustrations they have with doctors.

The priorities, in general, are totally fucked up. The top priority in the psychiatric ward, in the whole damn hospital, is for you, the individual doctor, to look good. If the patient happens to get better, then that's a nice coincidence.

I'm trying to stay out of that trap. I keep reminding myself, I'm here for the patients. I'm going to do what has to be done, and I don't care what people think of me.

One of the things I like to do is ECT—electroconvulsive therapy. A lot of people get squeamish when you talk about shock therapy, but I see how it works, how it helps the patients. I do ECT at least three times every week. It's a fascinating procedure. One doctor has to hold the electrodes on the head, and the other person does the switch. I like doing both. There's also an anesthesiologist standing by with some oxygen. And the patient gets a general anesthetic and a muscle relaxant. The general anesthetic puts them out. They don't feel any pain or remember what happens. It's a real benign procedure.

It's about the only procedure we have in psychiatry, and maybe that's why I like it so much. I like procedures. They appeal to that medically oriented, obsessive-compulsive part of me, where I like to do something. And that's the way we all are in medicine. I also like the fact that ECT is so effective. It's like magic.

And seeing a patient make progress is the best kind of thing that happens around here. The worst is when a patient commits suicide. That happens all the time. It hasn't happened to one of my patients yet, but I know it will. It happened to another resident about a month ago, a woman resident on the other ward. It was a stupid, pointless thing and it wasn't her fault. It was the fault of the parents, who took their son out on a weekend pass. They were told to bring him back up to the ward personally, not just drop him off. But they just let him off downstairs, and instead of coming back to the ward on the fifth floor, the patient wandered up to the eighth floor and jumped off. He landed on the pavement outside. It was gruesome. And the poor resident felt terrible, crying and real upset. We all kind of rallied to her support. She got the brunt of it this time, but it's an inevitable thing in psychiatry. It will happen to all of us sooner or later.

Psychiatrists think about suicide a lot. In psychiatric residency programs it's a known fact there's usually one person every year who does it. And that's just in the Bay Area. Sometimes we make jokes about it, like, "Who's it going to be this year?" Jeez, the chief resident on my ward—the senior resident—is a very knowledgeable guy who's obviously real depressed. He's the one who comes in and presses the button for ECT while I hold the electrodes. Well, he holds that button down *way* too fucking long! It's obvious that he's treating himself in some symbolic way. It wouldn't surprise me if he kills himself somewhere down the line.

In general, I think my busy schedule keeps me from thinking about my problems. I get depressed too, a mild kind of depression, like when I broke up with my wife or some girl I've been seeing. And I feel shitty and down and I don't like going in and paying attention to all these other people and their problems. But when I see these patients who are so much worse off, and start focusing on them, I stop thinking about me. That's why the higher-functioning kind of intellectual ones are the patients that give me the most trouble. They can do a lot of intellectualization and rationalization just like I do. They tend to get me thinking more about my problems, and I have to stop myself.

The worse patients of all are the oncology patients I see when I work for my father. I work for him every weekend and usually one afternoon during the week. I've been doing it for years. I need the extra bucks, since all they pay a resident is a thousand dollars a month.

All of his patients have cancer. They are all kind of depressed. And what happens is I spend more time with them than my dad does. It's part of his way of dealing with things that he just goes in there and out again. They don't get enough of him, so I come in. I spend more time because I don't know them and I have to kind of mull over things and make sure I'm not messing up. I tend to want to hear more about their feelings anyway, because that's my orientation. But if I don't really watch it, they latch on to me and I never get out.

It's real stressful, more stressful than my residency, and I don't like it at all. I don't like the patients and I don't like working for my dad. I have to set up limits and boundaries or else he'll just engulf me. He'll have me over there eating with him, and working for him, and spending all my energy as kind of an extension of his ego. I don't want to work for him anymore, and as soon as I can get some kind of psychiatric moonlighting job, I'll switch over and do that.

It doesn't mean that I don't like him. I get a kick out of the way he's so proud of me. When I work with him sometimes, we'll go in together with the first few patients so he can introduce me. He'll introduce me to anybody and everybody. He must have introduced me nine times to the maintenance man at his office. He always tells me how much he respects me and my intelligence. He'll come to me on a lot of medical questions and ask my advice. He always tells me that he thinks I'm smarter than he is, and I'll be a better doctor, and that kind of thing. Somehow, it has sunk in. I feel very confident. Not a hundred percent, but all in all, compared to other people, I agree that I'm very competent.

People often ask me if I feel competitive with my dad, and I usually tell them that I don't. He's proud of me. I'm proud of him. The more I know of medicine the better he seems. But I don't feel like I have to be the same kind of doctor or do things in exactly the same way.

Already, my father's started worrying about the third generation. He wants me to get married and have a son so he can live to see a grandson who's a doctor. I know he'll try to take over that kid, because that's the way he is, my father. And when I think about kids, just in the abstract, I think, yeah, I would really like it if my kid was a doctor. And then I think, maybe we're not so different after all, my father and me.

SHAPING UP

DR. BEN BRODY, Psychiatric Resident

The whole point of medical school is to change your personality. And about the first thing that happens is they give you a cadaver. It's supposed to change your attitude about the body. And that's how you're expected to learn gross anatomy, by dissecting this dead body. Everybody seemed to name their cadaver. Our cadaver's name was Abra—Abra Cadaver. I think it was stupid and silly, but that's what we named him.

I had this almost morbid fascination with it. The other three guys would want to cover the face while we worked, but I would always want to have it exposed and want to open the eyes and get up close and look right in the eyes. I guess I was pondering what it was like to be dead, what it must feel like to be a cadaver.

DR. STANLEY RUCKERT, Intern

A cadaver is totally different from a human body in that the skin is blanched white. It's been in this vat of formalin, it's ice-cold, it's rigid, and the skin feels like shoe leather. The first thing we had to do, first day of gross anatomy, was examine it. Then we had to strip to the waist and examine ourselves. Then we went back and got to feel all these landmarks on the cadaver.

I was a little smug going in because I grew up on a farm and we butchered, cut up cattle and slaughtered pigs and whatever, so I figured, well, this should be easy for me. But it wasn't easy because this was a body, a human body. And for two days it bothered all of us intensely. Maybe a week at most, but then after that we just got into it.

Then one day I remember very vividly, this was maybe four months or so into the dissection, I'm digging in the neck, looking for a little obscure branch of this nerve, or whatever, when all of a sudden I realize that I have my nose buried in there and that my hair is brushing across the face of this man that's lying there staring up into space. And I just pulled back! You know, my God! What have I gotten myself into!

DR. CHARLOTTE KIRKHAM, Hematology Fellow

I hated med school. It was tremendously cutthroat and I thought the men were very immature, very into one-upping everybody. Look, everybody's insecure. I mean, we're all insecure. It's just that on a continuum these guys were off the scale. I just did not want to be there. A lot of the things that are taught there are a complete waste and I've already forgotten most of what I knew. The professors wanted to intimidate us. It was like you were five years old, back in grade school.

The cadaver was bad for me too. I had a male cadaver, and my father had just died. I kept seeing my father. I remember cleaning out shit, just spooning it out with a spoon from the bowels. There was a lot of formaldehyde around and your eyes sting and there's crap all over you. You tend to be more grossed out than anything else.

DR. GARLAND LOCKWOOD, Obstetrician-Gynecologist

My roommate flunked out of medical school. We only had six guys flunk out, see, and he was one of the six. He was not that bright, and he didn't like what he was doing. I remember taking the final, second quarter in biochemistry. It was a three-hour test. Ten minutes into it this guy just stood up, went to the front, tore up the test booklet, and tossed it in the trash. He knew he would flunk out, so he just walked out.

At first I envied him. I hated medical school. In my second year I started seeing a psychiatrist, and that's the only time I've done therapy in my life. He told me I should start focusing energy on things outside school. And when I met my wife, see, I thought that getting married was a way I could develop some life outside school. I think that's why so many people get married in med school.

DR. BARNETT GOLDSTEIN, Plastic Surgeon

As a senior in medical school I worked as a clerk at county hospital. The students do odd jobs, or anything the residents permit us to do. And one night we had a delivery, with an extra-large baby, who tore through the soft tissue of the rectum. The resident delivered it and he says, "Does anybody know how to do an episiotomy repair?"

I stepped up and said, "I can do it." I had never done one in my life but I'd read about it in Eastman's textbook on obstetrics. And I was afraid I might never get the opportunity, and I wanted to learn, so I lied.

I went in there and started sewing. When I was finished I was very proud. It really looked good. The chief resident came in to do a quick check. He goes to put his finger into the rectum, but it was completely closed. I had stitched it closed. So the guy laughed and said, "Come on, Barney. Tell the truth. Had you ever done one of these before?"

I said, "No, but I read about them. I just wanted to have the opportunity."

44

So he said, "Well, that's great. No harm done." And he took out the stitches and we did the whole thing over. The patient was a big fat Mexican gal, and was screaming the whole time. She was yelling "Ouchy! Ouchy!" But I don't think she knew what was going on.

Anyway, it was really an educational experience for me. After that I knew how to do an episiotomy repair.

NANCY PROCTOR, Nurse

There's a new group of interns that starts every spring. What they say around here is try not to get sick in June or July because that's when they're green and they don't know what they're doing. They use the patients to train themselves, and that's not great for the patients. It always surprises me how little they know when they start. To tell the truth, some of the janitors know more than they do. But then you realize if they knew everything, they wouldn't be here in training.

DR. MILTON TESSLER, Cardiologist

My first day on call as an intern, I was assigned to the emergency room. It was the Fourth of July. As soon as I walked through the door, an ambulance comes screeching up and they wheel out a guy in a lot of pain, who's covered in white sheets and sponges. The resident takes a look at him and then he looks at me and he says, "Well, do you think you can start an IV?" All I could think of was, "Well, of course, smart-ass." So he unwraps the sheets from the guy's chest and hands me the guy's arm, which was severed above the elbow. The resident sort of smiles and says, "Why don't you take this arm into the next room and start an IV on it?"

So I carried the severed arm into the next room, put it on ice, and had the IV bag running into the vein and thought, how bizarre this whole thing is! The point is you want to try to keep this limb perfused while you get the surgeons in to see whether or not they can reattach the limb. So we called the surgeons in off the golf course but they decided that they really couldn't save that arm.

The resident obviously was trying to hassle me, but I said to myself it's all for a good purpose. This is going to be my life's work and I've got to shape up.

It kept up like that for the rest of the year, and it never really got easier. Once when I was an intern on the wards, a student nurse came up, a very pretty girl. The kind you always wanted to walk behind when she went down the hall. And she said to me, "Gee, I'm having a little trouble taking a blood pressure. Will you help me?"

Maybe if she wasn't so pretty I wouldn't have agreed right away. But I did go up, and I put the blood-pressure cuff on the patient and I figured, oh, this is terrific, now I'll show her what a good doctor I am. So I started taking the blood pressure and I couldn't get it. It must have been a minute, a minute and a half, I couldn't get any reading. Then I looked up and saw the patient wasn't breathing, and realized the reason the nurse couldn't get a blood pressure was that the patient had arrested. I felt like a real idiot. I yelled at her to go out and get someone, to call an arrest. We tried everything we could, but we couldn't get his heart back. We lost the patient.

The thing that bothered me was I should have known better. If someone says, "Come here and help me take a blood pressure," the first thing you do is assess the patient briefly. Just look and make sure everything's okay and then go ahead. You're not anyone's blood-pressure technician. You're not a toenail technician. You're a doctor, and you've got to do it all.

THE RELUCTANT
REBEL

DR. MILTON TESSLER
Cardiologist

DR. HARVEY FREDMAN, Professor of Gastroenterology

I remember him as an intern—a nice, quiet person who sort of faded into the woodwork. I was very surprised when he wrote the letter to the paper and started that whole controversy.

DR. BURTON WEBBER, Ear, Nose, and Throat

He's a young cardiologist who's just starting out but already has a big reputation. Most of it negative, I'm afraid. About a year ago he wrote a letter to the editor of the *San Francisco Chronicle* about the quality of health care at Memorial. He said, in effect, that the doctors are only interested in money and they're slaughtering the patients. Well, you can imagine the reaction. About twenty doctors wrote in to answer him. Then Tessler wrote back to defend himself. The whole thing went on for weeks.

In the middle of this episode I called up Dr. Tessler and asked him to come to lunch with me. As president of the County Medical Association, I wanted to meet him and hear what he had to say, and I was very pleasantly surprised when we got together. He's an articulate and courteous young man. This image of a rabble-rouser that's been hung on him doesn't really fit. The basic problem, I think, is that he's not temperamentally suited for private practice. He's more interested in cardiac research, in an academic position, and I think that's the direction he's headed.

GEORGIANNA HARLAN, *Ward Clerk, Translator*

I went out with him a couple of months ago. It took him weeks and weeks of flirting before he got up the courage to ask me. Then we went out to see a movie, some sexy French film, and we had coffee afterward. He wanted to talk about the movie in a very intellectual way. He reminded me of a character in a Woody Allen movie the way he took it so seriously. Then he took me home and shook hands. That doesn't happen very often, shaking hands! I never heard from him after that. Maybe it was just too much excitement for one night!

BECKY KRIEGER, *Nurse*

Milt Tessler is just wonderful! He was definitely one of the best interns we ever had. He was unusually sensitive to all the patients and they really loved him for it. I still see him occasionally, and I get the idea that he's lonely right now. He's very idealistic, and that makes it hard, and that's also why he gets disillusioned about working in the hospital. He has very high standards and not everybody can live up to them.

————————

I met Dr. Tessler at an atmospheric French café not far from the hospital. The waitress, who treated him like an honored and familiar customer, took us to a dark table in the back. Tessler apologized for the semipublic setting for the interview but explained that his bachelor apartment was far too disordered to receive any visitors and that this restaurant served as his home away from home.

With his long, thin nose, cool blue eyes, and shoulder-length brown hair, Tessler's appearance seemed to fit his image as a youthful medical rebel. His blue blazer and conservative striped tie were, however, the very soul of respectability. He seemed, in any event, particularly concerned to disavow all revolutionary intentions regarding his hospital and his profession.

THE WHOLE INCIDENT of my notorious letter was kind of a joke. What happened was the *Chronicle* ran a big article about cardiovascular surgery at Memorial. You know, the wonders of modern science, miracles of healing, that kind of thing. The whole piece could have been written by the hospital public-relations department. The thing is, I deal with cardiac problems every day, and, to put it bluntly, that's a big problem area for our hospital. And there's way too much surgery, particularly coronary-bypass surgery, and the records show that our surgeons aren't particularly good at it. So this article really bothered me, especially with its glorification of some individuals who don't deserve to be glorified. I didn't want to point my finger at any one person or even one department, so I wrote a very general kind of philosophical letter criticizing the whole cult of doctor worship. I raised some questions about this supposed utopia known as Memorial, and I hit particularly hard on the idea of the profit motive, you know, and how it distorts medical judgment. I don't know what I was expecting to accomplish, but I certainly didn't expect the response that I got. People were absolutely hysterical and there were a whole series of letters, calling me every name in the book. It showed very clearly that doctors really are a closed society. There is this idea that the public has to be kept in the dark or the whole system is going to collapse. It's the same way some of the older doctors won't discuss a case honestly with a patient because if he knows what's going on he might get in the way. It's a foolish attitude, but I should have known what was coming. Some people stopped saying hello to me in the halls. My referrals dried up—I was an outcast.

And the funny part is that I'm not much of a radical. I voted for Ronald Reagan, so how radical can I be? But I also went to Columbia in the sixties. I was never SDS or anything like that, but I was there for the riots and it left me with more of a questioning attitude, that I don't have to accept things just because they've been like that for a long time. And I have some very big questions about the way we organize health care in this society. It's too involved with money every step of the way. The thing is, it's become an enormous industry that thrives on human misery. The sicker a patient gets, the more money his doctor makes. Until the patient dies and then you can't bill him anymore. In a way it's set up like a double penalty for people who get sick. You not only suffer and lose time at work, but also end up paying through the nose. Even if your insurance covers most of it, you'll still end up paying something, and if you're too poor for insurance you'll get inferior care. Maybe we should arrange it just the other way around, so that healthy people pay a certain amount every year, but when they get sick they don't have to pay anymore. I don't know. But I do know that money is a factor for the doctor. If you're making a decision about surgery that is borderline necessary, and you know that doing the surgery will make you five thousand dollars richer, obviously that is going to influence your decision. Not that you're going to commit malpractice or mislead the patient, but it could definitely tip the scales.

I don't know what the answer is, but I'm interested in some of the ideas about group practice or community health systems. I wouldn't want to see a nationalized system like they have in England because I also believe that the personal contact between doctor and patient is important. It's necessary for a doctor's happiness and emotional stability to build up personal relationships with a finite number of patients. There's just a point of overload where even the best of us is going to go downhill.

I probably ought to go into academic medicine, where there's a little less pressure and more of an emphasis on research and creative work. Maybe I could teach people to have a different attitude. But the thing is, if you've been trained all your life to be competitive and to push for the top, it's hard to change overnight. It's hard for me to turn my back on a place like Memorial, even when I know what's wrong with it. There are certain values that I inherited from my parents, and they're just part of me, like it or not. My parents were both concentration-camp survivors. They were married to different people before the war, but both families were killed at Auschwitz. They met in a displaced persons' camp in 1946 and then they came to America together. My father is a successful businessman, but he really had to struggle to get where he is now. He raised all of his kids with the idea that we should be doctors, and I guess it worked, because he got three M.D.s. My one brother is a neurosurgeon and the other one is going to be an orthopedist. I'm the oldest and I'm also the black sheep of the family because I went into cardiology, which is a relatively low-paying specialty.

I made that decision in my third year of medical school. I found that I really enjoyed listening to heart sounds. There was something very romantic about cardiology. The idea of being able to diagnose heart abnormalities, of saving somebody's life as opposed to taking out their cataract or healing their acne. In cardiology, we don't cure anybody. We may ameliorate their situation with medications or we may send them to a surgeon to prolong their life. But in general, not many people die at your hands; if they do, then they were basically dying when you got there.

I remember when I was an intern, a guy came into the ER with a heart attack. He was sitting there waiting for somebody to see him and underwent cardiac arrest, and I came in with the surgery intern. We shocked him a number of times, but he wasn't responding. We tried to give him various medications. We couldn't get an intravenous line in the usual spot, so I ended up putting it in a very unusual spot, which is the femoral artery in the groin. I just jabbed it in. He was unconscious and it was very bizarre because we would shock him, he would wake up and look at me and say *"Stop!"* and throw up his arms like, you know, this is too much. And then he'd pass out again, and we kept on. After about ten of these shocks, the senior resident came and said, "We'll never get him back. Let's leave." But I just kept on going. I didn't want to give up. And after shocking him about twenty-five times, we pulled him out of it.

I remember him walking out of the hospital a couple of weeks later, and of course he was very grateful. He was a normal person, a laborer, about fifty-five years old. I remember his name and I still think about it. It made me feel terrific. Even if I wasn't the best intern in the world, and I couldn't get an intravenous line in, or I couldn't take care of all the work before morning rounds, I had a certain amount of stick-to-itiveness and persistence, and I happened to save this guy when somebody else would have let him die. That made me feel like someday I would really be able to do some good.

Maybe I define "doing good" differently from some of the other

51

people in this place. One time I was taking call for one of the other residents and I was covering his patients. There was one patient where it was clear that my colleague did not want her resuscitated, did not want her life prolonged in any way. But when the patient started bleeding out, I ordered blood for her. I knew it was just a palliative and she would die anyway in a couple of days. The next day the resident came down on me and said that I took the coward's way out. I told him that whatever he wants to do with his own patients is fine, but as long as I am there and I am responsible, I will prolong life in any way I can.

This job gives you two conflicting messages. On the one hand, you feel in control of the world because you have the ability to cure and you hold life in your hands. On the other hand, you are constantly exposed to death and illness and you are constantly reminded of your own mortality. I remember one case where we had this thirty-year-old delightful guy, who had just finished his Ph.D. in psychology, gotten a wonderful job at the university, had a happy marriage, a beautiful baby, a doting Jewish mother, and he had just gotten acute leukemia. And I had to go by and see him every day on rounds. Every time I walked into his room it was like getting kicked in the groin. The thing is, there are plenty of guys who are sixty-five and seventy and they have heart attacks or cancer and they die. But this one was inherently unfair and it threatened my whole concept of what my future should be like. I always had this conception that I'm going to be a doctor and someday, hopefully, I'll be successful and famous and have a family. I've been counting on that, but every time I saw this guy with leukemia, I thought, shit, I could end up here in this hospital and die an agonizing death along with him! We gave him chemotherapy and prolonged his life for six months. Just long enough for his family to fall apart and his mother to suffer beyond endurance.

And one of the things I carry around all the time is this feeling that things are going so well for me that it's bound to crash at some point. In a sense, I'm beating the odds by just being able to walk around and not have all of these maladies I see all the time. I have a strong sense that eventually one of these things will happen to me. It's like there's a big bloody monster out there who is out of control. He's putting all these people into the hospital and making them suffer and breaking up their lives and he's just waiting to get me. He's pushing against the door trying to break in and I can feel him getting close.

The situation with my parents' health has been very painful for me. My father had a series of heart attacks, so that's very close right there.

When I was doing my residency, he went in for heart surgery. He had four bypasses and he had an aneurysm removed. It was major, major surgery and I didn't want them to do it at Memorial. They did the surgery in New York and of course I was right there. My father had hallucinations after his surgery, which is not uncommon, and he felt that he was in a concentration camp and the nurses were trying to kill him. And I slept at the hospital for a couple of nights just to be around, to be sure that I could tell him that we were in good hands and that he was going to be fine. They did a superb job, actually.

Just when my father was getting better we started having problems with my mother. It was a terrible situation where over the course of two years she first had difficulty walking, and then couldn't hold her urine, and then lost her memory and became demented. It was a degenerative brain illness, but we couldn't be sure of its cause. At first, we sent her to a psychologist, who concluded it was a functional thing related perhaps to menopause. Then in a few months she couldn't walk anymore and it became clear that this was definitely an organic thing. We didn't really know what to do. We had a family conference and my two younger brothers, who were both in medical school at the time, came home to help us decide. And after talking with people in neurosurgery we decided to have an operation to try to relieve some pressure on her brain. It was just possible that with this operation her condition could be curable. You put a little tube in, and drain some of the fluid from the brain into a vein in the neck. If there were any chance that this would help, we all wanted to take that chance. But after the operation she got worse.

My father wanted me to move back home to complete my residency in New York so I could be there and take care of my mother. The thing is, that to work at the hospital and then come home and see my mother every night, that was something I couldn't handle. It was incredibly selfish of me, but I knew I couldn't do it. It's one point that I'm not real proud of, but it was really a matter of self-preservation.

I was flying back and forth anyway several times every month, so I was around. And there came a time near the end of her course when there was a question of whether to put her in the intensive care unit. I was standing there in the hall when some of the interns and residents were discussing her; they were saying she would never have a useful life and there was no point in putting her in intensive care.

Naturally I became emotionally upset and called the attending physician. I said, "I heard that there's a question of moving my mother into the intensive care unit but they're not sure if they want to free up a bed. What do you think?"

And he said, "Well, I can understand she's your mother, Dr. Tessler, but you can probably see their point as well."

It turned out that she didn't get admitted to the intensive care unit. I went back to Memorial and then about two weeks later I was calling in to find out how she was doing when her attending physician got on the line and said, "Your mother has just arrested. We're in there, a full team is working on her. Do you think we ought to put her on a respirator?"

When he said that I could feel my heart beating faster. I couldn't stand up. I didn't know what to do. So I said, "You're her physician. You have to do what you think is right." Then I hung up. They didn't put her on the respirator and she didn't make it.

Afterwards, I thought about it a lot. I think I did the right thing. If she had survived, her life wouldn't be anything that she or anyone else would have wanted. She didn't know her own name, she was incontinent, she was demented. The thing is, I wouldn't want to be in a position, given my philosophy, to deny her any type of life-prolonging measures. So I tried to take myself out of the situation, by telling her physician to make his own decision. If I had been there, I probably would have put her on the respirator. And maybe I would have been wrong. There are so many factors you have to take into account. The limited resources of the hospital, for one thing, and the limited time and energy of the house staff. If someone is really a hopeless case and they will never be a socially useful citizen, or have all their mental faculties or fit your view of what a human being should be, then you're apt to spend less time on them. I can understand that. I know it makes sense, even with my mother. But I don't want to face those decisions and that's one of the reasons I want to go to a different area of medicine.

Thank God my father is doing better now. It's been two years since my mother died, and he's adjusted to it very well. I wanted him to come to California and move in with me, but he has all his friends in New York. My brother just started a fellowship in neurosurgery in Manhattan and he's living a few blocks away, so I feel better about the whole thing. But I still worry about my father and I know that we could lose him any time.

The worse part is that he wants to see grandchildren before he dies, and I'm the oldest so the burden is on me. I'm looking and I'm serious, but it's not easy in my situation. There are lots of women who would go out with me, but I'm not sure about their motivation. I see what happens at parties when I'm introduced as "Milt Tessler" or when they say, "This is Dr. Milton Tessler." The "Doctor" makes a big difference in the way people respond. The title is a symbol of power and wealth, and I want to get away from that. Even when I've dated people who really liked me for other reasons, it's always a factor. One woman I was seeing came to visit me at Memorial. I was dressed in my surgical gown, and she said, "My God! You look incredibly great in your greens!" Well, I thought perhaps I looked better in a jacket and tie, or, if I were flattering myself, in a bathing suit! I mean, what is it about these greens? These things are worth about fifty cents. It makes me feel like I'm a policeman walking along in my uniform, carrying my gun, and that's what really turns them on.

Just because I happen to be a physician, women want me to be a take-charge person in all situations. And the thing is, when I get away from the hospital, I like to shed that role. I want another person's suggestions about shopping or clothes or what movie we're going to see. I go out of my way to bring the person into my life, and this makes some women uncomfortable, because here I am the big doctor, and I'm wishy-washy about what tie I'm going to wear!

I'm still looking for the right woman, but I've got to confess that I'm getting impatient. Medicine makes you impatient; you're used to getting immediate results. One of my biggest aggravations is waiting for phone calls, waiting in lines. If I go to a dentist's office and I sit in a waiting room for an hour, I rapidly go through the roof. My patients have to wait all the time, but when you're a doctor, you're not used to waiting for anything.

Sometimes I think I ought to get out of medicine, but I'm not really serious about it. I just have to figure out how to make a better place for myself, where I can have more of an impact on the overall scheme of things. One of my fantasies is to take a few years off and go to law school. I've never wanted to be an attorney instead of a physician, but I am fascinated by the law. Maybe I'll do it at night some time. When I get that law degree, maybe I could use it to write medical legislation. I'd like to have a role in that larger world outside of medicine.

But right now I'm staying where I am. The thing is, I have to build up more of a track record before I go to something else. Some of my colleagues think I'm a troublemaker and malcontent, but I'm actually very attached to this place. In a funny way, you could say that I love it. It's a source of my professional and my social life. So I hang around a lot of times, hours at a time, when I don't really need to be there. That's a common habit, even with the older physicians. When I was in medical school there was this one doctor who was just incredible. He'd be there night after night till after midnight, when he could have gone home at six. I could never understand it, but then I found out that he had a very sick child who was in terrible shape. At the hospital he was king; he was in control of the whole milieu. But when he went home, he couldn't even control his child's health, so naturally he wanted to avoid that kind of pressure.

Maybe it's the same thing with me. My social life is lousy and my apartment is a mess. My mother died and my father could die any minute. But when I'm at Memorial I don't have to worry about that and I can try to do good for somebody else. It's a very supportive environment for the doctors. There are nurses I have known for years and they have become like sisters to me. Some of them stick in the mind because they went out of their way to help me. Nancy Proctor is a good example; she just has that spark of life. She took me under her wing and helped me a lot when my mother died. She attracts a lot of attention because she comes on very brash and sexy, but she really cares about what she is doing. There's something about the hospital that brings out that kindness, especially if you're a kind person to begin with.

THE
CHEERLEADER

NANCY PROCTOR
Nurse

DR. BEN BRODY, Psychiatric Resident

Nancy is one of a kind! She has more energy than any human being I have ever known. She likes to do cartwheels and backflips down the halls of the hospital. She loves to play practical jokes, and she cheers up the patients with her wacky sense of humor. When I was an intern, she used to flirt with every single guy on house staff. One time I made some comment about the way she jumps around all the time and she said, "If you think I've got energy at work, you ought to see me in bed!" I'm sorry to say I never did.

DR. HARVEY FREDMAN, Professor of Gastroenterology

Nancy's not shy, that's one thing I can tell you! She always lets you know what she's thinking, what's on her mind. Sometimes she says things that she probably shouldn't say in public, but she gets away with it because she's an outstanding nurse. She has outstanding judgment and a good mind. She's very independent. In fact, she's one of the best nurses we've ever had.

57

Nancy is an excellent nurse. I recognize that, even though she sees herself as my enemy. During my internship year she tried to get me kicked out of the program. She said I was incompetent, and she got most of the other nurses to go along with her. She was gunning for me, maybe because she was an eligible female and I was a threat in terms of all the male attention.

Now she's married with a baby, so that element of competition doesn't exist. She's pleasant and friendly, but I could never trust her again. Not after what happened.

DR. CARL GORMAN, Neurosurgeon

Her husband is Barry Proctor, who is doing a fellowship in urology. I don't know him too well, but I always thought he was sort of a jerk. She struck me as being very nice, very sexy. I don't see how those two ever hit it off. She seems much more to wear the pants. Much more in control, much stronger personality. When I was an intern, she used to go out with everybody, she was very popular. She was very clearly in the market for a husband and she wanted to get a doctor. She got what she wanted, but I thought she could do better than Proctor.

———————

Nancy Proctor's work schedule brought her to the hospital four times a week for a full shift; I met her on an off day while she played at home with her baby, Max. An active, good-natured ten-month-old with jug ears and wispy blond hair, Max seemed to be primarily responsible for the innovative scheme of interior decoration employed in the Proctor living room. Dozens of toys and soiled baby clothes covered every available inch of space, along with old newspapers, dirty dishes, and overflowing ashtrays. "I'm not much of a housekeeper," Nancy said. "I'm also a lousy cook. Barry must have married me for my other talents."

She wore snug white shorts and a halter top, an outfit which seemed perfectly suited to her boyish, athletic frame. Her face, which was pert rather than pretty, featured a broad, turned-up nose, wide-set brown eyes, and straight brown hair worn in bangs with a ponytail. While Max crawled back and forth across the carpet, Nancy crossed her bare legs on the sofa and began describing her illustrious ancestors.

M Y GREAT-GRANDFATHER WAS a horse thief in Ireland. Then he ran away to America and became a whiskey smuggler. A very resourceful guy.

His daughter, my grandmother, is also interesting. Her husband was an alcoholic and used to beat up the kids. One night he came home drunk and she locked him in the closet and set him on fire. But in the meantime my grandmother had been seeing the TV repairman, who she later married. He's my grandfather now, a real nice guy.

My dad reacted to all that by becoming a policeman. He's been a cop for thirty years. He's the deputy chief in the little town where I grew up. It's a farming community in the Central Valley, north of Fresno. The biggest excitement in town is watching the vegetables grow.

My high school wasn't very academic. We used to have fire drills every day because people liked to set trash cans on fire. We were about half white, half Mexican. It was one of those schools where we weren't allowed to play certain other schools because everybody knifed everybody else.

I was a cheerleader my senior year, not because I was pretty but because I was an acrobat. I did a lot of flips to show off my underwear. That was very popular. I was known as Miss Megaphone Mouth, a very loud, shrill voice. Didn't do a lot of dating. I was very backwards. When I look back on myself now, I just laugh.

I spent most of my time on sports. I was the only girl in the history of our high school to be named athlete of the year. I held some track records there for a while, don't know if I still do. For a while, I thought I wanted to be a gym teacher, but I found out that I didn't. Got a hernia catching fat girls flying off the equipment.

After high school, I went straight into nursing. I had to figure out some way to get away from home. There was a junior college in San Francisco that had a nursing program. I signed up and moved to the city. My parents didn't want me to move out, so they wouldn't let me take my bed. I slept on the floor the first couple of months.

I finished the program in two years and then I was a registered nurse at age nineteen. That was pretty exciting, and I had no trouble getting a job. There's always a shortage of nurses, especially nurses who are willing to work nights. I started off working night shift at one of the Catholic hospitals. I used to come in at eleven and go home at seven in the morning. A hospital gets pretty wild at that time. There's not a lot of doctors or supervisors around, so the nurses pretty much have the run of the place. Most of the other people on night shift were about my age, maybe a few years older. We had some old folks on the floor, and we used to play with them. They were completely out of it. We used to put up their hair in braids, with all kinds of little ribbons. Some of the old folks had these big old bedsores. We had to lie them on their sides and tape their butts apart because they're so saggy. You have to pull the cheeks apart and coat 'em with Maalox to heal the bedsores, and then you put a lamp on it. So here we've got these old ladies with pigtails and pretty bows, and their cheeks spread apart and a spotlight on their ass. We thought it was sort of funny. They actually got better nursing care from us because on the other shifts people would try to get them out of the way, but we had 'em right out there on display.

Sometimes the patients really gave us a rough time. We had one guy who needed a barium enema. This guy was totally out of his mind. Four of us were holding him down and we shoved the enema hose in there and he just turned around and whacked us. And this was after we'd gotten about a quart and a half inside this guy. He just went crazy so we all ran out of there and we came back a little bit later. Here was this guy, sitting at the edge of the bed, diarrhea running down his leg, and he was taking the hard chunks and throwing them against the wall. That was nice. We had to get security in there to hold the guy down so we could clean him up and finish the job.

Even things like that never really bothered me because of the positive feelings with the other people who worked there. We were wild, we stuck together, we had a great time. Usually, everybody tries to get off the night shift, but we were so nuts that for two whole years nobody left that shift.

The only problem was the social life. You work nights, and you're so tired on your days off that all you want to do is sleep. I was still a virgin and totally inexperienced. It wasn't until I got to Memorial that things began to change.

It was a better job all around. More money, for one thing. And Memorial is a teaching hospital, so there are always lots of interns around. Right away, I got into the spirit of things. If anyone asked me out, I accepted. This one intern took me to the movies twice, so I decided we should get more serious. This was 1973, I was twenty-two years old, and I decided it was time to lose my virginity. I asked him over for dinner one night and my thoughts were that I was going to get laid. Well, one thing led to another and I did get laid. Some people say the first time is painful, and all this kind of crap. Well, it was fine for me. He didn't even know it was my first time.

After I screwed him I thought for a couple of days that I must be in love. Then he told me he was screwing one of the other nurses, and that didn't bother me at all so I figured I must *not* be in love. Then I decided I'd better get on some birth control. After that, things just took off.

I went wild, actually. I decided I'm going to screw everybody I can and I'm going to have a wonderful time. I was working pediatrics, and the group of interns was all single males and one female. They were just terrific. We used to go drinking every Tuesday; we'd go over to JoJo's and play darts and have drinking games. One night a week we'd all go into the city and go dancing and drinking. Then every other weekend I'd invite everybody over to my apartment and we'd have dinner and then we'd either go to a movie or ice skating or something like that. We'd always do things together. It was sort of like having brothers, but better. You can't have sex with your brothers.

One time we had a slumber party for the nurses and the doctors. We showed stag films and we had crazy games like "Pin the Cock on the Male Pin-Up" and "Pin the Tits on the Female Pin-Up." And we played music and we went out and wrapped toilet paper all over the front yard of one of the older doctors.

With all the parties, I was always the ringleader. I always did most of the organizing. A couple of times I thought I was madly in love with some guy, but the group always turned out to be more important. Then I met Barry, and I found something better and I started staying home.

He was an intern—naturally—but he didn't make much of an impression at first because he was very quiet and sort of shy. Then one night a whole group of us went out for pizza and I was sitting between Barry and another guy. The other guy asked me out and I said sure. Then Barry said, "Well, if you'll go out with him, will you go out with me?" I said, "Yeah, I go out with anybody."

So I went out with him three times and the only thing I let him do was kiss me. I did not want to get involved right then, because I had just found out that I had borderline CA of the cervix. I was going to have to go in for a D and C, and for a cone biopsy. It's a pretty serious operation, and I was scared.

The night before I went into the hospital I went out with Barry. I was feeling very melodramatic, like I might die tomorrow or something like that. And Barry took me to an expensive restaurant with flamenco dancers. We were watching them dance after we finished eating and we decided neither of us like flamenco dancing. I had ice in my mouth and I said to Barry, "You want some ice?" He said, "Sure," but he didn't know what I was talking about. So then I started kissing him right there and we started passing ice back and forth from mouth to mouth. Then we went out to the parking lot and got into my van and I whipped off my bra and we got very involved. We didn't screw but we did other things and I orgasmed a couple of times and he came a couple of times and I decided this is the guy for me.

Then I went in for surgery and everything turned out fine. I wasn't going to die. Barry was the very first person to visit me, and he brought three dozen roses. All the interns from that class came to see me. Not one of the nurses, but all the doctors.

I went out with him again the night after I got out of the hospital. We couldn't screw because I just had the D and C. But we went out and he ordered steak and I ordered fish. My fish turned out lousy so I told him to share the steak with me. He said okay. Then I said, "Why do you do everything I tell you to do?" And he looked at me and said seriously, "I'd do anything for you."

When he said that, I knew this wasn't a guy who was going to screw me over. This was the guy for me. I decided then and there that if he didn't ask me to marry him in a week, I'd ask him. I waited a week and nothing happened, so I went ahead and asked. He said yes. And we got married two months later.

Once we settled down a lot of people were thankful. I used to be very rowdy and loud and obnoxious. On my evaluation it says that I made chicken calls in the ICU. I'm very good at chicken calls: *Buck-buck-buck-bee-yuck!* But after I got together with Barry, he liked to screw so much that I was too tired to carry on like before.

We started trying to have a baby right after we got married. We tried for three years, but nothing happened. Then one of the guys at work told me that if you screw and stand on your head afterwards you'll get pregnant right away. So far seven people have tried it and all have gotten pregnant within a month. Being acrobatic, it was sort of a pleasure to stand on my head. And right away, it worked.

Max is a wonderful healthy baby, but since he was born it's been a strain. We never have enough hours in the day. Barry's really considerate about everything. I usually don't feel like cooking, and he never complains about that. We usually get Chinese take-home food, or go out to a Mexican restaurant. He doesn't care. If the house looks a mess, and he doesn't like it, then he'll clean it up himself.

The biggest problem is Barry's schedule. He leaves the house at seven in the morning and he comes home at eight or nine at night. He's always tired. He enjoys his work, but sometimes it's frustrating for me. One night he came home around midnight and we started fooling around right here in the living room. I was sucking him off and he was hard as a rock and then suddenly he started snoring. Right in the middle of getting sucked off! I woke him up and he said, "Oh no, I wasn't sleeping. I was just playing." Well, he'd been snoring for ten minutes!

My parents thought I was absolutely nuts to go back to work after the baby was born. But I couldn't stay away, because I love nursing. I'm one of those crazy people who really enjoys all of it, even the scut work. I used to come in on my days off just to see how the patients were doing. I still do that, and I bring Max with me.

Some of the things that have happened at Memorial are just unbelievable. We had a little girl once, four years old, with a brain tumor. They removed the tumor, but they also did some nerve damage, so she developed some very serious respiratory problems. They put her on a respirator and the doctors told us, "It's too bad. She's not going to make it." But the nurses all said, "Yes she is!" We all loved this little girl. She was just bright and adorable and her parents were wonderful. At Halloween she was really sad because she wanted to go trick-or-treating. So a bunch of us went out and bought her a whole bunch of candy and we made a little costume for her. There she is on the respirator, sitting up, wearing a little princess costume, looking at her candy. She couldn't swallow, but she loved M & M's. So we let her eat some M & M's, even though they went bubbling out her nose, and she just thought it was wonderful.

Well, we just really sat on this girl. We weren't going to lose her. And little by little she got stronger. They didn't think she'd ever be able to walk, but we really worked with her and her parents and now she walks almost like normal. And she finally got out of the hospital after being there for eighteen months.

Just a couple of weeks ago I got a letter from her mother. Every nurse has a box full of notes and letters like this. The mother told me that one night her daughter was saying her prayers and blessing her grandparents and her sisters and everybody. Then she said she had to thank someone for getting her better. And the mother said, "Do you mean God?" And the girl said, "No, I mean Nancy."

You get a letter like that and you know that this is the best job in the world. At Memorial, we get miracles all the time.

Sometimes it goes the other way, of course. You lose kids when you shouldn't lose 'em and nobody understands why. Or you get kids who are so sick you can't do much for them. For two years, I worked the intensive care unit, the pediatric ICU. A lot of those kids were accident victims, or near-drownings, or meningitis, and they were really in bad shape. They just sort of lie there unconscious. You never really know if they can hear you or not. So I always talk to them and caress them and hold them and rock them, just in case something is getting through. I encourage their parents to keep talking with them, or bring in tapes and play them for the kids, so if they do hear anything it's something familiar and not so frightening for them.

The saddest kids for me are the ones with cystic fibrosis. It's a disease that affects your lungs. What happens is they fill up with mucus and slowly rot away. You end up drowning in your own mucus. Those kids are real sad because you just watch 'em wasting away. They are usually very special kids. Kids who are full of love and life and are very giving, very bright.

We have a special cystic fibrosis unit, and those people spend all their time working with those kids. Marian Donahue, the CF social worker, gets really involved. She's a beautiful girl, but she chases all the men away because she just wants to give everything to those kids.

That's part of working at the hospital, meeting people like that. Barry and I talk about it all the time. We've got all kinds, we've got every extreme. There are people like Dr. Fredman, who's pretty crazy but also sort of a saint. He spends all his time at the hospital and never does anything to enjoy himself.

And then there are other people who are really selfish and go into medicine for the money and the prestige. A lot of surgeons are like that.

We have one neurosurgeon, Carl Gorman, who is just about the worst. Last Thanksgiving Day we had a kid whose brain was swelling up and she needed a screw put in to relieve the pressure. Otherwise she would have permanent brain damage. So the nurses on the ward called Dr. Gorman, who was the neurosurgeon on call, and told him to come over. He just out and out refused. He told them it wasn't a real emergency.

Then I got on the phone and started begging him to come. It took about ten minutes to persuade him. Finally he said he would do it, but only if I got everything set up ahead of time and if I put the football game on TV so he could watch it while he was doing the procedure. He put the screw in, and the kid turned out okay. And he watched that damn football game the whole time.

When you talk about the selfish people in medicine, that's the kind of guy you're talking about. And when you meet him, you'll find out he's not even embarrassed.

THE COLDEST CUTTER

DR. CARL GORMAN
Neurosurgeon

DR. STANLEY RUCKERT, Intern

He's a young guy, a loner, and most people don't like him. He's in his own little world. He's not a very smiling, happy sort of person. He has this reputation that he's a real bastard, but I haven't seem him live up to that. I mean, he's been available if I've needed him.

DR. HARVEY FREDMAN, Professor of Gastroenterology

He has the typical personality of a neurosurgeon. They are all cerebral types, and that's why I call them "cerebral surgeons." If you look at their role models, the people who are training them, they all have a very stern look about them, and Carl is very much like that. But despite this seeming aloofness, he is more than willing to talk when asked about the patients.

DR. CHARLOTTE KIRKHAM, Hematology Fellow

We were interns together, so I got to know him. This guy is totally obnoxious. He is also the original male chauvinist pig. I used to think my ex-husband, David Anzak, was pretty bad, but Gorman makes David look like a liberated man! A couple of times when I've seen him in the hall, Gorman's tried to pat me on the bottom. It's not sexy or affectionate, it's just patronizing. I get angry when he does it, but he doesn't even notice my reaction.

———————

The most notable feature of Carl Gorman's apartment was the human skull prominently displayed on the mantelpiece. In response to my questions, he assured me it was genuine—a souvenir of his neurosurgical training.

At thirty-three, Gorman maintained some of the awkward diffidence of an adolescent. Dressed in black slacks, white shirt, and a narrow black tie, he seemed to have a difficult time settling his gaunt frame into the living-room lounge chair. He told me several times that he felt uneasy about the interview and explained that he had never before participated in a tape-recorded conversation.

As we began, it proved impossible to extract articulate answers; in responding to even my most innocuous questions he offered only a few reluctant grunts and brief evasive phrases. After ten minutes of frustration, I decided to change tactics. I turned off the tape recorder for a few minutes, described my conversation with Nancy Proctor, and repeated her criticism of Gorman's response to an injured child.

As he listened to my account, Gorman's entire attitude changed abruptly. His crew-cut red hair seemed to bristle, his blue eyes widened behind the rimless glasses, and words poured forth.

Nancy Proctor is a good nurse, but unfortunately she gets hysterical. A lot of people in pediatrics get hysterical. They get so focused on their kids that they lose sight of the big picture.

I remember this incident very clearly. I was a resident at the time, and Nancy filed a complaint with the head of my department. Nothing ever came of it, because I didn't do anything wrong. The way I handled the patient was entirely appropriate.

This was a young girl that fell down roller skating and went into a coma. I put a little pressure monitor in her head. A few days later, she came out of the coma. But when Nancy called me she thought the patient was in trouble. I was home that afternoon watching the football game, a college game of some sort. I knew those nurses very well and they are always disorganized. Every time I go over there, I'll be cruising along and then I'll say, "Get me a syringe." And it's "Just a minute, doctor . . . we don't have one . . . we'll have to go up to the ward." And you have nothing to do but stand there and wait.

This time, I didn't want to wait. I wanted everything to be ready before I got there. There's nothing wrong with that. I wanted to teach the nurses to do it right.

I also wanted to see the end of that football game. I was sitting at home really enjoying it, and I don't get much chance to relax. If I had to go to the hospital before the game was over, I wanted them to put it on TV. The procedure with the little girl was totally mechanical, and I work better if there's some entertainment in the background. It helps my concentration.

That's standard procedure in the operating room, if you want to know the truth. Maybe people don't watch TV, but many of the surgeons bring cassette players and they listen to their favorite music while they work. We had a resident who finished up two years ago, an excellent neurosurgeon. He was from Texas and everybody called him Buffalo Bob. He was famous for listening to Elvis Presley and Johnny Cash while he worked on brain tumors.

I bought a good cassette player last year and I always listen to tapes when I'm in the OR. My favorite is *Die Walküre*. I love Wagner. The nurses hate it, but I tell them not to listen.

I learned music from my mother. She wanted to be an opera singer when she was younger, but she never made it. Today she's a housewife. My father is an attorney. They live in Minneapolis, which is where I grew up.

Looking back now, I can see how I got involved in medicine. When you're a freshman in high school you go to see your counselor and she says, "Well, what would you like to do with your life?" I had to think of an answer, quick. And I said maybe I'd like to become a doctor. And there was instant reinforcement. "Oh, that's great." After that, I didn't think about it but the idea stuck with me.

For college I went to Princeton, which was part of the family tradition. My father went there and my grandfather too. I worked hard and I did well and in junior year I met my girlfriend, Joyce. That's the most serious relationship I've ever had with a woman. She was a commercial artist in New York who did advertising illustration, layout. We saw each other every weekend, and when I went to medical school in Philadelphia, we kept up the relationship.

After med school, I got the offer to do my residency at Memorial. There was a good deal of prestige attached to that. I decided to go out to California, and she came with me. Then we got an apartment and moved in together.

In many ways, Joyce was my opposite. She is a flaming liberal. She is a very warm, very caring sort of person. I think I'm more analytical. I don't have a lot of patience with stupid people. She complained about that and said you have to be nice to everybody. I think I'm civil to most people, but I'm more direct than I am nice.

We lived together two and a half years, but there was always a strain. She wanted to be more a part of my life than she was. She wanted to come over to the hospital, meet me for dinner and whatnot. She wanted to know more of my deepest thoughts. I'm not sure I had a lot of extra-deep thoughts to lay on her. She felt that I was always holding back.

The relationship was obviously going downhill. Long about last spring, things weren't too good. Nothing was said, but I was sort of considering my options.

Then I got a two weeks' vacation in the month of June. Joyce wanted to get away to some romantic place, like the Virgin Islands.

I wanted to go home to Minneapolis. That's one of the most enjoyable things that I do. My mother waits on me hand and foot. We have a pool in the backyard and tennis courts right across the street. Joyce was welcome to come along, but she'd been to Minneapolis before and she didn't want to go.

So I went by myself, and when I came back she met me at the airport and said that she had moved out. It didn't bother me that much, because it didn't surprise me. I had sort of decided that we should chat about splitting up. So when she moved out, she was really saving me some hassles.

Since she left, I've gone out with several different people. I go out about once a week. Even if I'm tired, I try to make a point of it. I want a woman with a good head on her shoulders. I don't like women who are very quiet. I'm quiet, and if they don't say anything it's going to be a real dull evening.

The social occasions I enjoy most are when old friends from Princeton come to visit. I don't really have a lot of friends who I knock around with and whatnot. But I don't miss it because I'm so busy, and because of all the time I'm in the OR. The feeling there, when you're doing surgery, is just something hard to describe. I hesitate to say it, but it's almost a romantic sort of thing. In some respects it's very mechanical. But you've got a patient with a brain tumor, you take the brain tumor out, close it up, and have the patient wake up and recover. He's forever in your debt. It's like magic, but it's something you can really put your hands on. I like to use my hands. The operating room is a great place, for everybody except the patient. I mean, there are times when things don't end up right. Maybe the patient was so far gone by the time you got him that Jesus Christ himself couldn't come in there with a scalpel and save his life. But when things work out, and you do an elegant operation on somebody, it's such a high it's just incredible. You go out there whistling and you feel like you're right on top of the world.

We do all different kinds of operations. There are various kinds of openings in the skull, limited only by your imagination. You can do anything you want. Here, let me show you.

He took the skull down from the mantelpiece and brought it over to the couch. As he sat down beside me, he rested it on his knee and used the forefingers of both hands to trace imaginary lines on its surface. He explained surgical details with boyish enthusiasm and displayed more passion and excitement than at any other point in our conversation.

You can make a window over here or a window in the back. Take out a big hunk of bone. Both sides sometimes. Usually leave a strut here in the middle. You can take off any part of the skull that you want.

You're the surgeon, so you do it from start to finish. First you have to shave the head. You have to wash it, and then you start with a scalpel to open the scalp itself to get down to the bone. You make sort of a horseshoe and then you pull the scalp down over the face. Then you start working on the skull by drilling some holes. They are what we call burr holes. We have electric drills now and you go clean through the skull, but you have to be careful not to go too far on into the brain itself. That's call plunging.

Once you've got the holes, you're ready to saw. The hand saw we use is like a wire with teeth on it. You pull it through these holes and then you can cut out what's between them. And once you've done that, you can elevate the bone flap, like so. Then you outline an incision which eventually will get you down to see the brain proper.

You can take out a big portion of the brain, depending on the kind of tumor you're working with. You can take out part of the frontal pole, everything above the ears. You can also take off a lot of the occipital lobe, and the only problem would be blindness in half of each eye. But if you take out all of the two frontal lobes, you'll end up with a patient in a so-called lobotomized state—sort of a dull, dim-witted person.

For the most part, our patients don't die, at least not in surgery. Last year, my partners and I did operations on four hundred patients and we only had three operative deaths. In general, we patch 'em up and we get 'em back to their families. Or if they're dying of maligant tumors, they go to a nursing home and there are other physicians who take care of them from there. Sometimes we see a long downhill course, but it's not very common that we follow a patient to his demise.

I think we're getting pretty good in this business. We don't make a lot of mistakes. Once in a while you think, Jeez, we should have done a little better job on that fellow. But usually if he doesn't do as well as we'd like him to, it's because he had a malignant brain tumor that was going to kill him anyway. We tried our damnedest and we failed.

We get paid a lot for what we do, even in comparison to other doctors. I'm in my second year out, after finishing my training, and I'm expecting about two hundred and fifty thousand dollars. I'd say a good, established neurosurgeon in this area makes seven hundred and fifty thousand a year.

That's a lot of money, and that's one of the reasons that people don't like us. A lot of people you run into will say that the neurosurgeons are assholes. Maybe they say it about surgeons in general. I know they say it about me.

It's based on interpersonal relationships, more than anything else. We're just so busy. We don't have time for a lot of nonsense. And that's all you get around here most of the time, is a lot of nonsense. Somebody has a headache, and the medicine docs want you to come see if they have a brain tumor. It's true that a headache is a cardinal symptom of brain tumor, but it's also a symptom of stress or getting hit on the head with a hammer or whatnot. Most of the time it has nothing to do with brain tumors.

I don't go out of my way to make enemies. I just try to do my job. But I remember a couple of years ago when I was a resident, I was between cases in the operating room. I just had a few minutes and I ran down to the cafeteria to get some coffee and yogurt. One of the social workers came up behind me in the line and said, "Oh, Dr. Gorman! How nice! Could I eat lunch with you?" I said, "No," and ran straight back to the operating room. And I heard some comments about that—that I was stuck up and thought I was too far above her to be nice. That wasn't the case at all. I just don't have a lot of time to sit around and chat.

In some ways it's more difficult because I'm single. When the nurses find out, they are very nice to me until they figure out that I'm not going to take them out. I suppose I try to defuse some of their aspirations right at the beginning, by not being particularly warm to them. I try to be businesslike.

My mother used to say that I guard my words as a miser his gold. I have never been a very carefree sort of individual. Surgeons aren't supposed to talk much. We're not supposed to be happy and accessible. That's the stereotype. And I try to live up to it.

SPECIALTIES OF THE HOUSE

BECKY KRIEGER, Nurse

Of all the people in medicine, surgeons are the most action-oriented. They're very sure of themselves and very overbearing. The kind of guys that used to play varsity football and stuff like that.

This weekend, I had a little two-year-old who was going to have a minor but very painful procedure. To get her ready for surgery I thought they really needed to sedate her so she wouldn't move, but the surgeon said, "No. You just hold her down and we'll give her a local." Then they got this big eighteen-gauge needle in order to give her the local anesthetic. And I said, "My God! You're not going to use that needle to inject this poor child!" And the surgeon just started laughing and said, "That's right, honey, we're all barbarians! We all eat red meat for breakfast and use eighteen-gauge needles on infants." He thought it was really funny, and went right ahead.

DR. JACK BUCKMAN, Director of Emergency Medicine

In surgery, you have to live with your decisions. Once you're at the operating table there isn't an opportunity to fall back on anybody else's judgment. It's like a submarine commander. You get used to giving orders and keeping everybody moving along. It doesn't mean that there can't be levity or humor, but you know you're the guy in charge. Since you're living by your own judgment almost all the time you get very distrustful of anyone else's judgment. And that makes surgeons difficult people to get along with.

DR. ARNOLD BRODY, Director of Medical Oncology

As a group, surgeons are not too smart. Those are guys who learn how to put on a complicated pair of shoes and they can do it real good. They charge about four times what they should. The more benevolent among them often reduce their fee by a third or sometimes a half, which results in their being regarded as God's gift to the patients. At that point they're still being paid twice what they should.

There's a real macho streak in the surgeon's personality. These guys just love to operate; they really get their rocks off cutting on people. And they get a real bang out of walking out of an operating room with their greens on, a few bloodstains, a sweat-stained cap and neatly manicured nails. Coming out and telling the family, "We just got in there in the nick of time and we got it all." These are statements which bear relationship to the truth approximately five percent of the time.

Cardiologists are another strange breed. They're very technologically oriented. They get you plugged into so many gadgets so quickly it can make your head spin. They have a certain amount in common with other internists. And there's a witty definition that says an internist is the doctor that carefully documents the downhill course of a patient. They write real good notes on the chart—when they happen to be good doctors. When they're not good doctors they don't write good notes. The downhill course is inexorable and occurs anyway.

DR. STEVEN EBERSOLL, Radiologist

The internists have a very rough time. They just work harder than hell, you know. They deal with the dregs of the patients, a lot of old people, very sick. And these are probably the smartest guys in medicine. They're working really hard, and they're just tired. They get into kind of a trap, some of them, and they're not even making that much money. So a number of these guys come by to talk to me. They want to know how they can get into a residency in radiology. Because they're really unhappy where they are.

DR. ALLEN BARSAMIAN, Staff Psychiatrist

There are two kinds of men who go into obstetrics-gynecology. Some of them have a particular sensitivity and caring for women. But then there are others who do it precisely because it's difficult for them to identify with female patients. In other words, every disease he treats is a disease or a process that could never happen to him. When he's helping a woman through a painful labor, or ovarian cancer or breast cancer, he can have that detached stance because he knows he'll never be sick that way.

DR. REUBEN PESKIN, Director, Hospice Project

Since I've been active in our organization of gay physicians, I've gotten a good perspective on which specialties are most heavily represented. Of course, there are a lot of gay psychiatrists. There's an old joke that a gay man's two best friends, and his two worst enemies, are his mother and his therapist. Psychiatry has always been important in gay culture, and a lot of people went into therapy looking to be "cured." Naturally, gay physicians are attracted to that field.

Pediatrics is also an area where gay people tend to cluster. I think that a lot of gay men would have been very good parents. And one way, at least, to get some of those same satisfactions is to be a pediatrician.

DR. CHARLOTTE KIRKHAM, Hematology Fellow

The nurses are the ones who are constantly with the patient. We kind of whiz in and whiz out, and if we establish a close relationship during the time we're in the room, that's unusual. But in terms of laying on the hands, the nurses do it more than the physicians.

There's a stereotype of nurses, which is true for the most part. They're kind of flighty and not all that bright. A lot of them are there to get a doctor, and they work really hard for that. But meanwhile, they do a good job. They are decent, direct, emotional sort of people.

GEORGIANNA HARLAN, Ward Clerk, Translator

I know all the different specialties. I work on the pediatrics floor, where all the teams make rounds, because kids have everything there is. It's like a parade almost when they come through. And I don't even have to make an effort, but the doctors notice me. I've dated every kind of doctor. I can tell you there are some very big differences, very basic differences in personality. I never need the doctor to tell me what specialty he is, because I can tell. If we become intimate, I can tell for sure.

I've had the most experience with surgeons, and my ex-husband was a surgeon. They are very mechanical and very selfish. They have nicknames around here . . . we call them blades, or butchers. And that's just the way they are in bed. Wham, bam, thank you ma'am. Very fast and efficient and they act like the woman is under anesthetic.

Internists are the opposite. They are very bored and very easygoing and very intellectual. They always want you on top, they always want you to do the work. One time I went out with an internist, a resident, right after he got off work and we went to his place and I was up there just riding away and he just got limp all of a sudden. He said he couldn't help it, he was thinking of his patients, and then he fell asleep. He left me hanging there. Just hanging there.

Pediatricians are like big babies, but I haven't had so much experience with them. I meet lots of them but they don't go out with me so much because I have small boobs, and they all crave big boobs. They want to suckle there for hours, just returning to the state of babyhood.

Gynecologists are also funny. You would think they'd get bored looking at all those vaginas, but what they really like to do is go down on you. Every gynecologist I ever met, that's what he wants to do. It's like they have a relationship to women where they perform a service and they want to continue performing a service. Regular sex isn't so interesting to them.

I've only gone out with a psychiatrist one time, and never again. He just went completely limp, he couldn't get hard. We had to lie there and talk about it until I made him feel better and he could explain the whole thing. Not a very pleasant way to spend the night.

But then doctors in general aren't so great. I don't know why women go after them. It doesn't matter what specialty they are, in general they are lousy lovers.

THE SWEETHEART
OF WARD THREE

GEORGIANNA HARLAN
Ward Clerk, Translator

DR. CARL GORMAN, Neurosurgeon

She's a clerk on Ward Three. She attends a design school at night and she wants to be a clothing designer. I think she's a pleasant sort of person. Very earthy. I went out with her once. We had a good time, but nothing serious or intense.

DR. ALLEN BARSAMIAN, Staff Psychiatrist

I went out with her once or twice. I had a very good time but I don't think it's appropriate to say more than that. Let me put it this way: She is very free in her attitudes, very fun-loving.

DR. STANLEY RUCKERT, Intern

Georgianna is friendly and somewhat flirtatious, but she is also very selective. I've seen a lot of guys try to come on to her. She plays the game with them. They think they're really getting somewhere, but they're probably not. She's very good at shooting people down and sort of puncturing their egos, and that can be a lot of fun to watch.

I know Georgianna. Bright. Gracious. Relates well with people. She does all the translating for the pediatrics floor and she speaks a beautiful Spanish. She's not outstandingly pretty, like Charlotte Kirkham, but she is very sexy in how she relates to people. The way she walks, the way she smiles at you. Very intense. There's another side to Georgianna, with more of an attitude of cynicism. I know she's somebody who's had a lot of trouble in her life, but she's a very strong person.

———————

Georgianna Harlan lives in a tiny studio apartment decorated in classic bohemian style, with bean-bag chairs, a coffee table shaped from a redwood slab, and Picasso "blue period" prints on the walls. The room is dominated by a huge bird cage in one corner, which houses a cantankerous, continuously squawking parrot.

Despite her laments over the small size of her breasts, Georgianna Harlan nevertheless makes a voluptuous impression. Her hips and thighs were so generously sculptured that the thin cotton of her bright print dress strained visibly in the effort to contain them. With her thick black hair cascading to her waist, her pale translucent skin and huge brown eyes, she was a woman who would attract attention in any setting.

She served jasmine tea in tiny china cups, leaned back in one of the bean-bag chairs, and gathered her knees up to her chin, exposing a broad, smooth expanse of powerful thigh. Fiddling with a box on the coffee table, she withdrew a neatly rolled marijuana joint and lit it with a conspiratorial smile.

HARLAN ISN'T MY family name—that's my ex-husband's name. My real name is Dadarrio—which is just impossible. I'd like a new name, because "Harlan" isn't me. And I'm going into fashion design, and most designers have a little catchy name. So I'll think up something.

My father is a chemist who works for one of the lumber companies in Oregon. My mother is an obese, neurotic housewife in Kansas City who I haven't communicated with in the last thirteen years.

I was seven years old when they split up. All four of us kids went with my mother. She remarried and moved to Kansas City and we lived with my mom and stepdad and I was extremely unhappy living there. I ran away from home when I was fourteen. I went out to Oregon and moved in with my dad.

I was very mischievous in those days. I have always been real curious and I'm willing to try anything once. When I was fourteen I was smoking a lot of dope. Junior high school, ninth grade, I was getting high three times a day. I hung around with the gangs—though I always got good grades. But my dad found out what was going on. He took me down to the jail and said, "Look at this. If you get in trouble, that's where you end up."

So I quit. I quit all my friends. I quit doing everything. I had no friends at all. I had to make a transition. And that's the time that I met my husband. I was fifteen years old.

I got a job that summer working at Der Wienerschnitzel hot dog stand, and Eddie was working there too. I didn't like him at first because he was very much a playboy, very handsome. He was suave and intelligent, a very dominating personality. So I was really surprised when he asked me out. And we kind of hit it off from there. We'd steam our buns behind the bun steamer at work there, at Der Wienerschnitzel. We went on to other jobs after that, doing many different things, but we stayed together. Ended up living together when I was nineteen. I was in junior college by that time. My father was having problems with a woman he was seeing. Poor old Dad never did have good luck with the ladies! It was very unpleasant, so I moved out and got this little apartment near school. Eddie would stay with me one night a week. And then two nights a week. And then pretty soon it was seven nights a week. We lived together for three years without much responsibility on his part. He'd just show up whenever he felt like it. He was attending the University of Oregon, and majoring in biology, premed.

He was interested in medicine from the time he was a little boy. He always said he either wanted to be a doctor, or a bum on the beach, or a rich dope dealer. And these days he does a little bit of all three! Part of what appealed to him in medicine was the idea that doctors are kind of a sex symbol. I have great visions of his just screwing his way through the wards. At the same time, I know the girls are pretty disappointed. Which makes me feel pretty good. When we got married, when I was twenty years old, Eddie was the only person that I'd ever had sexual relations with. Since then, I've sampled a couple of others, and they sure are a hell of a lot better than he was.

Eddie had a really tough time getting into medical school. The only place that would take him was Guadalajara, in Mexico. That meant we had to move to Mexico, and before we moved we had to get married. We had a big dream of our future and how it would be. Our agreement was that I would put him through school and then he would put me through school. This dream is what kept me going. That when he was all done I could go through school and study fashion design and we could have a family. I always wanted a nice house and six little kids.

But it started to go wrong as soon as we moved to Mexico. I got a job as a seamstress, but it didn't bring in a lot of money. That was our only income, except for my father, who provided a little bit of help. So I had to work about fifty hours a week, and then I got a job teaching English.

We couldn't afford a place of our own, so we had to share a house with another medical student. That was okay. I can compromise. But it got to the point where I was playing housewife to both of them. I had to cook for both of them, do dishes for both of them. I even did the other guy's laundry by hand on a scrub board. Just having him there was very difficult. We'd get into bed and watch TV at night and there was this third person in the bedroom watching TV too.

That went on for a year and a half. Then I just exploded. I told Eddie I was going to go looking for another house, and if he wanted to come, fine, if not, that was also okay. I was the one paying the rent. So we moved far out into the country, and it was exquisite. We got a huge three-bedroom house to ourselves and paid forty-seven dollars a month for it.

He was in med school all this time and staying late at the library or the hospital, and I didn't see him too much. That was okay, because I was really busy and I was really enjoying my job. I still had these naive visions of him cherishing my love and being very faithful to me. But now, at twenty-seven, I know he was fooling around the whole time, and it's very disillusioning.

The second year we were in Mexico, Eddie sent me back to the States for the summer. He was going to stay and earn some money translating the ECFMG Course, which is for foreign medical students who want to get back into the States. So that summer I came up to San Francisco and worked. I had friends and they got me a job in a fancy dress shop and I could earn a lot more money working there for a few months than working in Mexico. I started going out at night with my girlfriends, going out dancing a little bit. Trying to be a human being. Otherwise I was just a machine, working to pay for Eddie's medical school. So I'd go out with my girlfriends, and one night, I felt that I needed something and I propositioned someone.

It was like Eddie sent me away to do it, almost. I really don't know what went on with him that whole summer. He could have done anything and everything he wanted to, and he probably did. But it was a turning point for me when I met this guy and I asked him to go to bed with me. I was very needy for some sort of physical affection. I just found someone that looked very attractive, but I knew that I wouldn't become involved with him. Physically, it felt good, but it also made me feel real bad because it was something I never wanted to have to do. In the whole three months I was there I probably slept with this guy maybe three times. But wouldn't you know it, I got pregnant, and went back to Mexico, and had to have an abortion.

Eddie never found out about it, because I was very careful to keep it a secret. He thought we could come back together and everything would be just the same. And it was the same, but that meant it wasn't very good. I was thinking a lot about my life, and I had big second thoughts about our arrangement. I didn't trust Eddie to live up to his promises. I struggled with our relationship for another six months. Then one day I was doing the dishes and Eddie was in the living room watching the old boob tube and sucking up a six-pack of beer, which he did a lot of on his time off. I walked in and told him that I wanted to go to school next semester and live by myself. He was just flabbergasted, shocked. He tried to talk me out of it, because I was his meal ticket, but two days later I packed up and went home to the States.

I went to San Francisco, because of my friends and because it sounded like a good place to live. The sister of our old housemate from Mexico worked for Memorial and she suggested that I apply there. Being that I spoke Spanish and they have a need for that, I got a job easily.

My official title is Unit Service Coordinator Number Three. Basically, I'm your ward clerk or secretary. I transcribe all of the doctors' orders onto a file that the nurses can refer to, to see what sort of procedures have been done on a patient and what sort of treatment they need. I schedule all the different procedures that have to be done. I work the desk area, which is the center of activity for the whole ward. I answer the phone and kind of run the show. I also do all the translating. I translate admission orders, or surgical and anesthetic consents. And instructions between nurses and mothers and the patients themselves. I've worked there two and a half years, and I get paid six-fifty an hour.

I like the constant hustle and bustle at the hospital. I like the contrast with my home environment, where I'm so relaxed and everything is much more easygoing. I like getting to know the nurses. It's the first time in my life that I've had a lot of girlfriends. There's a real feeling of closeness that grows up with the people who work together at a hospital, and I'm part of that team.

I haven't seen Eddie since we broke up—it's been more than two years. I took out a couple of loans to help pay for his medical school and I'm stuck paying them off all by myself. He's a resident in surgery at a hospital down in Los Angeles, but he won't help me.

I started dating doctors right after I came here. Basically, that's who I meet in this environment. There's something about them that I'm attracted to. There's something fascinating about a person who can function as a doctor with so many people and handle so many different situations.

The man I'm seeing now is a surgeon. He has atrocious hours, but he has a lot of plans for doing things in the future that I'd like to share with him. At the same time he diffuses his energy between so many different women that it's unsatisfying for me. He doesn't come close to meeting my needs. I would like some sort of secure partner, and he can't offer that to me. His medicine cabinet is full of different toothbrushes, including mine. No way is he ready to settle down.

I'm beginning to feel with this man the way I felt with Eddie. I'm just starting to think he's plain immature. Basically, our relationship is a one-way street. For his birthday, I embroidered the pocket of his lab coat. I put little billowing clouds around the name, with some sunshine on top, and there's a seagull sort of flying across the sun. And it has his name on it and "Department of Surgery." It was a lot of fun for me. Nobody else in the hospital has anything like it. I really expected when I gave it to him that I would get more than "Oh, thanks."

I support him in what he does but he doesn't support me. I'm under a lot of stress right now. I'm going to design school at night and I'm planning to leave the hospital in a couple of months so I can make my living as a designer, so there's a lot of pressure on me.

Smoking dope is like a release. I see a shrink periodically and she says it's perfectly fine for me right now. I don't need to worry about it at all. Every afternoon, I get a break a couple of hours before I get off work. I have three or four friends who are nurses, and we go out to the parking lot and get high. Sometimes a doctor will come over and join us. One fellow was a good friend, an intern who was on surgery at the time. In fact, he was covering neurosurgery in the emergency room that evening. And he wanted to talk to me about his girlfriend. So we went out to the parking lot and sat down on the ledge and got high. Just laughing and talking and smoking dope. Then he was paged to the emergency room. He was really stoned and he had to go in there and perform some minor surgery. He told me afterwards that he did just fine.

I'll miss the hospital, but I need to satisfy a whole other part of my life. There's no sense of personal accomplishment. But I get really involved, emotionally involved, with some of the people, and it's going to be real hard to give that up.

One example of that was a fifteen-year-old boy who came up with his mother from Nicaragua. He needed open-heart surgery, and I ended up translating for them for a couple of months. This boy was really delightful. They were also very loving when they were together. That was something I never had at home with my mother, so I enjoyed seeing it. They used to tease me about my Spanish, and correct me whenever I made a mistake. We really loved each other an awful lot. The boy and his mother brought me

Christmas presents, and I used to bring them little things whenever I could. Even on my days off, I'd call or come in just to keep up with him. The surgery seemed to go okay so he was discharged and then we said goodbye.

He came back the next year to have an adjustment on this artificial valve they had put into his heart. He was at the hospital for a good month before this second operation, and we got back together and visited a lot. His mom always came looking for me to translate, and the social worker came looking for me, and the cardiologist, and the surgeons, so I was there a lot of the time.

This time, the boy was scared shitless. So was Mom, although she never showed it to him. She'd come back to where I was working in the infant area at the time and let me know how scared she was. Then we'd go back to the room and she'd be real strong with her son, real confident. She was a short, very chubby mother, always giving him a lot of love, and a lot of prayer going on there, too.

He had his second surgery and afterwards they put him on an adult floor. I'd go up and see him every day at my lunch break. And I would even bitch at him if he was being too ornery.

And so I'd gone up one afternoon to visit, and it was three days post-op, and he was looking so much better, but he was really bothered with some pain in his shoulder. Anyhow, I went back downstairs and I went back to work. About half an hour later I heard a STAT page for 7 East ICU, which is where he was. That means it's an emergency, it's somebody's life or death. I knew there were six patients in that ICU so I tried to think it wasn't him. Then I heard them STAT page the pediatric cardiologist, and I knew it was him. I asked somebody to cover for me, and I got in the elevator, almost crying with worry. When I got to the unit, one of the nurses came rushing out and they opened the door. All I could see was a mass of people standing around. It was like red, solid red all around. They'd opened up his chest right then and there, and blood was over everything. They did their best. They were doing cardiac massage on him, but he was gone. And I couldn't work for the rest of the day, I was so upset. It really hurt me an awful lot, the way he died.

I've had a number of situations like that, where I've gotten real close to the patients and things just go wrong. I know it's changed me. You get more of a sense of perspective on life. I think I'm a more mature person than I was when I started. I think I'm a pretty mellow woman overall.

The only problem is hooking up with the right kind of man. I'm still waiting for my Prince Charming to come along and sweep me off my feet and make me live happily ever after. My shrink told me I was meant to be a princess.

One thing I know for sure is that it's not going to work with this fella I'm with right now, and I'm going to have to start looking outside the hospital. I've finally come to the point where I almost refuse to go out with a doctor. I don't even look anymore. I'm not interested. I know some women who have gotten so frustrated that they've tried relationships with other women, just on an experimental basis. It's crossed my mind too, because I've seen a couple of sexy movies and you keep hearing about it. It wouldn't really interest me at this point, but I don't know about the future. I really enjoy sex an *awful* lot. In fact, I'm horny *all* the time, but I've got to have quality at this point in my life. And I'm definitely having a very dry spell.

That doesn't mean that the doctors are giving up on me. They still come around, they still show an interest, especially the new ones. The only one who's never approached me in that way is Dr. Fredman. He's just about the only one, married or single. And I like him for that, but you can see that it's just part of his personality. He's not really interested in dating or partying or friends or anything else outside of work. He's kind of a mystery man around here. You see him cruising through at three in the morning. Even though he's been around for years and years, nobody understands what makes him tick.

THE MAD MONK

DR. HARVEY FREDMAN
Professor of Gastroenterology

DR. STANLEY RUCKERT, Intern

Dr. Fredman just looks crazy. He's tall and he's got these wild eyes and this gray hair just shooting up out of his head. This is a gentleman who puts the capital O and the capital C in "Obsessive-Compulsive." He may also be the best all-around doctor I've ever met. His patients get the best treatment of anybody in this hospital. He never lets go, he's working all the time. He's famous for sleeping on a cot in his office; he's here seven days a week when he's not off lecturing in Japan or God knows where.

NANCY PROCTOR, Nurse

My husband, Barry, is doing his GI fellowship under Dr. Fredman, and he comes home every night very depressed. Fredman is such a slave driver that Barry can't take it. This guy doesn't have anybody to go home to, so he doesn't want any of his fellows to get home either. He just started psychoanalysis and I think it's helping him. For the first time, he's going out on dates. He's called me up on occasion and asked me if I thought certain nurses would go out with him. It's kind of hilarious. Here's a man in his forties, a world-famous doctor, and he's calling me to try to line up dates!

Women in general don't want to get involved with him because he has no time. It would be like emotional suicide, marrying him.

BECKY KRIEGER, Nurse

The patients he treats are real train wrecks. He does very, very aggressive treatment with them and a lot of times they wouldn't live if it weren't for him. All of the nurses, and the interns too, are scared to death of Dr. Fredman. He can be very abrupt, and he throws tantrums when he gets mad. But the longer I work with him, the more I see his concern. You can see by the way he stops and talks when he's making rounds. He's really a very gentle, caring man.

DR. HARRISON O'NEILL, Gastroenterologist

Harvey is a freak, a deformation. Thalidomide babies are born without arms—Harvey has arms, but no personality. As a doctor he's about the best. He's in all the journals and textbooks, and he lectures all over the world. But he's just a sad kind of guy who's a failure as a human being. So he runs and hides by being a super doc.

Dr. Harvey Fredman resembled the popular caricature of a mad scientist—including bald pate with a fringe of unkempt gray hair, horned-rim glasses perched on a bulbous nose, and ill-fitting lab coat.

His office displayed the same air of eccentric disarray as his person. Before I could be seated on the one chair available for visitors, he had to clear away a stack of papers, books, and journals. He fumbled with a hot plate, kettle, and Styrofoam cups, preparing instant coffee for both of us. As he spoke, his full lips drew back to reveal a set of widely spaced teeth twisted into a shy smile. That smile remained constant even during the most painful aspects of his narrative.

We met at eleven P.M. on a Thursday night, when the only other person on his floor of the medical office building was an elderly cleaning lady. As she passed Dr. Fredman's door, she greeted him like an old friend.

SHE KNOWS ME because I stay late a lot of the time. Usually I'm the only one. But it's not true that I sleep in the office! You can look around. There's no cot, there's no couch. For the last two years, since I started analysis, I haven't slept here once. Before that, I would stay all night maybe once a month. Sometimes you just can't help it. I'd be here till four in the morning with a sick patient and it didn't make sense to go home.

I still get difficult situations but I handle them differently. On Tuesday night I had three critical patients and we were here till three in the morning. But I did go home afterwards, because I've learned to trust people more than I used to. If I get good colleagues around me, I can leave them alone and trust them to do what needs to be done. Now I can get away from this place, without thinking about it every minute while I'm gone. I used to call up all the time whenever I went away. I didn't trust anybody, but I'm not like that anymore. I'm going away in December for three whole weeks and I have no qualms about it. I'm going back to Cleveland for my nephew's bar mitzvah, then after that I'm going to a cousin's wedding.

That shouldn't give you the wrong idea. I'm not really tied to my family. I've thought about them a lot in analysis. My parents were both born in America, but their parents were immigrants. They were sort of that in-between generation. My father spent forty years in the fruit and vegetable business in Cleveland. When we were growing up, we always felt more comfortable with my mother's family. They were younger, more educated, more middle-class.

My parents have been married forty-eight years. The first twenty years were very rocky, and God, it was terrible. I swore that if I ever got married I would never fight like my folks fought. They used to fight about money. My dad made a reasonable income, but it was never enough. He gambled a great deal. I think he was driven from the house. My mother was always nagging him, plus the fact that her three sisters used to live with us. And my mother was foolish, because she used to side with her sisters and not with my father.

Money was always a big issue. When it came time for me to go to college that was the main consideration. I was a good student in high school, so I could have gone anywhere, but my parents wanted me to stay in Cleveland so they could save money. I did what they wanted, but when I decided to go to medical school it was the same thing all over again. I wanted to go to the University of Michigan, but they wouldn't help me if I went away from home. They wouldn't even give me a loan. But I knew I had to leave Cleveland. I decided then and there that I would not let a major decision be affected by the question of dollars. When I told my parents what I was doing, my mother was terrible for a couple of weeks. Carrying on about leaving home and rejecting them. But I broke the ties. And the ties have stayed broken.

I'm not close to any of them anymore. To this day, my brother and I compete. He's four years older than I am, and he's a very successful businessman. A multimillionaire. If I'm speaking someplace, then he's going to speak in three places. If I'm in *Who's Who,* he was in *Who's Who* first. It's gone on like this for years. I know that I'm more internationally famous than he is, but I'm not sure he acknowledges that. We're on speaking terms, we see each other a few times a year, but that's it. My parents still hold him up as an example to me. They just can't say that he's successful in his way, and I'm good in mine.

I see their effect on me in a lot of ways. Money is an obvious thing. I have a tendency not to spend it, even when I have it. I feel guilty if I go out and spend money on something for myself. At the same time, I don't think about money when it comes to my professional decisions. I get paid by the medical school on a straight salary. I make sixty thousand dollars a year right now. In terms of patient fees that I bring in, the medical school collects about a hundred and eighty thousand every year. So you could say I make a sacrifice to teach here, but I don't see it that way. If I went out and set up my own office, I would not have the same opportunities I've had here.

I enjoy teaching young people, trying to influence their career choices. That is something you cannot measure in dollars and cents; it's something I can only measure in my head and my heart. When someone says, "That young doctor you trained five years ago is just terrific," I feel good, because he responded to my ways, and he's doing the kind of job I expect from him.

I used to feel I was in competition with people that I was training, but now I never have that feeling. Maybe it's because I've crossed the forty line and the people I'm training are in their late twenties, early thirties. Maybe it's because of analysis. I have come to realize that I don't have to prove myself anymore. I still write more than any of the people that I train, even now. And a lot of it has actually helped prolong life in a productive manner for people who formerly would have died or would have had a miserable existence. There is nothing that makes you feel so good as for a treatment to work out well and the patient to get better and to feel better and to look better. I get a big kick out of it.

In my area we get a lot of patients who are very, very sick. I have an official title as Chief of Parenteral Nutrition. We work with central venous catheters, these plastic tubes that we feed into the patient's heart as a means of giving them their nutritional needs. It's an area that I sort of fell into when I first came here in '73. I was seeing a lot of problems with our patients getting infected in the hospital, because the technique was new. The doctors and the nurses didn't know the optimal way to care for these catheters. I just took it upon myself that this was going to be something I was going to straighten out. There was nobody else to do it, and I didn't wait for a committee to tell me what to do. I set up my own protocols for care, and I worked with the nursing staff and I went floor by floor showing people how to take care of these central lines. Over a year's time, the infection rate came down dramatically. I wrote an article, and now most of the hospitals in the world are using these techniques I developed.

If I died now, I know that some things I've achieved are going to stay in the medical textbooks indefinitely. Maybe somebody else would have done what I did, but most people aren't as hard-driving as I am. The absence of a family, the absence of my being able to relate to women readily, created a situation where I gave all my time and energy to medicine. So I could do three weeks' work in one week. And I don't have any guilty feelings about outside hobbies or interests that I haven't pursued.

But I always had a very hard time relating to women. I went out a very limited extent in high school and college. I went to some dances, I went to parties. But I could never get close to any of the women.

My wife was probably the only woman outside my family that I've had a close relationship with. She was an only child in a very wealthy family. Her father was a doctor but he died when she was twelve years old, and she was raised by her mother, who's a very lovely and very educated woman. They lived in South Africa, they were South African Jews. And one of the hardest things for my wife when she was growing up was the idea that she had a physical deformity. She had one leg that was shorter than the other so it was difficult for her to walk. Other than that she was an attractive woman with a pretty face. She was also very intelligent. She went to medical school in South Africa and then came to the United States to do her residency. She was working as an anesthesiologist when I met her.

I was doing a fellowship in a hospital in New York. I had a painful ganglia on my wrist, so I went into surgery to have it cut out. She was the anesthesiologist on duty, and I liked her right away. It was a very lonely time in my life, so when they were getting ready for the operation I asked her if she would go out with me.

I went with her a little over a year before we decided to get married. Now I can admit to myself that I didn't really love her, probably just liked her. I thought that whatever discomfort I had with her would probably pass. She had never been with a man before. I went on one trip with her to Canada, trying to get her to sleep with me, but she wouldn't.

We got married in Johannesburg and then we went to Europe for three weeks on our honeymoon. Right away, she started to have hallucinations; she started to have delusions of me as her father, who had died when she was twelve. It was bizarre, especially when I was having intercourse with her. She wasn't kidding, she really thought I was him. It was very frightening, and it persisted. I had to give her injections of antipsychotic drugs in London, and the last two days in England I had to hire a nurse to help take care of her. I finally got her back to New York, put her in the hospital, and went through group therapy with her. Then she came out of the hospital and seemed to settle down.

She went back to being an anesthesiologist at the hospital, but something happened that made me decide that I just didn't want any part of it anymore. I was supposed to go to Boston for three weeks to attend a specialized and highly competitive course in immunology. I thought she was well enough so she could come up and join me on weekends. Well, she just became very depressed and tried to get me to give up the course. She said she was going to kill herself, and I was afraid she meant it, so I gave up my trip.

After that I decided I couldn't let my career get ruined by staying with this woman. I knew I had to bail out before I ended up getting her pregnant and getting myself caught. We stayed together for a while longer but I isolated myself sexually. Then I got the offer of the job at Memorial. I wanted to move to California, but she wanted to stay in New York. One night she said, "If you don't change your ways, I'm going to go home to South Africa." So I said, "I'm not asking you to go, but if you walk out now, you're never going to come back." At about five o'clock that morning she left for the airport, but three hours later she called and said she wanted to come back. I said no, I don't want you back. After that she was rehospitalized and as soon as she got out I filed for divorce.

That was eight years ago. After that I left New York and I was feeling a lot better. I came to Memorial, and I thought everything was okay. But in 1978, Reuben Peskin, who's a psychiatrist on staff, came up to me and said, "You know, you ought to go into analysis. I've been noticing how exhausted and irritable you've become. What's driving you to work so very hard?"

I thought about it then, but I didn't have time for analysis. I was working till three and four o'clock in the morning every single day. But then something else happened that got me worried about myself. There was a very successful surgeon, killed himself right here in his office. I kept thinking that something like that could happen to me. Then in September and October of '79 I began to get precardial chest pain. I said to myself, what am I doing to myself? I don't want to put myself in a grave, so something's got to give. Why am I working like I'm crazy? I want to know why, and I want to alter my behavior.

That was how I really got started in analysis. It's been two years now, and it's been very useful for me. Analysis is restructuring; it takes a long time. I got the way I was over many years. But I've started to change.

I make a big point now of getting out of the hospital. A lot of times I'll still work late, but on Friday evening I get out of here at six o'clock. I go home, take a shower, and put on some music; later I get dressed and go out. I've got some friends, a man I knew from high school in Cleveland, who's a lawyer with a nice wife and three kids. I go out to dinner with them or we eat at their home. After dinner maybe we'll go to a movie or maybe I'll go alone. Or else I'll come home and do some reading. I get the *Wall Street Journal* now so I'll be aware of things outside medicine. I save my *Journals* from the week and then I read them all on Friday night.

I get up late on Saturday morning, and I go shopping and do some of the things that I have to do to keep my life going. I stay away from the hospital until Saturday afternoon, so I have a pretty good break away from here.

I also go out on dates. Almost every week. I really want to meet someone and get married again. I want a family. I haven't met anybody yet, but I'm not giving up. It's extremely difficult to meet people outside of the profession, and most of the people who go out with me are nurses or doctors. That's a problem, because people from the hospital know all about me. They know what I've done, and they don't respond to me as just Harvey Fredman, man. It's like they are looking at your résumé and not really looking at you.

But my relationships inside the hospital have gotten a lot better. Most people call me by my first name, which I think is a good thing and to me means I've managed to bridge the gap. Sometimes they tease me and I know they make jokes about me behind my back, but I don't mind it. It makes me feel sort of like I'm accepted.

Fredman became suddenly quiet and stared out his office window. He began to weep softly with a hand over his eyes. I shut off the tape recorder and offered to leave, but he insisted that I stay. "In two minutes I'll be fine," he said. "It's just hard to talk about all this." He reached into his desk drawer, removed a box of Kleenex, and blew his round nose three times with savage force. Then he returned to his narrative as if nothing unusual had occurred.

Like I told you before, the students are very important to me. I figure I'm a good role model in terms of my involvement with the patients. What we need is more people to show them what a physician is really supposed to do. I don't think doctors spend enough time talking and listening to their patients. It always surprises my fellows and the students when patients come back to visit me after a couple of years. I always remember the patient and his family. I ask about his kids and what they're doing, and I ask about his job. I remember all kinds of little things. I'm sincere in it, but it also shows the patient that you care about him as an individual, and not just some Joe Smith with chart number so and so.

That concern is something you can't teach. I have a hard time getting the house staff to sit down for two hours and take a detailed medical history of the patient and the family. Often, that will give you the answer to your problem, and save a patient several days in the hospital, and thousands of dollars in tests. But young doctors just don't want to do it. They're impatient. When we get one who really cares, it's more of an exception than a rule. Right now there's only one of the interns I can think of who really fits that description. His name is Stanley Ruckert and he's very bright and very concerned and sort of a special friend of mine. He has the right kind of involvement with the patients, and in this current group, he's the best of the bunch.

THE TEDDY BEAR

DR. STANLEY RUCKERT
Intern

DR. MONICA WILKINSON, Chief Resident, Pediatrics

He's a teddy bear. He's really sweet. He's also a very capable intern. A lot of times the interns get very arrogant, like they already know everything they need to know. Stanley's not like that at all. He seems like he's more vulnerable.

DR. LANNY BUCKMAN, Pediatric Resident

He's married to Kathy Merkin, who's also an intern. She seems about twenty years older than he is and twenty years more mature. She's more formal and businesslike. He's more outgoing and more smiling and warm. He's from Indiana, and sometimes he pretends that he's just a country boy who doesn't understand what's going on. But he's actually very smart, though I do think his wife is much smarter than he is. She certainly is more sure of herself.

BECKY KRIEGER, Nurse

Dr. Ruckert is one of the nicest interns in that new group. You see it when he talks to the patients, and you see it when he talks to other people on house staff.

The other night one of the women was having a rough time. She's an intern, but her husband's not in medicine. She was saying that he started complaining because she's never at home. She was feeling sorry for herself. And then about an hour after she came onto the wards, she just went into the ladies' room and burst out crying. When she came out, Stanley was walking down the hall. He saw she was upset so he just came up and they put their arms around each other. They started comforting each other. Afterwards, she told me that just the fact that he put his arms around her, and patted her on the back, and said he was going through the same thing, made her feel a whole lot better.

———————————

Exhausted after twenty-four hours on call, Stanley Ruckert leaned back on the sofa and sipped at his Diet Pepsi. With his barrel chest, curly blond hair, and large, slightly mournful brown eyes he seemed to live up to the teddy-bear image. He explained that our interview happened to fit comfortably into a gap in his schedule. Having just left work himself, he had to wait another three hours before his wife finished her work at the hospital. He wanted to stay awake so that they could take advantage of one of their rare opportunities to eat dinner together.

In the late-afternoon light, their modest apartment appeared to be unusually tidy. The magazines were stacked neatly at the edge of the glass coffee table, and the carpet had been freshly vacuumed. In response to my question, Ruckert said that he, rather than his wife, took primary responsibility for keeping the place neat.

THAT'S THE WAY I am. I've very compulsive about my work and my environment. Everything has to be in place or I can't handle it. Let me put it this way: I have gotten where I am today only because I worked real hard. I really respect people who can read things once and then remember them. We had people like that in high school, but while they goofed off I was hustling. I had to study all the time to stay at the top of the class. Then I got to college and I was really afraid of all the brilliant people. But I found that by pushing myself and putting in a couple of extra hours every day, I could do as well as they could.

College meant a lot to me, and I took my classes really seriously. I got a lot of ribbing from a lot of people because of that. But to me, college was important. I grew up on a farm and went into the city to go to school. My father works as a maintenance man and my mother is a housewife. All four of my grandparents were immigrants from Austria. They all came over in the years just before World War I.

It was my mother who decided I was going to be a doctor. She has a genetic disease, retinitis pigmentosa, and she is blind from it. My mother is a very bright person, and she is very frustrated and stifled because of her blindness. She always thought it would be wonderful if her son could be a doctor and maybe cure some of these diseases. My father came to the same idea from another direction. To him doctors were upper-class people who made lots of money and had good lives. I think these two things combined and I was pushed into it. When I excelled in school at an early age, they both said, "Oh, you ought to be a doctor."

I went to the University of Indiana. I was the first person in my family who ever went to college. I worked my way through, and money was always a big factor. Then I got a scholarship to go to medical school in California. Since it was free this is where I wanted to go, but I was sort of disappointed after I got here. I didn't like the people I was thrown in with—my classmates at med school. I guess I expected them to be knights in shining armor or whatever. I at least expected them to be what I would consider regular people. But a lot of them were very egocentric; some of them didn't even say hello. They were just cocky people, and I don't like cocky people. I remember thinking, when these guys become doctors, I don't want them working on my family!

I see some of the same traits in some of the doctors at the hospital. There's a callousness, a lack of concern. I see people working for their own ego, not for the patient. These people are more into how a certain chest operation is going to affect the outcome of their research project than how it's going to affect the patient.

One example sticks out in my mind. We had a fifty-year-old schizophrenic gentleman, who waxed and waned, and was not really mentally cognizant by any legal standards. He had cancer of the colon; he was going to die from it and there was nothing we could do. He'd had chemotherapy, radiation therapy, the whole shot, and it was time to lean back and let him have a dignified death. He was cared for primarily by his eighty-year-old mother, who was a very sweet old lady. It really turned my stomach the way they kept this guy going. They should have just fed him, put him on a morphine drip, and let him slip under in a dignified manner. He didn't know what was going on anyway. But the residents would not let him go. They wanted to keep working on him for their own sake. There was one resident in surgery who convinced the patient's mother that he could do an operation which would relieve the obstruction of his bowels. "We can take care of the problem," he said. He really led this little old lady, who wasn't too with it herself, to believe that her son was going to be cured.

This resident wanted to do an end-to-end anastomosis of the bowels, removing a big section and then reconnecting it. He'd never had a chance to do that operation before. He went ahead and prolonged this poor guy's agony with this horrible operation. I wanted to stop him, but I'm just an intern and there was nothing I could do. The patient died about four weeks later, but the resident got the chance to do his big operation.

I was really appalled by that. I couldn't stop thinking about it. I don't want to sound corny, but working with the patients still feels like a privilege to me. To enter people's lives, to do your best to help them, that really makes me happy. Maybe I'm just too sensitive over the few bad apples that you meet. I'm still young and eager, and whatever, but I hope I'll never change and start looking at everything as another part of the job.

When I lose patients, I hurt for them. At the same time I recognize the cycle for what it is, for life and death and birth and all. I know there's only certain things I can do, but it doesn't stop you from hurting.

Sometimes we get patients who are right on the borderline. There's a man here now who's been here for eight months, and it's hard to decide whether he's better off alive or dead. The patient is sixty-three years old, one of the wealthiest guys around. He's a lawyer who used to be on the city council. He always liked to live a fun life, and about three years ago he left his wife and his three daughters and jetted off to France with his twenty-five-year-old mistress. When he was in Europe he got a case of diverticulosis, which is an infection of the gut. He was too busy having a good time to get treatment, so he wound up with bacteria in the bloodstream, which finally settled in his brain. He had this huge brain abscess, and he was in a coma when they brought him in. His family brought him here because they didn't think he would get such good medical care in Europe, and they had to sort of kidnap him away from the mistress. When he came in, we put a hole in his skull to see what was there. We nicked the dura, which is the covering of the brain, and green pus shot up maybe seven, eight inches. We evacuated just a ton of pus out of there. Now he can move his eyes, but that's about it. He has total amnesia. He has very limited brain function. He has a vocabulary of about thirty words, but sometimes he can't speak at all. He can't swallow, so he has to be fed by a tube and he's wasted down to eighty-nine pounds. I must have spent a hundred hours with him, but he still doesn't recognize me. He doesn't know his own name.

In the time he's been here, I've seen his wife and his daughters age about ten years. Because even with everything that happened, they still care about him and they visit him just about every night. I think maybe it would have been better if he had just expired. It's not just a question of his pain and what he is going through, but also the suffering of the people that are involved with him, the family. And I think that's very real and very significant.

When you work at a hospital about a hundred and twenty hours a week you start having a whole new attitude toward death. You start to realize that it's not always the worst thing that can happen. The first time I lost a patient I was a third-year medical student here at Memorial. This gentleman had come in because all of a sudden he got hoarse. We did a chest X-ray, and there were cannonballs in his lungs. That's a term we use for these huge tumors. This guy was pretty happy when he first came in, he looked good and he was working full-time, but once we checked him into the hospital he started going downhill in a hurry. He had big-time metastases from these cannonballs, with the cancer spreading all over his body.

I was the one who had to tell him he had cancer. I was only a medical student, but the intern and the resident dodged the issue and left it up to me. And right away, the patient asked me how long he had to live. I told him we didn't know. For every person who's going to die on schedule there's two who defy the odds—they either go more quickly or they just go on and on, and, as they say, miracles do happen. So I told him yes, he was terminal, but he had a fair amount of time, and I called his wife and she called the rest of the family. They were good people, working people; I could relate to them very well, and the family started relating to me as their personal physician.

And one day as I was sitting with him, he started having a seizure. I sent him down for a brain scan, but after that he deteriorated quite rapidly. He had his first seizure on a Thursday, and by Saturday he was out of it most of the time, and starting to have some difficulty breathing. I had to give him Valium intravenously, and the family understood that it looked pretty bad.

On Saturday night my wife and I were supposed to go out to dinner. We got dressed up and we drove to the restaurant, but on the way I said, "Oh hell, I want to go by the hospital and see this guy." The resident was shocked that I came in on my own time and he said, "There's really nothing you can do." I said, "I know that, but I wanted to hold his wife's hand for a few minutes and talk with her."

Then the next day I came in and he was completely comatose. On top of everything else he had a superimposed pneumonia. He was on oxygen and he was having a really tough time breathing. I went in to see the resident and said, "Look, cut the oxygen." I knew that would allow the patient to die, with a respiratory arrest. He was end-stage disease and the family had expressed a strong interest that nothing be done of a heroic nature. They didn't want us to do anything except keep him comfortable and reduce his pain. The resident said, "We could intubate him, and put a tube down his throat and maybe we can get him over this pneumonia." But then the intern came in and he agreed with me, and the resident finally said, "Okay, if that's what you want to do."

This was Sunday morning. It's funny, because I can even remember the time. It was eleven-oh-five, and everything was real quiet like it is sometimes on Sunday morning, and I went in there and turned off the oxygen. Then I sat down and stayed around until he died at twelve twenty-six. One hour and twenty-one minutes. And during the last part his wife came in, and he opened his eyes and saw her. Then he took two deep gasps and closed his eyes and very quietly died.

It was so gentle and calm, it just didn't bother me. But something else got me upset and took my mind off what happened. Because I was just a medical student, I couldn't pronounce this man dead. An intern came in who was pretty much a stranger to the family and did the job very matter-of-factly. He checked the body, then went to the family and said, "Well, he's dead." It got me mad because any fourth-grader can learn to pronounce a patient dead, and it was like my special place with the family had been usurped.

I do wish I got more recognition, more appreciation than I do. People very rarely express their gratitude for what you've done, the extra work and the concern and the devotion you show for a patient. And it hurts. When people are leaving the hospital after four or five weeks, they barely have time to say goodbye. But that patient has been a big part of your life during that time, that family has been very important to you.

You know, none of these people has ever paid me a cent directly. They pay their private physician, they pay the hospital, but the people who really sweat over them and are there at three in the morning don't get any money and don't get any recognition either. I get paid less than fifteen thousand dollars a year. That's a typical intern's salary, and my wife, Kathy, gets the same thing. I accept the situation, and I try not to get depressed. I think one of my strengths is that I can practice medicine as it has to be practiced without letting other things interfere. I can shut out whatever else is going on in my life. If things aren't going that great, and you don't feel your life is going right, you can still be somebody special in somebody else's life—you can still be a doctor.

That's why some people like to hang around the hospital even when they don't have to be there. As many hours as I have to work, I still spend extra time just by choice. Sometimes I stay late just because I need to gear down from the pressure. If it's been a very rough day, it's good to take some time talking to people and just having a chance to relax, rather than rushing right home to collapse.

Kathy feels the same way, and a lot of times I'll be expecting her at nine o'clock, and she won't be home till ten-thirty, maybe eleven. That's what you get for marrying another doctor! I knew from the beginning there were going to be trade-offs. We met in med school, first year. At first I didn't like her, because she seemed egotistical and competitive and I didn't think she had a sense of humor. Then I saw she was really dedicated about medicine; she's more intense, more hard-nosed than I am. We still didn't go out together, because she was about three inches taller than me—in fact, she still is taller than I am! But that didn't matter after we started doing things together and talking about our work. We've been married now for two and a half years, and the only problem is the time we have to spend in the hospital. Right now Kathy is in the nursery, so she's on call five nights a week. And on those nights the only chance we have to see each other is at dinnertime. We have dinner together at seven o'clock at the hospital cafeteria and then we have to go back to the wards right away. I'm usually asleep by the time she comes home. Saturday is her day off, but she's usually so exhausted that she sleeps straight through. Then Sunday, I'm on the wards until three. It's been four months since we spent a whole weekend together!

A lot of times I'm really glad that we're both in medicine. It's nice that when I come home and I'm upset, and I want to bitch and complain, that the person at home really understands. But sometimes I think how I'd like to come in and sit down to dinner and have somebody pamper me. Right now, with Kathy and me, every little thing turns into a major production. I mean, going to the post office to buy stamps, or stopping at the bank, or cooking dinner, whatever it is, we have to schedule it and decide which one of us is going to do it. The way it's worked out I take most of the responsibility for washing or cleaning or whatever.

And there's a problem with our sex life. It stinks right now. If one of us is turned on, then the other one is turned off. I find sex is a release from pressure, but Kathy doesn't get into it when she's pressured. So I'll come home really upset and really want to get into it, but she'll be feeling down and she'll say no. Other days she'll really be up for it but I'll have a ton of things to do around the house or I'll want to go jogging or go out to dinner and get out of the apartment. It works out maybe twice a month, sometimes less. And that's no good. I'm twenty-seven years old and I've got a normal sex drive, so it's frustrating.

I do want to be married to her, but sometimes I wonder. I think about what it would've been like if I had married some pretty nurse who wanted to be a housewife. What's so terrible about that? I'm really a warm sort of cuddly person, so I wouldn't mind having some cute little wife who just adored me. Maybe it wouldn't seem as exciting as being married to a doctor, but what's so exciting when you never see each other?

The worst part is worrying about the future. When we first got married we talked about having kids when Kathy finished her residency. She'd be thirty then, and we wanted two or three kids. Then, in the middle of the internship, she changed her mind. She decided she didn't want babies because she didn't want to interrupt her career. She decided to go into pediatrics and get exposure to children in that way, and get better satisfaction because you have a lot more kids to deal with than just two or three.

I respect that and I accept it, but where does that leave me? I always wanted a family. To think that I'll never have one gives me a lonely feeling. A lot of times medicine gives me a lonely feeling. You're taking care of people all day, but who's going to take care of you?

I think that loneliness is part of the job. We learn to live with it. But that's why so many people get involved in affairs, and having sex right in the hospital. It's a way you get companionship, a way you get relief. It's not something that appeals to me, but I see it all the time.

SEX SYMBOLS IN WHITE

DR. STANLEY RUCKERT, Intern

Outside the hospital, it always impresses people when you say you're a doctor. It's a great way to start a conversation in a bar or whatever. I've got a friend who's got his line all worked out. He meets a girl, and he says he's a plastic surgeon. He's really a urologist, but he starts talking about tummy tucks and boob jobs and then he'll say, "Gee, you have nice breasts," and he'll go on from there.

Inside the hospital, everything is so highly charged that people are thinking about sex all the time. Last Wednesday this one nurse goes walking past while I'm sitting down real tired and the way she swings her hips sort of wakes me up. Later on, at about four in the morning, she helped me put in an IV. I said she was really nice, and she said, "Thank you, but I was really upset with you a while ago." I asked her why, and she says, "Because a picture came out of all the new interns, and I looked at your picture and I thought you were really a doll. Then I found out you were married to her, to Kathy Merkin!"

It was very flattering, but I don't think the nurse really cared that I was married. I'll admit I was a little tempted. But things are too close. I mean, my wife could walk onto the ward at any time. It'd just be too dangerous.

BECKY KRIEGER, Nurse

I would be very nervous being married to a doctor. They work in an environment where there are so many women around, and I see how some of them behave. It all comes back to power. Doctors are calling the shots. A lot of women want to hook themselves on to that. It's often said that the guys who are the biggest studs at Memorial, you wouldn't even look twice at them out on the street. But within this atmosphere, they are hot stuff. We work in the kind of situations where barriers break down quickly.

PEGGY HAGERTY, Head Nurse, Delivery Room

Two weeks ago I helped my aunt check in for some cardiac surgery. She was pretty upset, so the whole family took her up to her room. But when we went through the door there was a man sitting on the bed. He was wearing a white coat and he had a beeper on, which made me think he was a resident. He said, "Excuse me. I didn't know anybody was checking into this room. Would you wait a minute, I need to use the bathroom." Then he went into the bathroom and locked the door.

This is all very unusual, so I took my family down the hall to the nursing station and told them to wait there. I got back to the room just as the guy was coming out of the bathroom. He says, "Don't worry. I'll go get someone from housekeeping to clean up the bathroom. Just sit tight for a few more minutes." Then he exits stage left. About two seconds later a woman comes out of there, sort of brushing her hair. And she says, "Ah, I didn't know anybody was checking into this room. Excuse me." Then she disappears. My aunt couldn't believe it. This is her entrance into the hospital. These two strangers in her room. Hospital personnel no doubt using it for good and noble purposes.

DR. MILTON TESSLER, Cardiologist

There's a whole camaraderie that develops on the wards. You and the nurse are working side by side, saving a life. Now that the work is done, it's time to pause . . . for a beer . . . or some sex . . . or something like that! You've denied yourself for so long to take care of these patients, now it's time to have a good time. Let's not worry about tomorrow because tomorrow there's just more of this tension and this grief.

Then there are other times when you're really up. You've done something really terrific and you think you're Superman. Maybe there was a cardiac arrest and you saved a life, and you feel like you have life and death in your hands. It's an incredibly exhilarating experience, not just psychologically, but I'm sure there are also physiological reactions, a release of substances that stimulate you. It can make you sexually supercharged, or at least you think you're supercharged, and you're ready to prove it to the world.

DR. HARRISON O'NEILL, Gastroenterologist

Sometimes the sex at the hospital can get pretty blatant. One time I did a liver biopsy on a gal that I had found very attractive. She came down for the liver biopsy made up beautifully, and dressed in a lacy black nightgown, as though she was some sacrificial maiden.

As an intern, I also had some pleasant surprises. One time I was asleep in the on-call room when I felt someone get into bed with me. I tried to figure out who it was but it took me a few minutes in the dark. Then I saw it was this nurse, an older woman, married, who was absolutely naked. She had these enormous breasts, and that's how I recognized her. We never had a particular friendship, before that night or after. But it was all right at the time. It made me feel good. But nothing special.

107

DR. DAVID ANZAK, Obstetrician-Gynecologist

When I'm in the examining room, I wouldn't say that I don't notice what a woman's body looks like. If she's particularly good-looking, that does occur to me. But the next step, a feeling of personal attraction, that doesn't take place. I may think, yes, this is a beautiful woman, and yes, she's sexually attractive, but I don't get turned on. It's just that there's no connection between my objective appreciation of her looks and a feeling of personal interest.

That doesn't mean that the patients don't try to get my attention. They come on with me all the time. I have one patient who is very, very attractive. She's a gorgeous woman, a professional tennis player, with a magnificent body. I know she'd love to sleep with me. She'll touch me on the hand when she leaves. Or send me little thank-you cards after a routine examination. I understand what she's saying. There is a temptation there, but I just won't do it. I think it would be wrong to give in to that.

A lot of my colleagues will justify getting involved with patients, like they're doing the patient a favor. They pretend that a harmless little affair is really part of the therapeutic process. As if they owe it to their patients not to turn down those invitations. I don't agree with that at all. The potential for abuse of one's position is so great that absolute rules have to be set. Even if the patient wants it desperately, and knows what she's doing, it's wrong for the doctor to go ahead. I think that sleeping with patients is a form of malpractice. In a sense, it's like an adult sleeping with a child.

But we still notice things. Anybody who believes that a gynecologist stops noticing women is just dead wrong. When I was a resident, we used to have grand rounds on Friday morning, and it was a very big thing, a big auditorium, with dozens of gynecologists from all over the city. Here is this large room, filled with about forty board-certified gynecologists, and in walks a secretary, a very attractive-looking secretary. She walks up to the professor and bends over to tell him something. She was wearing a very tight skirt and when she bent down it emphasized her rear end. And everyone in the room turned around to look, almost in unison. And when everybody realized that everybody else was looking, all of us, this whole group of gynecologists, started laughing. You may be a doctor, but you're still a man.

DR. JACK BUCKMAN, Director of Emergency Medicine

When I first took over the department, we had a problem with faggot nurses. We had quite a few of 'em in here. I weeded out most of the swishy kind, because they were propositioning patients. That's a personality aberration I don't permit, not even among heterosexual people. If I catch a nurse or a doctor hitting on a patient, I call 'em right out in the hall and say, "Hey! None of that bullshit around here! Make your dates elsewhere." If I catch 'em again, they're gone. I'll fire 'em before they can turn around.

When you handle come-ons from patients, it's a different story. If one of them is acting even remotely seductive to me, I'll just say, "I feel uncomfortable with you behaving like that. I'm here to help you with your medical problem and I'd just as soon let you save that for another day, another person." It happens to all doctors. But it's part of the Hippocratic oath, you're not supposed to have sex with your patient. There's some guys, like this black guy Garland Lockwood, who make trouble for themselves. They strut and behave in such a way that it advertises they're available. But I don't do that. I never have.

I don't want to give you the idea that I'm a saint. I've fucked a lot of nurses in my time, but if you're an insurance salesman out visiting companies on the circuit, you get a lot of secretaries too. The point is not to get involved with someone you work with every day. You don't want to shit where you eat, in other words.

DR. GARLAND LOCKWOOD, Obstetrician-Gynecologist

Whenever you ask doctors about sex, you always get the same answer. "Maybe some other people step out with patients, but I'd never think of it." Well, I won't try any of that bullshit. See, I've slept with some of my patients. It happens. You can't help it. One of them actually sued me for it, and made a big stink, and we had to settle out of court for a lot of money. So now everybody looks down on Garland Lockwood, bad boy, shame on him. They are a bunch of hypocrites. Most of them are worse than I am.

Everyone goes out with patients. It just happens because you meet people that you like. Or let's say they like you. I would never ask a patient out if my life depended on it. But they ask me out all the time, and sometimes I decide to go along.

For a lot of doctors, it's different. See, they're not attractive guys and they have to use some sort of power position to get women. A lot of gynecologists have sexual relations with their patients right in the office. I know guys who are proud they can get away with it, even with the nurses around. And there are a lot of weird women who come on to us. You're doing an examination, with her legs spread open, and she gets excited and starts breathing heavy and closing her eyes. I've heard stories from my colleagues, of these women who are there for a pelvic exam, with their feet up in the stirrups and their ass at the edge of the table. Instead of sticking a speculum in, the doctor sticks his penis in there. It happens. And supposedly the women get turned on by it. The sexual side of medicine is just amazing, because the women keep coming at you all the time and you start thinking you can do anything. So maybe I did get involved when I shouldn't have, but I'm still a lot better than some other people I know. I never did anything really gross.

DR. BARNETT GOLDSTEIN, Plastic Surgeon

I remember the first time one of my patients suggested that we have sex together. She came in to me for a little cosmetic surgery on her rear end, and she was a beautiful girl, very seductive. After I examined her, and I told her the price, she said, "Can't we work this out? You can do something for me that I want, and I bet I can do some things for you that you want." I said, "The only thing I want is that you should pay me in advance." Which she did, and she became a very good patient of mine.

This sort of thing happens all the time. A lot of other doctors will go for it. But it's not a good idea, because you get started with the girl herself, then after you get involved you're doing all kinds of little favors, or giving surgery, for all her family and all her friends. I know guys who do all kinds of stuff. I had this one gal who needed a very specialized piece of surgery, so I sent her to somebody else. She came back and told me what happened. When she told this other surgeon that she couldn't afford his price, he told her that he'd make a deal. If she gave him a blow job in the office, he would do the surgery at a reduced rate. So I asked her, "What did you do?" She said she gave him the blow job. "Well," I said, "I wish you would have told me that before. If I knew you were that flexible, you wouldn't even have to worry about a bargain rate. I know some guys who would have done it for free."

NANCY PROCTOR, Nurse

What makes doctors attractive is the money. But physically, they certainly aren't as attractive as lots of other people. Doctors—a lot of them, anyway—are sort of wimpy because they're like moles. They sit around in the dark and study and work and study and work and they're sleep-deprived most of the time.

DR. CHARLOTTE KIRKHAM, Hematology Fellow

Right now there's a cystic-fibrosis kid who really has a crush on me. He comes from a really screwed-up family and he is very wanting. He's fourteen, a bright kid with a good sense of humor, and sometimes he makes these remarks that are kind of suggestive. It makes me sad. I'm sure he's going to die before he ever gets laid. Sometimes I start thinking about the book *Johnny Got His Gun*, where the nurse has pity on this soldier who's completely paralyzed so she gives him the little bit of sexual satisfaction that he can feel. And I think that I could give him the experience of getting laid, just once, before he dies. He's a good-looking kid, and very sweet. Obviously, I'd never do anything like that. But sometimes the idea goes through my head.

DR. CARL GORMAN, Neurosurgeon

When you're a doctor, and you're single, people are going to take an interest in you and there's not much you can do about it.

Just the last couple of weeks I've been getting anonymous notes, with a woman's handwriting. One of them said, "I hope to see you at such-and-such a party." And then the next week there was a card with Snoopy on it that said, "Rats! We didn't get to talk at that party! You didn't stay long enough." Then a week later, somebody sent me two dozen roses, also anonymous. With a little card, "We'll have to stop meeting like this!" And I still don't know who it is!

DR. MONICA WILKINSON, Chief Resident, Pediatrics

Lately I've been getting some strange phone calls. It's not too bad, maybe once a month, but it's the same person every time. He comes on and says, "You're so fine, I saw you in the hospital, you turn me on." I don't know who it is 'cause he always hangs up, but it's probably some kid who came through as a patient. Whoever it is, it doesn't bother me that much 'cause he's not mean and he doesn't get dirty. But still, it makes you think, and I see now why a lot of people get unlisted numbers. If I wasn't a doctor, he'd probably never notice me. But as it is, I play into some fantasy he has. When you're a doctor, that's a price you have to pay.

MISS GOODY TWO SHOES

DR. MONICA WILKINSON
Chief Resident, Pediatrics

BECKY KRIEGER, Nurse

She is right up there with the very best doctors that I know. She's so smart and so good that all of her patients do real well. She is also a good organizer. She has an excellent relationship with everybody in the hospital, from janitorial up to attending—she has such respect for what every person does. She's one of those people who will ask the nurses what *they* think—and that doesn't happen all the time.

DR. GARLAND LOCKWOOD, Obstetrics-Gynecology

She is Miss Goody Two Shoes. She knows how to play the game. She's very slick and she's made herself a big favorite with the hospital power structure. Whenever somebody's attacking me, they talk about her to show they're not prejudiced. You know, "Why can't that Lockwood be more like Monica Wilkinson? She's black too, but she's a good girl."

She's a sleeper, that girl. During her first year here she didn't make such a great impression. I think she suffered from having gone to a black medical school that wasn't good enough. But she's shown just tremendous growth over the three years she's been here. All she needed was an environment where she could thrive. She's already above average and she's going to be an outstanding pediatrician.

———————

I spoke with Monica Wilkinson during her lunch breaks on three successive days. We met in a small conference room down the hall from the nursing station so that she could be readily interrupted for questions or emergencies. A tall, slim woman of twenty-nine, she wore jeans and platform shoes under her white coat. Her large gold-hoop earrings emphasized her close-cropped hair and long neck. She smiled continually during our conversations, and two slightly crooked front teeth gave her expression an appealing, irregular and somewhat mischievous flavor.

MY MOTHER WAS a nurse, and when I was a youngster I never wanted to touch anything in medicine! My dad died when I was five, and Mom was always working. She had to work nights for some of the time, and my brother and I hated it. But in retrospect it worked out quite well. I am of the school that believes it's not the quantity of time you spend together, it's the quality. I can honestly say that the quality of time spent with my mom made up for all of the problems. Also, there were extended family relationships, as in many black families, so we really didn't feel like we were out there flapping alone.

In high school I was very interested in women's athletics, track and field. I did the broad jump, high jump, some of the middle-distance running. At first my mother was proud of me but then she turned negative. She said, "If you do athletics, you're finished before you're thirty. If you do medicine, you go on for a lifetime." I didn't care about medicine 'cause all I ever heard was the way my mother complained about being a nurse. And it came down to it, and we had a big blowout my senior year, 'cause she said I had to cut out track team to do better in my classes. I didn't want to quit, but she won and I did it her way. I look back now and I wonder if I could've done both.

For college I had a scholarship to Vassar. It was the first time I ever lived away from Washington, and it was a big jump socially. At first I was really shy but then I became very politically active, you know, the whole black-student thing. It took up a lot of my time, and that's one of the reasons I decided to come home to go to medical school at Howard University. I did not want to put myself in another predominantly white situation where I felt I had to be politically active from a racial standpoint and it would interfere with my learning medicine.

It was my third year when I decided on pediatrics. I was working one night in D.C. General Hospital and I had to lavage an alcoholic all night long. That's where you put a tube down into the stomach and dump in icewater to stop him from bleeding to death. Then a week later he came back with exactly the same problem. At three in the morning I'm lavaging this same GI bleeder and I say to myself, "I'm not going to be doing this forever." This man is on his own path of self-destruction and I have very little empathy. Adults are too hardheaded. After about fourteen you cannot make an effective change or an improvement in a person's general health status. If Joe Blow has been smoking for twenty years he'll continue to smoke. If he eats the wrong kind of foods, he'll continue to eat those foods. But with children, there is some hope, some chance with parental intervention, that you can have an impact on their lives.

There's also more of a chance to fantasize and explore the imagination. You know, sometimes I'll go and talk to kids in the ICU or something and I'll say, "Okay, we're right out on the beach right now. We're sitting on the sand. And here comes a dolphin right out of the water and he's going to come and talk to us." With adults you have to be more serious and more pretentious and more austere about medicine. But in pediatrics, I will stop them when they're wheeling down the hall on their tricycles and ask to see their driver's license. It's the only specialty where when you go on rounds, you might reach into your pocket and find a gob of Green Slime. I have this one little boy who has a can of Green Slime and every day while we are talking he tries to stick some of it into my pocket when I'm not looking.

That doesn't mean it's all fun and games around here. We get plenty of kids with tumors and all kinds of serious diseases, and even though the cure rate is better than it is with adults, we still lose them all the time. Sometimes you feel it more than others. Last summer there was one boy who was fourteen who came in with aplastic anemia, which is a bone-marrow disease. He kept telling us to fix him up in a hurry because he was starting high school in the fall and he wanted to try out for the freshman football team! But within a week he went from being very alert to just lying there unconscious on the respirator. The whole family sort of fell apart at his bedside. It was a hardworking, lower-middle-class black family and they were all wrapped up in this boy.

I remember how I registered that loss. All of a sudden I caught myself crying when I was sitting at my desk and writing a note. I was swept up into the whole family constellation, imagining how I would feel. Maybe the fact that he was black was part of it. It's not that I'm less upset if a Caucasoid or Asian patient dies, but for some reason this young guy reminded me of a brother or whatever, subconsciously. That's one of the reasons, I think, it's important to get more black physicians out there, just because of that extra level of concern and empathy we're able to give.

After going through a black medical school and then working at the D.C. hospital where about eighty-five percent of the patients are black, it was an adjustment to come to Memorial. I never had any problem with out-and-out prejudice from any of the patients, but sometimes their attitude is a little casual, you know, or condescending. Sometimes they're real snotty when they think I'm just a nurse, but when I say I'm Dr. Wilkinson and I'm chief resident of pediatrics, you can see their attitude change.

But there are still some people who will want to call in somebody else. I've had several patients who've wanted an older physician. They never say we want one who's white, or we want a man, but I can feel what's on their mind. If they say, "We want somebody who's more experienced," then I say, "Fine." I think every

116

patient should have the right to request the type of physician they want, even if it doesn't make any sense to me.

If there's no feeling of comfort between parents of the patient and the physician, you're asking for trouble. One time I was in the nursery, and this mother who was real hyper had twins who were real sick. She didn't like me and I should have been smart enough not to talk in front of her, but I wasn't.

And what I have to explain here is there's a special word we use, and that word is "crump." If you say that a patient is crumping, it means you did something that didn't help, he's turning bad, he's getting into trouble. It doesn't mean he's going to die; it just means he's going the wrong way. Anyhow this mother was standing there when my intern came up and asked me how to dial the respirator for these two kids. I told him to try one setting and see what happened. And I said, "If they crump, we're right here, and we can just redial them up. So if they crump, they crump, it's not so bad." Well, the mother heard that and she got hysterical. She just went crazy, thay had to give her Valium. She thought I was trying to kill her kids.

She came back that night and I tried to explain it, but she wouldn't listen. She wanted to get me fired and it didn't die down until her babies left the hospital. Thank God, they were both in one piece.

It's funny some of the ideas that people have about doctors, and there is almost this background of hostility. Like the money aspect. People think we're just rolling in it, but for pediatricians especially, that's not true. This is my fourth year in the residency program and I'll be lucky this year if I eke out twenty-one thousand dollars. My boyfriend is a law student. After three years of law school he'll come out and he'll be getting thirty thousand dollars and here I am, nine years after college, and I'm still struggling!

He has a hard time handling my schedule, and last year we broke up because of it. Now we see each other twice a week and he's a lot more understanding about my hours. I'm always late, wherever I'm going. Sometimes he'll be sitting in a restaurant waiting for me and I'll show up two hours late and he'll say, "Oh, don't worry about it," but then, an hour later, I'll get another call and I'll have to go back to the hospital.

I wear this beeper twenty-four hours a day, because I'm chief resident. Sometimes I'm called at weird hours, and on one occasion the call came at precisely the wrong time, if you know what I mean. My reaction was like Pavlov's dog. You hear a bell, you jump up. Your boyfriend thinks you're crazy, but you've got to answer it. The next time we were together he put the beeper under the bed and covered it with a pillow.

He's a black guy, with a similar background and a good sense of humor, which helps when you're going with a doctor! He's six years younger than me, but maybe we'll get married anyway. I'm thinking about it more and more because I'm approaching thirty—and I've got to have some babies.

If I get pregnant now I think I would have the baby even if I didn't get married, which is different from the way I felt a couple of years ago. I could support a baby on my own. I could raise a child at the same time I'm working, just like my mother did.

I don't worry too much about the future, because I know some things are just set. Like I know that one day I'll be a patient in a place like this. I'll be stuck with multiple tubes and needles. I think about that and maybe I worry about it more than I should. I know, inevitably, I will have an IV in my lifetime and there's a good chance I will die of cancer. I wonder how it feels to be getting some of these procedures that we do all the time.

The part I really worry about is if I have kids and something happens to them. Of course, that's what I see every day, but I still don't know that I could handle it if it happened to me. The scary part is the terminal kids, where you know darn well there's nothing anyone can do and the parents have to sit back and watch them die. The CF kids are just about the worst, because cystic fibrosis is a slow disease, but it's going to be fatal every time. We have a special CF unit at Memorial, and the people who work there really take a beating. There is one social worker who gets totally involved with these kids, and I can see what she goes through. That's one job I would never want to have.

THE AMAZON

MARIAN DONAHUE
Social Worker, Cystic Fibrosis Unit

DR. BEN BRODY, Psychiatric Resident

Marian Donahue is six feet tall and she seems like kind of an Amazon, a real man-hater. All of the doctors are afraid of her because she goes crazy if she thinks they're doing a bad job with her patients. She thinks she knows more about medicine than they do, but she's only a social worker. She likes to put people down.

BECKY KRIEGER, Nurse

A lot of the social workers check in and check out, like punching a time clock, but Marian stays late all the time. She plays games with her kids, she reads stories, she holds hands. I've never seen anybody so totally devoted to her patients.

DR. ALLEN BARSAMIAN, Staff Psychiatrist

What's Churchill's line about Russia? "It's a riddle wrapped in a mystery inside an enigma." You could say the same thing about Marian Donahue.

On the one hand she is a very intelligent, competent social worker who makes a big contribution to the conferences about the children in the cystic fibrosis unit. She's not the easiest person to get along with, but everybody respects her for what she does. She also happens to be a beautiful woman who looks like she just stepped out of *Vogue* magazine, and is always very elegant and formal.

On the other hand, she will say things in the conferences that indicate that she has walked on the wild side. There will just be these off-the-wall comments about picking up people at bars and things. I haven't felt comfortable talking to her about it, which is unusual since I talk to social workers quite a bit. Maybe I'm a little intimidated by her.

Marian Donahue freely admitted that friendships play no important role in her life; her most significant relationships, she insisted, are with horses. She owns two of them, a mare and a foal, and rides every morning at six. Photographs of the two animals and of their mistress, dressed in formal riding clothes, covered every inch of available wall space in her dingy studio apartment.

Lying back on a threadbare sofa, wearing a white cashmere sweater and a green tweed skirt, she was a remarkably handsome woman—long-legged and graceful, with high cheekbones and a sensuously curving neck. She relaxed with a Scotch on the rocks and patted her nervous Doberman in an effort to reassure him about the presence of a male stranger in the room. In describing herself, she turned immediately to the question of her height.

WHEN PEOPLE ASK me, I like to tell them I'm five feet, twelve and a half inches tall! I've been that tall since I was fourteen and at the time I weighed about a hundred and twenty pounds, so I was a stick. I was pretty enough, but not dating material for any of the boys in my age group because I was much too tall. My father wouldn't let me go out with older people, so I was essentially shy. I was everybody's best friend. All the guys would call me up to tell me about their problems, but when it was time to go out, they would ask somebody else. I think that's how I got into social work.

The counseling role came naturally from my experience as a teenager. It was something I was always good at.

I grew up in the suburbs of Baltimore. My father is vice-president of a marketing company, and we've always been upper-middle-class. My family is Irish on both sides, and we had a very strict Catholic upbringing. My father dominates the scene at home and he's a very devout Catholic. I believed in it myself, and practiced it, until the very end of high school.

In college I partied hearty. It was the first time I was away from home, the first time I knew what it felt like to be attractive. There were plenty of guys who were tall enough for me and everybody wanted to ask me out.

My boyfriend was your typical macho football player—rough and tough and constantly getting into fights. He was totally possessive and he was also the first person who ever had sex with me. He raped me, as a matter of fact. He left bruises all over my body. I hated him but we kept going together for two years. He was always rough with me and I never enjoyed it, but I thought that was what I deserved in life. It was the typical Catholic attitude of beating yourself for having a good time.

The only good thing from the relationship was a paper I wrote about the psychology of the football team as a cultural entity with its own folkways and all that stuff. It helped get me into graduate school. My boyfriend was furious about it, but by that time we were breaking up anyway. I wanted to stop partying and concentrate on grad school. I went for a master's in psychiatric social work and I wound up with one of the best records in my program.

After that, I had plenty of offers for a job, but I wanted to move to California. I love the beach—as a kid I went to the shore every chance I could. I'm definitely an outdoorsy person. So California was what I wanted, and I took a job at a veteran's hospital over in Oakland.

I had responsibility for one whole floor, and the majority of the patients were returning Vietnam vets. This was 1971, so we got new patients all the time. These were psychiatric inpatients, people who had really broken down pretty badly in the war. The physician on the psychiatric ward was scared to death of the patients and he used to lock himself in his office. So I was writing the orders for medication and doing a whole bunch of stuff that was highly illegal. That was very typical of the VA. An incredibly political place with a lot of deadwood around.

It was very depressing, and you really began to get a helpless feeling. There were a couple of guys who I poured hours and hours into, really doing everything I had ever learned in school, but there was nothing in school to prepare me for really helping them. There was one young man who believed he was Jesus Christ, and another one who thought he was speaking to Hitler. And then there was a young black guy, an MP who had had the job of guarding some top-secret planes out on an airstrip. He was the only one out there for eight to ten hours a day, and finally he just flipped. The stress of knowing he was responsible for forty million dollars' worth of hardware just flipped him out. It was sad, because he was so bright and had so much potential. To see him flip, when he flipped, was something I'll never forget. He'd be looking at you and then his eyes would flicker to the side and he'd look back and suddenly he'd change from rational John to totally psychotic John. And he would attack you. One time I was playing pool with him, and he flipped, and he almost killed me with a pool cue. It took the other crazy patients to hold him off and to get me out of there.

There was another one who thought he was in love with me. He was tall, good-looking, and sexy. It was kind of flattering, you know. He used to follow me around the hospital. One time he kicked down steel doors, double-locked steel doors, to get into my office and give me a kiss. Then he escaped from the hospital and came to my house one night. I had to call the police to pick him up.

I spent three years at the VA and I got very burnt-out by it. I was just fed up with psychiatric social work, and I wanted to get into medical social work. I got a job at a hospital in San Jose dealing with the pediatric patients and their families.

That was a lot less demanding than all the crazies at the VA, and I started developing my social life. Right away I met Doug, who was a psychology intern at the hospital. It's really difficult for me to remember what it was about him that attracted me. He's not my type at all. He's very, very nice—almost too nice. Very well dressed, drove a Corvette. Came from a rich family. He was all the things my parents thought I should have. A few months after we started going out, his internship was over and he had to go back to graduate school in New Mexico to finish his Ph.D. Going with him meant getting married, so that's what I decided to do. For one thing, the idea of living out in the desert really appealed to me.

We stayed married for almost three years, and most of the time it wasn't bad. We had everything in common except a sex life! I had no desire for him physically. Which was really sad, because he's a very good-looking man, but we just didn't have it. At first, I thought it was a sexual dysfunction on my part. I had so many years of Catholic upbringing that it was normal for me not to enjoy sex. I never was sexually satisfied. I never had a climax or any of that. But it was pleasant with most people. I didn't have any trouble getting aroused. But with Doug, after we got married, I couldn't even get aroused. It was painful for me and it was also miserable for him because of his own self-image and his own needs. I wanted to get into sex therapy for a while, but we knew all the therapists in this small community and there was just a sense of embarrassment about going to them with our problems. Doug was doing a postgraduate fellowship in clinical psychology, and he didn't want to go to someone he worked with every day.

After the first couple of years, I couldn't fake my way through anymore. We decided to get divorced, but we couldn't split up right then and there. Doug was going to take a job back in California and I wanted him to take me along. I didn't want to be stuck in New Mexico on my own, and I needed him to help support me until I could get my own job out on the coast. He was really a good sport and we stayed married for six more months even though we had separate bedrooms. After that he helped me get my job at Memorial. Then I moved out. Right away, things got better.

I was twenty-nine years old and for the first time I was going to go out and have a real social life and start having a good time. One of the girls at work introduced me to JoJo's and all the local singles' places.

I didn't sleep around a lot when I first got divorced. I didn't have the confidence to do that, and I wasn't quite free of the shackles of Catholicism. But I found out that I enjoy that scene. I enjoy the wittiness, the playfulness, the feeling of being attractive and everybody desiring you and you're kind of laughing to yourself. So I did that for a while and then I got into the disco scene. I started doing a lot of dancing and I was up to all hours every night, partying.

And naturally, my sex life got straightened out. It was almost like a miraculous lifting of guilt. And it happened practically

123

simultaneously with my thirtieth birthday. I can't tell you exactly what happened, because I don't know. All I know is it was like feeling free, all of a sudden.

I still remember the first time I climaxed. I was really surprised and in a way it was kind of *anti*climactic! It was just some guy I had met that night and we were just going along and then all of a sudden, there it was. It was very pleasant, and it was really nice to know I could do that. I still don't climax all the time. But I get as much satisfaction just from physical closeness, from togetherness. So at this point, it's not a big thing.

My work is really the biggest part of my life. My official title at Memorial is Clinical Social Worker with the Cystic Fibrosis Unit. The CF population is mainly children and teenagers. I start when they're diagnosed and I follow them through till the day they die. CF is presently incurable. The best we can do is prolong life by a couple of months or a couple of years. In the past six years, we've had a big improvement. When I started, the average age of death from CF was eleven or twelve. Now it's fifteen, and it's rapidly climbing towards twenty.

I run groups for the patients, for their parents, and for their siblings. Part of the job is helping these kids prepare for death. I get them to talk about it. Some of the younger ones can't really talk about it, so I just hold their hands. I help them say goodbye as best they can. CF is particularly devastating because the kids are gorgeous. Some doctor did a study on whether or not their eyelashes were longer, because all the kids have the most beautiful long eyelashes. Any kid who's sick and frightened can become very sweet and appealing, but these kids really are a special group.

Right at the beginning, I had a difficult time. Especially the first time we lost one of the kids. It was a beautiful little blond girl who was so bright and so good and so healthy—everybody expected she would last for years. But then all of a sudden she got this virus and she was gone. That's the first time it really hit me: This is terminal, and there's nothing I can do. The next summer we lost four kids. These kids were super-special—they had a bond. We knew that once the first one died they were all going to die. There was just dread, waiting for it to happen. The last one who died was my favorite of all time. I carried her picture in my wallet for years. She knew what was happening, and she could handle it, even though she was nine years old.

I never cry after a child dies, but oh, God, you cry before you lose

124

them! You cry with the kids, because the kids know the doctors won't be straight with them. They depend on me; they know I'm not going to lie to them. The kids talk about how their families are going to feel after they are gone and how much they're worried about their moms. Or how much they are going to miss watching their little brothers grow up. I try to get the parents to participate, but most of the time they can't handle it. I don't have a family and I don't relate what happens to them to anybody in my life. I think maybe my biggest advantage is that when I go home, I can really be alone.

I come into work every morning around nine o'clock, pick up my beeper, my books, grab my bran muffin and a cup of coffee, and I head up to the floor. My rounds are going from patient room to patient room. I try to be as cheerful as I can. Unless someone is actually dying, when you can't walk in and go, "Hi there! How are you this morning?" Some people do that, but I don't. I'll say, "I'm glad you're still here."

Usually, I'll spend between fifteen and forty-five minutes with each patient, and that takes up the whole morning. In the afternoon I have meetings with parents, conferences of all the staff assigned to our unit. Later I go down to the clinic—we have an outpatient clinic three times a week. After that I usually go back and make more rounds, see the same patients again. Usually I go home at five o'clock. But if somebody's really sick I can put in sixty, seventy hours a week. If things are quiet, sometimes I only put in thirty.

Even though the hours are flexible, I take more of a formal attitude toward the job. A lot of the social workers come to the hospital looking like slobs, but I feel that I owe myself and the patients something more than showing up in thongs and no stockings. And so I dress. I make all my own clothes and I'm proud of the fact that I'm an excellent seamstress.

But if I'm going out at night to a bar or a disco, I put my work clothes away and put on my jeans. I want that real clear distinction between work and my personal life. That's why I won't date anybody from the hospital.

Since I got divorced most of my relationships have been sort of casual, but one of them lasted for almost three years. The guy was black and he kind of drifted in and out of my life. He'd been married twice before and he had a son. He worked for a tire company and he'd never really gotten his life together. We tore at each other's souls a lot. An awful lot. We made a lot of demands on each other, and towards the end it got bad. He hit me a couple of times and one time he really beat me up. The worst was when he hit me with his son there. We used to take the little boy with us on the weekends, and we'd get into these verbal sparring things and I'd always get the best of him. We were in the car, and we were having this discussion, then all of a sudden he slapped me, really hard. He knew there was nothing I could do about it because I was driving and he knew how angry it made me. He just sat back and watched me get angry. I wanted to hit him back, or crash the car, or do something violent. But I never raised a hand against him, because I thought he'll probably kill me. It was that kind of destructive relationship.

The man I'm seeing now is a lot better. He's twenty-five—ten years younger than me—and he works in construction. I met him at the gym where I go to work out. He's a very good-looking man and very exciting to be with. We see each other once a week. We have dinner, go dancing, and have sex. In between, we don't even talk on the phone, because there's really not much to talk about. I guess you could say he fits my pattern. The guys I am attracted to are rough and tough and not very bright. My husband was an exception and I wasn't really attracted to him. It's just that the things I really like doing are dancing, riding, being outdoors. It doesn't take a lot of brains to do that.

I'm not uncomfortable with people who are intellectually my equal. I'm just not interested, I find them boring. Like the doctors at Memorial are. I'd never go out with any of them. They're shallow and predictable. I've made a lot of enemies because I don't let them push me around and I won't let them step on my patients. A lot of them just have this attitude that the hospital's there for them, for their convenience and education, and not for the good of the patients.

When I'm not there working, I stay as far away as possible. Most of the time, I'm with my horses. That's been a big part of my life for the last eight years, since we lived in New Mexico. Riding is just fantastic. I love feeling the wind in my hair. I love riding in the mountains or on the beach. I love the discipline and beauty of it. It's something you can do alone and yet you're not alone. You've got the company of the horse and the communication is just fantastic. And training the horses gives me a real sense of accomplishment. If I didn't do the riding I'd be paying some shrink seventy-five dollars an hour, three times a week.

I get up every morning at five A.M. and I'm down at the stables by quarter to six. First thing, I'll take care of my baby. That means getting her out, grooming her, and feeding her. Then I take out the older horse for an hour of riding and training. By eight o'clock I'm done and I take a shower at the stables and drive straight to work.

It costs me six hundred dollars a month to keep those horses and my apartment only costs me three hundred! I earn twenty-six thousand dollars a year, and I spend over half my take-home on the horses. I can't think of anything I'd rather do with the money. I have a lot of goodies from that part of my life. I have a whole group of friends down at the stables, a whole group of horse people. I'm known all over the Bay Area for my riding, and I'm proud of the fact I'm really good.

I don't know what the future's going to bring. In terms of my work, I know there'll be more of the same. In terms of relationships, I'm not expecting anything great. I'm much less willing to go through the emotional ups and downs of any kind of serious involvement.

I know that I'll never have children. That's a decision I made four years ago. I've never really been interested in having children, and I had a tubal ligation right here at Memorial. Even back in high school, I never had any interest in having children. I don't want to take that responsibility. I could never be a totally giving, totally loving person. I'm very critical, very judgmental. I enjoy working with the kids at the hospital, but I can go home every day at five o'clock.

There's not that much that I really look forward to, when I stop to think about it. I look forward to my young horse being grown up. I look forward to riding her. I look forward to going down to the stables tomorrow morning. And maybe in the next few years I look forward to professional growth, to writing down some of my ideas of working with the CF kids.

That is, if I decide to stick with it. Sometimes I think I ought to get out and become a professional horse person, raising horses, teaching riding. But there's a lot I'd be giving up if I left my job. There's an emotional intensity that is hard to reach, and I don't get it a lot in my personal life because I don't have an ongoing relationship like a family. Right now, my patients give me an awful lot. They become my friends, they become my children.

There are a few people from the staff I would miss, but not many. Most of the people there are selfish and egotistical. Allen Barsamian is one of the exceptions. He's very sensitive and very committed to his patients. He's had a terrible life, but he keeps coming back for more.

THE WILD
ARMENIAN

DR. ALLEN BARSAMIAN
Staff Psychiatrist

DR. LANNY BUCKMAN, Pediatric Resident

If there's such a thing as a typical psychiatrist, then Allen fits the mold. He's very nervous and very intellectual. He's analytical about everything. He's good with patients, and he makes them feel better when he goes on rounds, but there's something sad about him. He was that way even before his wife died. We call him the Wild Armenian; it's a way of teasing him because he's always so serious and concerned.

GEORGIANNA HARLAN, Ward Clerk, Translator

Allen is a very pleasant man, very sweet. He wants everyone to call him by his first name—he doesn't like "Dr. Barsamian." He's very anxious that everyone should like him because he's not very sure of himself.

128

DR. HARVEY FREDMAN, Professor of Gastroenterology

Psychiatry suits Allen very well, because he could never deal with crisis medicine. He has a tough time taking responsibility, making decisions. He is more attuned to the sensitivities of the families and patients. He is just extremely kind. That's probably the first word I'd use when I think of him—he's just unusually kind and decent.

DR. CHARLOTTE KIRKHAM, Hematology Fellow

He once showed me some poetry that his kid had written. The peoms were about his wife dying. I read the poems, but I never got beyond the superficial with him. Then a little later he got married to some woman about ten years older who was the ex-wife of one of the surgeons. I started thinking about the time he showed me those poems. Maybe it was his way of saying he was interested in me. It was during my internship and I wasn't paying much attention to other people, but looking back on it, I wonder how far it could have gone. Allen is someone I really respect.

———————

Allen Barsamian found it impossible to sit still for an interview; he repeatedly leaped out of his chair, paced around his desk, and gestured enthusiastically to emphasize his words. He has a long face, high forehead, thinning crest of wiry black hair, and wire-rim glasses, tinted purple. His pear-shaped body struggled against snug jeans and plaid shirt. As he began describing his work, he offered a somewhat wistful apology.

I DIVIDE MY time between the hospital and a private practice I'm trying to build up, and sometimes I feel guilty about my private

129

practice. It often occurs to me that I make a living off other people's misery. I guess that's a problem everywhere in medicine: The sicker people are, the more money we take in. If you're saving someone's life in the operating room, you don't worry about that. But when you're talking to people in your office and charging seventy-five dollars an hour, naturally you're more sensitive.

That's why I like my job in the hospital: I'm part of a team where I'm really needed, where you can really see direct results from what you do. My official title is Director of Consultation Liaison Services to the Department of Pediatrics. Some of the sick children do things which are not really in their own best interest. Their reaction to the illness interferes with their getting proper treatment. Maybe they're racing around the floor in a wheelchair, pulling out their IV, chewing out the doctor, not taking their medicine. I try to help them get in touch with their anger or their depression. Then I help them find alternative ways of dealing with those feelings.

I meet with the physicians and the nurses first, to find out what their concern is. Then I meet with the family and later with the child. If it's a preschooler or younger child, I play with him and through doing that I try to find out what's fueling the behavior.

Most of the time we try to help the kids by manipulating their environment. That might mean getting doctors to be more sensitive. For example, a surgeon will spend maybe two minutes in the room with the kids. He'll take a pipe out of his pocket, and bang it on the weights in the traction apparatus and the tobacco will fall on the floor, and he'll say, "Well, the alignment is fairly poor; he may require a second pinning," and then he'll walk out. I actually saw this. The ten-year-old kid was sitting there and he knew what it meant and he was furious. No attention, no opportunity for reassurance; the surgeon is only there to write a note on the chart. I advise the surgeons to spend at *least* five minutes at bedside. The kid's not going to ask him to do that, so I act as the child's advocate, and I make that demand.

Another part of my job is working directly with the doctors, providing psychiatric care to the department of pediatrics. Every large department in a hospital, especially in a teaching hospital, keeps a psychiatrist around for themselves to deal with interpersonal as well as the personal problems. Every week I lead seminars for the house staff, nursing staff, social-work staff, about issues in child development and psychiatry. The people coming to these sessions are encouraged to be very candid about their own lives, their own feelings. All kinds of feelings come out, about having to deal with children who are dying or severely ill, or dealing with babies that are born very badly damaged. People will sometimes break down, and the discussions can be very exhausting.

An intern came to me last week whose father had died recently and she could not handle taking care of children who were dying. The whole idea of death in a hospital was too much for her; she would go into a closet and cry for maybe half an hour. I told her I had the same kind of reaction after my wife died, but you have to get over it, you have to create a distance. That's one of the most important things you have to learn in medicine.

Many people have been critical of doctors using humor to achieve that detachment because that doctor no longer reacts as, quote, "a human being." But if you're working in an emergency room and you're reacting the way normal people do, you could not effectively care for anybody. You get that message from the very beginning of medical school. In the first week, you're introduced to your cadaver and people vomit and have all sorts of severe reactions but right away there are defense mechanisms, like grim humor and other psychologically distancing reactions, that begin to occur. You begin to detach yourself more and more, and you don't have the reactions you used to have.

In every situation, there are many possible reactions. For example, your wife burns your dinner: You can get angry, you can be sympathetic, you can laugh about it. You have to choose. And just having the first reaction that comes to you is a primitive kind of thing, which your dog does when someone tries to take his bone away. A doctor has to choose the reaction that's going to allow him to help the patient, and that's a very distant, detached reaction. The average physician would bawl his head off if his own son came down with a life-threatening disease, but he can't let himself get upset when he sees eight kids who are wasting away with cancer. He's criticized for being heartless, but he's actually doing what he has to do.

Psychiatrists are supposed to maintain more of an intimacy and a balance, and that's why we get the reputation for being confused. The house staff also has the idea that a psychiatrist may be a doctor who couldn't hack "real medicine" so he went into a different and easier field.

In my case, I never had any interest in regular medicine. I went to Princeton in the sixties, and with my friends and the people I knew it wasn't considered such a great thing to become a doctor. Psychiatry, at least, was more identified with humanist values, and that's the way I wanted to go. My father was an attorney who made a lot of money and lived all his life in Fresno. He died when I was two, and I was the only child, so my mother spent most of her time with me. She always had a strong bohemian side and a lot of enthusiasm for astrology, for palm-reading, and for psychiatry.

In college, I never had to worry much about my classes and I worried more about getting laid. I was still a virgin in my junior year and just about to turn twenty-one. I had done a lot of petting, but I never had the experience of coming inside.

My roommates thought it was ridiculous and I thought it was ridiculous and for my twenty-first birthday we decided to do something about it. I was seeing a girl from Vassar, so she came up for a weekend and got a room at the motor inn a few miles from campus. We all went out to a movie and then afterward we all went back to her room and had a birthday party and got fairly drunk. Then my roommates left with their dates and there I was with my date and I remember having intercourse and being very clumsy at it. I was so drunk I can hardly remember.

When I woke up, I realized that I wasn't in love and I was never going to marry her. I also realized that I had used no birth control, and I went through a few hours of incredible depression. . . . Oh my God, what if she gets pregnant? And I turned on the TV and they were playing cartoons, it was a Sunday morning. I thought, my God, this is what the future has in store for me! I'm going to have to marry her and raise kids and move off-campus. I'm going to be listening to these goddam cartoons every Sunday morning!

During breakfast at my eating club some of the other guys' dates began talking about the effects of birth-control pills on acne, and my date said that it had helped her quite a bit, and that's why she stayed on the pill constantly because it was good for her complexion. And I sort of looked up and said, "Oh, you mean you're taking birth-control pills?"

And she said, "Of course! Do you think I would have made love if I wasn't?"

At that moment the bells in the carillon started ringing, and the sun came out and I felt wonderful. Like I just returned from the dead! It's ironic, because I used to be so afraid of children and marriage, and now my whole life is children.

I met my wife, Vera, right after this time I'm talking about, the summer between junior and senior years; we were both volunteers at one of the California state mental hospitals. A few days after I arrived for the summer I saw her walking across the lawn and she had long blond hair and the wind was blowing. I remember just thinking she was extremely beautiful, and the next day I asked her out for coffee. We talked all night and three days later we made love. She told me she wasn't using birth control, and I said, "Look, if you're pregnant, I want to marry you. And if you're not pregnant, I also want to marry you." Two weeks later I gave her a ring and she accepted it.

We still had to get through senior year, but we got married right after graduation. Her parents gave us a big, very traditional wedding here in California. We had to be out here anyway, because that's where I got into medical school. Medical school turned out to be easier than I thought it would be. Early on, I didn't have to make too many sacrifices. Then in the third year it got a lot more demanding, but it still wasn't unbearable. I worked hard, but there was nothing else I would rather have been doing. I feel that every educated person should know as much about his heart as he knows about a foreign language or German history or raising lima beans. So even though I knew I was going to be a psychiatrist, I never minded learning all the physiology. It increased my own hypochondriasis, but that was still an acceptable price to pay.

Internship was really a difficult year. Every third night I was away from Vera. She worked as a kindergarten teacher, so she had her own life, but the separation at night was difficult. The sense of sacrifice got even stronger when Rebecca, our daughter, was born in the middle of that year. There was this wonderful baby waiting at home and this beautiful wife, and I hardly got a chance to see them. Sometimes, on my way home from being on call, I would start crying. I've always done most of my crying, if I have to cry about something, in the car. I'd be so tense with the sheer emotion of working at the hospital that I'd cry on the freeway on my way home. I resented being forced to be away from her so much. Then

133

she died a couple of years later. She never lived with me when I wasn't on call in some way! And she never benefited from all that.

Vera used to worry a lot, and it upsets me to think of how much time and energy she wasted. She worried about entertaining friends. She worried about Rebecca, who was a very healthy baby. And she worried about our trips, making sure every detail was perfect. We traveled whenever I had time off, and when Rebecca was born we took her along. We had four trips to Europe during the time we were together. I had a small inheritance from my father, and we pretty much wiped it out with all our trips and vacations. It seemed childish and irresponsible at the time, but I wish we had done even more.

Then I finished my residency and started a special fellowship in child psychiatry. I knew I would be ready to practice within a year and the money would start rolling in. Rebecca was three years old and turning out to be a gifted child. Vera stopped teaching when Rebecca was born, but she went to school at night and she had just finished her master's degree in special education. We wanted to have another child, and she got pregnant right away. We felt like we were in control of our lives and it was just a very happy time.

And then when she was five months pregnant Vera got a postcard saying she should have her teeth cleaned. She went to a very fancy dentist in San Francisco. That was the way she liked to do things, everything really elegant and luxurious. But a week after this dentist's appointment she started feeling tired, and she went in to see her doctor. He didn't examine her, but he ordered a blood test. It turned out that she was quite anemic, and he put her on iron and he had a discussion with me over the phone about what could be wrong. We were both a little alarmed, but the obstetrician said the iron pills should take care of everything.

During the next couple of weeks Vera just got worse and worse. She was tired and distraught, and I became more and more irritable, and we began to fight. She decided to see a psychiatrist. She got a referral to a very analytically oriented psychiatrist with an excellent reputation, and he felt her problem was physical, not emotional. He insisted that she get a complete physical exam. Vera didn't believe him, and she didn't want to bother her obstetrician during the Christmas season. She was actually making a Christmas gift for him, a knit tie. Then it was a week before Christmas and we were still fighting and I said, "Look, the psychiatrist is insisting,

134

and I insist. You're not well. You're ending up with fevers and with a sore on your hand.'' That sore really worried me, so I called the obstetrician myself and told him he had to see her right away. He didn't like the idea, but he said to have her go into the emergency room at Memorial.

That was the morning of Christmas Eve. She drove herself in to the emergency room. I went with Rebecca and my mother and Vera's parents to a special Christmas Eve luncheon at the Hotel Fairmont. I called the hospital in the middle of lunch and an intern from Germany got on the phone and said, "I think your wife has bacterial endocarditis.'' That's an infection of the heart that you can get after bacteria gets into your bloodstream. The bacteria need a place to stay, and they usually can't find that unless your heart is already damaged in some way. So I said, "That's impossible. Her father is a doctor, I'm a doctor, I've listened to her heart millions of times. She never had a murmur. It must be something else.'' He said, "We'll see. We're drawing blood cultures and we want to put her into the hospital for a while.''

So Rebecca and I went directly to the hospital and Vera was sitting there laughing. "It's ridiculous,'' she said. "They really think I've got something serious.'' And I said, "Well, I'm sure you'll be okay, but it's best we do everything we can.''

I came back to visit her late that night and they had given her her own room, in Lerner Pavilion, which is a real ritzy part of Memorial. She was frightened by this time and she was crying. I was frightened too, but I felt very secure that she was getting the best care in the world.

Next day the blood cultures came back and they were positive— she had bacterial endocarditis. They figured that the bacteria must have gotten into her bloodstream when she had her teeth cleaned and her gums bled a little bit. As treatment, she would require four to six weeks of intravenous antibiotics. These IVs were very painful, and she would cry when she got them. But she was in a very nice room and she made a lot of friends with the nurses. The meals in the Lerner Pavilion were prepared by a chef who gave you whatever you asked for. Rebecca and I visited every day, and Rebecca would roller-skate in the corridors. Vera got lots of special treatment. The obstetrician that failed to make the diagnosis, that failed to examine her, felt really guilty about it. He came in constantly to talk with her, and she was crazy about him.

She did so well that they decided she could leave early. There was no sign of any problem. One of the nurses stopped me in the hallway and said, "You know, you guys are really something. I really envy you. We've got plenty of doctors' wives, because this is a special pavilion, and they're so unhappy and they're always complaining. But Vera is so happy about her life. She talks about your future, she talks about the new baby. She really feels like she's gotten her life together."

And that conversation was a Wednesday night in January. She was supposed to come home on Monday. And then the next night, Thursday night, Vera insisted that I go home early. I was overwhelmed with work because I continued to do my fellowship and she wanted me to get some rest. She said, "You know, I'm never alone while I'm pregnant, because I have *him,*" and she was pointing to her stomach. She said, "I'm really happy." I talked to her on the phone that night, around ten o'clock, and she felt great.

About four in the morning I got called by an intern saying she was having a grand mal seizure. I talked to the intern very calmly, and then I hung up and just started to scream. I called her parents and said, "Oh my God!" I just kept saying, "My God!" I started to cry and scream while I was getting dressed. Rebecca woke up and said, "What's wrong, Daddy?" And I rushed down there, but by the time I arrived she was already unconscious.

She was in a coma for two weeks. The only way I handled that was my roommate from Princeton flew in to be with me. He is an attorney but he left his practice just to help me through. I would spend maybe three hours a day at the hospital, but the rest of the time I let myself just be intensively with my friend. We went to the ocean and jumped in and splashed around, even though it was freezing. We ate at the best restaurants and we had one-hundred, two-hundred-dollar meals. We'd go to the steambaths, sometimes with Vera's father, and we'd get beaten with eucalyptus leaves and we'd sit there for hours.

Over at the hospital I accepted that she was going to die. She had the seizure because she had blood in her brain. She had what we call a mycotic aneurysm, which developed as a secondary result of having bacterial endocarditis. She was sick for weeks and weeks before she ever went into the hospital and the aneurysm must have been growing in her head all that time and it got bigger and bigger until it finally burst. The night after she went into a coma, a neuroradiologist showed me the Polaroid of her brain. One half of her head was filled with blood—the left half, the important half. At first I denied what I knew intellectually, and I thought that she could recover completely. It's the same problem I have now with these children who are dying. The problem of not wanting to give up hope because you feel you might be cheating them of a last chance. My friends and her father kept insisting that she was going to live, and it was hard for me. It taught me a lot about how to work with families with kids who are dying, because you don't want to give up hope, but at the same time you want to help them accept it. I found myself trying to help her father and mother accept it, trying to help my friends accept it, and all the time wondering what the hell I was going to do with Rebecca.

Vera was never conscious again after that first night. She moaned and groaned, but she wasn't conscious. They chose a form of treatment which was experimental, but which now has become routine. They gave her a gram of phenobarbital, which stops the seizure activity, and then they drilled four holes into her skull to get the blood out and to relieve the pressure. They cooled her body down, and after that she was no longer restless, she was just completely still. I would come in and these nurses in the neurosurgical ICU would just walk out and start crying. I kept talking to Vera, every day. I would try to talk her out. I was saying, "How can you do this? Don't go! Don't leave me! I can't live!"

Then they were deciding whether to turn off the respirator because she had no EEG activity and they were explaining to me all the medical alternatives for saving the baby. That was a bizarre experience, because these people who were talking to me had been my teachers in medical school. It was as if they were talking to me about some patient, and I was the intern. That may have helped me to get through it, because there were life-and-death things to decide. I wouldn't let them try to save the baby if it meant hurting Vera. They still thought they had a chance for the baby, but it turned out we lost him too.

When I finally saw her dead and they turned everything off and she was prepared by the mortician, I decided that this body had nothing to do with her. We all have this myth that after a person's prepared like that and buried, they are actually preserved in some way. She did look rather pretty, and we selected a nice casket and she's buried in a very beautiful place. I had an image of her sort of

137

resting there and I clung to that, which I think most people do after a loved one dies. But years later I read a book on death that tells what really happens. People who are buried become rotten in just a few weeks. After a few months, they're unrecognizable. They're just filth. It was a couple of years after she died when I read that, but I cried again when I thought about it.

During the time we were getting ready for the funeral, I was surrounded by friends. And older people too, and all my Armenian relatives, everybody. They were all there at the house. And the meals, we had these huge meals! They'd all bring food and there was a strange kind of festive atmosphere. I cried for hours every day, but every time I cried I felt better. I was getting my distance. I realized that people can die, and you feel awful, but life goes on. And I realized it's only a matter of time before something horrible happens to all of us. Either we get sick, or we lose somebody we love. It's only a matter of time. I mean, the nicest thing that can possibly happen is that your wife will die of a heart attack in her sleep when you somehow don't need her so much anymore. But how in the world is that going to happen if you have a good marriage? I mean, even old people still need each other.

When Vera died, I went right back to work. It was surprising that work felt so good and I could get involved with other people's problems. But about two weeks after the funeral I went to the mountains with a friend and we went fishing and I was cleaning some fish and I realized that some of them weren't quite dead yet. And right in the middle I started thinking of Vera and some of the incredibly brutal procedures she went through. I had to see her, and my daughter actually saw her at one point, with holes drilled in her head and tubes coming out full of blood. And I thought of that and I said, "My God! If that can happen to Vera, what does it matter about these fish?" And I remember just chopping right through their heads and mutilating them in a way I never would have done before. I noticed a whole change in my attitude toward life.

When I went back to work I had some of those same angry feelings. For example, one girl came in, who happened to be single, and she said she had gotten pregnant and then had a miscarriage. Well, here I was, having lost my wife when she was five months pregnant with a highly valued child and being left with a three-year-old daughter and not knowing what to do. And I was sitting there listening to this girl who came in and told me she couldn't work for six weeks and went on disability and needed Valium because she had lost her baby. Before Vera died, I would have been very sympathetic. I still *acted* sympathetic, but I felt just completely ripped apart to have to give her medication so she could deal with her stress. It was very hard for me to become enthusiastic about dealing with other people's minor problems after suffering such enormous problems myself.

I finished my fellowship that June and got my job with the department of pediatrics. I was earning more money, so I bought a little house, and my mother moved in to help take care of Rebecca. I did a number of things to help deal with the loss. I wrote a story about what happened to Rebecca and me and it got published in a local magazine. I helped Rebecca write some poems about her mother. I tried to spend lots of time with Rebecca, but I also enjoyed being single. I did everything I possibly could do as a single man—both sexually and romantically.

I could not believe how many sexual proposals I had! Nurses, social workers, friends, the wives of friends, everybody wanted to comfort me. But sooner or later, they all wanted the sense that you cared about them, or wanted to marry them, or give them a baby. So it wasn't exactly living out a sexual fantasy, because there were always strings attached, and I didn't feel like giving any kind of commitment, until I met Janie.

I met her at work, where she was a social worker on the obstetrics floor, and right away I thought she was beautiful. But she was forty-two, which is eight years older than me, and she had three boys from her first husband. I had tried to date younger girls for the most part, but I found out that I couldn't talk to them and they also weren't into sex as much. Women, I found out, have huge sexual appetites in their late thirties and early forties and they are much more free than women in their twenties. A friend of mine who's a surgeon in his fifties goes out with girls who are nineteen, twenty years old. I told him he just couldn't handle a woman his own age. So anyway, despite the fact that I never wanted to get involved with an older woman with a lot of kids, I found myself falling in love with Janie. But I still felt it might be too complicated because of her boys. I didn't like them the first time I met them. They were smelly and dirty and there were too many of them and they liked their dad too much. But I started going over there every afternoon after work and I began to fall for the boys too. I also saw that Janie was a good mother, and she could be a wonderful mother for Rebecca.

I'm a psychiatrist, so nobody has to tell me there's an obvious Oedipal pattern right there. I fall in love with a woman who's eight years older and who has three boys of her own, and I obviously want to become one of the boys and have her mother me. I lost my mother figure when Vera died with the baby, and now I'm trying for a replacement. I've got this burning need to be accepted as a father by my stepsons, because of the old Oedipal struggle to supplant the father archetype, to take over from the boys' real father.

But whatever's going on it seems to work, and we've been married now for ten months. We wanted to have a baby together, so she got pregnant right away and she's going to be a mother again at the age of forty-three! That's sort of risky, but one thing I learned when Vera died is that you have to take risks. You can't be cautious and cringing, because you never know what's going to happen tomorrow. With Janie, I may not have the sense of carefree happiness I had with Vera. On the other hand, there are some things about this relationship that are much better. We're older, we're more mature. Sexually, we're very compatible. I was compatible with Vera too, but we were like kids compared to the way I feel now.

And I really enjoy my stepsons, though it's a painful situation at times. They see their father every weekend. He's a very successful orthopedic surgeon on the other side of town, and they really worship him. They call me Allen and sort of treat me more like a big brother, though sometimes they call me Dad by mistake. We do a lot of things together, and sometimes, when we're together as a family, I'm happier than I've ever been in my whole life. Like last summer when we all went camping in the Sierras. Tommy, my roommate from Princeton, said that one of my problems during my whole life has been my need for playmates. I love to play. Vera was a great playmate while we were married, but now I've got all these kids, and it's wonderful.

The only problem is finding time to fit everything in. I'm really trying hard to build up my private practice, but it's not going so well. Part of the problem is that I'm too honest. Most children who are emotionally disturbed don't really need a psychiatrist. There's very good epidemiological evidence that children outgrow their emotional and behavioral problems without any intervention. Less than ten percent of the people who have emotional problems as children end up having emotional problems as adults. So I get a child referred to me, say, after a divorce, and maybe I'll see him three or four times to talk about some of the heavy things that went on there. But after that, what he may need more than anything else is to be on a good Little League team, or to be with other children, or to visit his uncle more often. He doesn't need a psychiatrist, so I won't continue seeing him and charging the parents seventy-five dollars an hour.

That attitude has made me much poorer, but I think it's immoral the way other psychiatrists try to hold on to patients and keep them coming back when it's not really accomplishing anything. There was a little girl who I saw six times who had a mild depression, but basically she was fine. I told the parents their daughter was perfectly normal, but they didn't believe me, so they took the little girl to another psychiatrist. This guy recommended psychotherapy twice a week and now he's been seeing her for two years! That's a hundred and forty dollars every week for a hundred weeks, so it's fourteen thousand dollars! That's money I could have made except for my own sense of integrity. My wife, my friends, they've all accused me of letting go of patients too easily. Maybe it's true, but at least I can live with myself.

My income, unfortunately, isn't very good. My job at the hospital pays twenty-four thousand. Theoretically it's a part-time job, but it ends up taking most of my time. Last year my private practice brought in another fifteen thousand. But that's not a lot to live on with all those kids and all those responsibilities.

This is a bad time for psychiatry in general. People don't take it seriously. The other night we went out to dinner with some friends, and both of them are attorneys. And they were saying something about their two-year-old and I told them it was normal, all two-year-olds do that. But the mother said no, it wasn't normal, she had two other boys and she knew. Well, I was furious. I've gone through nearly fifteen years of training and this is my field. If I were a stockbroker and I said convertible bonds are a good thing, she wouldn't have said, no, municipal bonds are much better. But in psychiatry everybody's an expert, everybody knows better, even your own family. When it comes to dealing with my stepkids, Janie just assumes she knows better because she's the mother.

But even with the problems that crop up, I'd have to say I'm very happy. Of course I still think about Vera, but now it's only once a day, and then usually for two or three minutes. Occasionally I think about her a little longer, but I'm just totally immersed in what I'm doing. I know I'm entering a new period in my life. Up to now, I've had experiences, I've been absorbing things. But now I'm at the time of my life where I want to be generative. I want to produce something in the world. I have this family which I feel I'm generating, and even my stepkids are part of it, because I know if I die tomorrow, they will have some of me in them. I'm generating a new baby with Janie, and that's very exciting. But also my work. I want to write academic papers, and maybe someday I'll write books. I want to take care of patients, I want to give something back. I feel like I'm ready to take off. In one way or another, I know I'm going to make a contribution.

MARITAL BLISS

DR. ALLEN BARSAMIAN, Staff Psychiatrist

Doctors and their wives are supposed to be happy, they're supposed to have it made. People never look at the other side and consider all the problems you get when you marry a doctor. I see some of it in my practice, where a lot of the children who come to me are from medical families. They're severely disturbed, they have terrible behavior problems, they need to be hospitalized. There's one kid now, whose father is a big internist, and the boy refuses to eat. He's eight years old and he's trying to starve himself to death. Another kid, the son of a nephrologist, tried to shoot himself last year. Twelve years old, and he picked up his father's gun and wounded himself in the shoulder.

And the denial behavior from these parents is incredible. "My son couldn't do that. It must have been an accident." It's like someone else I know, who said, "How could my wife possibly leave me? I'm a doctor and I'm chairman of my department." A lot of doctors have bought into the idea that they're supposed to have good marriages and nice families simply because of who they are. Because of all the prestige and the security associated with medicine, a woman will put up with a lot before she walks out on a doctor.

NANCY PROCTOR, Nurse

It's horrible being married to a doctor. You've got to share your husband all the time. Let's say it's your anniversary and he promised to come home early. You make a special dinner and put on your sexy underwear, and everything's warmed up and ready to go. But somebody's really sick and he can't leave the hospital. The evening's spoiled but you can't even blame him.

DR. REUBEN PESKIN, Director, Hospice Project

Women have been programmed to believe that doctors make the best husbands. You can almost hear the mothers saying it: "Why don't you marry a nice doctor who'll always take care of you?" A doctor is supposed to be strong and nurturing and protective. He's supposed to be a superman who can take care of all the woman's needs. But maybe he comes home at night and he wants to sit and read the paper. He's been with patients all day and he's absolutely exhausted. The wife gets jealous and says, "You love your patients more than you love me." That's not true, but it is true that he wants to have a different relationship with her than he has with them. It's just it's hard to make her understand, because part of what attracted her in the first place is the fantasy of living with a doctor. As a result, the wives often become hypochondriacs. They develop all kinds of imaginary illnesses to get their husbands' attention. They feel it's the only way they can get him away from his patients.

DR. LANNY BUCKMAN, Pediatric Resident

During the last years I was married to Jack there was a feeling of competition between the hospital and his family. He was running the emergency room at Memorial. He's very good at what he does, and the patients and the people who worked for him gave him so much adulation and respect that his wife and kids couldn't possibly compete. At home, the expectations were a lot more complex and the family wanted him to give a lot more. It got to the point where he started saying, "Everybody else admires me, but you're the only one who's critical, who doesn't appreciate what I do." Well, I did appreciate him but I couldn't treat him like God. He was supposed to be my husband, not just a brilliant surgeon.

JOE RIVERA, Emergency Care Technician

I don't think doctors know what love is. They're competitive throughout life—they've got to be tops. In medical school they're taught that you're the doctor, this is the patient, remove the feelings and just look at what's going on. So this is what they do when they leave the hospital; they've been doing it so long that they can't cut it off. Only one or two of the ones I've worked for were normal or loving people. The rest of them have problems. Big problems.

DR. CARL GORMAN, Neurosurgeon

Everybody expects a doctor to have a divorce or two. It's part of the pattern. It usually comes when you're about forty and you're rolling along with your practice. You're entering a period of maximum earnings. Got a big house, drive a Rolls, a Mercedes or whatnot. And what else is the big status symbol in life? A beautiful young woman. But you've got some old battle-ax. Been a good wife, and maybe even put you through school, but she's not quite what you're looking for in status. Doctors are very status-conscious, or else they wouldn't have gone into medicine. So you start to look around. Your wife finds out, she's pissed off, divorce. And the truth is, it's becoming more acceptable.

DR. BURTON WEBBER, Ear, Nose, and Throat

There are certain recognized danger points for medical marriages. Especially in the transition from the days of residency and making relatively little money to the days of private practice and adoring patients. All of a sudden you begin making money and you begin making it very fast. There's a sudden sense of power that can

145

be very hard to handle. I think it leads to a kind of confusion about yourself and your values.

I find it sad when I look around at my colleagues and their family situations. We have, for example, the "Yes, doctor" syndrome. A physician works all day long with patients who hang on his every word, nurses who hang on his every order. This whole life we lead outside the home builds up our sense of power. Everybody says, "Yes, doctor, yes, doctor," all day long. Then you come home, and your wife says no. She says, "Go take the garbage out" or "Why are you late?" or "That was a foolish thing you said." The kind of thing we never get during the day.

That contrast does foster some very genuine difficulties in terms of a marriage. But that's part of the challenge. In my opinion, none of the negatives about this profession can take away from the sense of privilege and satisfaction that it gives you. At least that's my conclusion from my career and my life these last thirty years, and I don't think I'm so unusual.

THE PARAGON

DR. BURTON WEBBER
Ear, Nose, and Throat

DR. ARNOLD BRODY, Director of Medical Oncology

There may be a good more substance to Burton than I give him credit for. He and I and Eddie Ferraro were all premeds together, and even way back then Burton was very involved with the premed society, and all those prissy little things. And doing it right! Always into the most prestigious fraternity. Neither Eddie nor I would have anything to do with it. To us, guys like Burton Webber were a royal pain in the ass. He's probably a decent doctor but he's not one of my favorite people.

DR. EDWARD FERRARO, Medical Oncologist

I first met Burt when we were both premeds and we took embryology in summer school. He was really a handsome guy, very suave, tremendously popular, and I guess I must have envied him somewhat. He seemed to lead this romantic, wonderful life and all of the best-looking women always wanted to go out with him. He was probably stuck-up, but he went to a lot of trouble not to show it. He was really sweet, and pleasant to everybody. Bright too, but not real bright. He had to struggle to get into medical school. He chose a specialty—ear, nose, and throat—which doesn't involve a lot of real doctoring or brain power. And I always saw him as just this decent sort of mediocre guy.

I sort of lost touch with him over the years but then I got an ear infection, and my doctor was away on vacation. So I decided to go to Burt. And I went to his office and I just couldn't believe it. I mean, there must have been two dozen people sitting around in that waiting room. Sitting there for two hours, just waiting for a few minutes with the great Dr. Webber! Suddenly I realized how successful he had become, how he had gotten to be a much bigger doctor than I was. Then later he even ended up as head of the County Medical Association. He has it all—the big house, the big car, the rich practice, membership in all the right fraternities and clubs. That's how I think of Burt today—the classic image of a very successful doctor.

DR. DAVID ANZAK, Obstetrician-Gynecologist

When I was in medical school, Dr. Webber was a very well-known leader of the medical community. I heard him speak at a forum on medical ethics, and I thought he was pompous and smug. He was so gung ho for medicine, and so politically conservative, that my attitude as a medical student was pretty much negative.

That's changed over the last few years as I've gotten to know him. We've become friendly through social events and some of the internal politics here at Memorial, and I found out that Burton Webber is a delightful person. He and his wife are two of the most charming people I've ever met. With his warmth and his concern he's sort of an old-fashioned, Marcus Welby–style doctor. He just strikes me as a happy man. I don't know if it's because of his professional life or his family life or both, but that's just the impression he gives. He seems like he's in a situation where all the pieces fit together.

———————

When I called Burton Webber to arrange an interview, he insisted, though we had never met before, that I come to his home for dinner on the night of our conversation.

Three days later I joined the doctor and his wife for a delightful meal of barbecued salmon steaks and corn on the cob. The cozy dining room, paneled in maple, struck a note of rustic simplicity. The entire home, in fact, suggested a colonial New England farmhouse incongruously transplanted to a hilltop in Northern California.

Dr. Webber's wife presided over the meal and gave instructions in Spanish to a white-uniformed maid. A slender, handsome woman in her mid-fifties, Fran Webber wore her graying brown hair in a neat coil at the back of her head. Her somber demeanor offered a strong contrast to her husband's lighthearted jocularity. Having just arrived from the office, Dr. Webber still wore his immaculately tailored blue three-piece suit and bore more than a passing resemblance to Spencer Tracy. If central casting wanted an actor for the role of an eminent yet compassionate physician, they could hardly have done better than Burton Webber.

I'VE ALWAYS KNOWN that I wanted to be a doctor, as far back as I can remember. The only problem was getting into medical school.

As a premed, I spent too much time on my social life and my grades were never that hot. Two years in a row I applied to medical schools but they didn't want me, so I entered a graduate program in zoology. I went on to my master's degree, and then I got a job teaching zoology at a state college. I did research, and I was good at it. I published a few papers, but I just didn't feel at home as a researcher in the laboratory. I wanted more of a direct human contact. So at age twenty-eight, I decided to reapply to medical school. This time, with my M.S. and my publications and so forth, I looked more impressive to the medical schools, and I was accepted.

By that time I was already married for four years and we had two little kids. I met Fran when I was in grad school in zoology. She was doing research for the man who I later took my Ph.D. with. I've always thought she was more intelligent than I am. My skills are dealing with people, but Fran is the real intellectual in the family. We met in the laboratory, and four months later we got married. Exactly nine months after that came our first child.

149

We had to struggle when I was in medical school, because we had the kids and we didn't have much money. My parents were in the furniture business in Oakland, but by this time they were retired. They had used up their savings helping me through college and graduate school. Fran's parents were living in a duplex, and they gave us the apartment upstairs where we only had to pay fifty dollars a month. But other than that we were on our own, so I taught anatomy and I did research and so forth, just to make some extra money.

I didn't pick my specialty until senior year in medical school. When we took our rotation in ear, nose, and throat, part of the assignment was spending a day with one of the attending doctors in that specialty. This was around 1958, and the whole science of ear surgery was just beginning to blossom. And that morning I came in and put on a green scrub suit and I went into the OR. The attending doctor said, "Sit down. You can look into this little eyepiece and see the operation." Well, I can't tell you! Through that microscope you could see everything—the whole anatomy of incredibly beautiful, fine little blood vessels. There was no bleeding at all, and at the end of the operation the patient's hearing had been almost completely restored. It was surgery that was creative, with results you could measure. I came home to Fran and said, "I had the most exciting morning watching surgery and I decided I'm going into ear, nose, and throat." And I never wavered.

I set up my own practice after residency, and right away the money came rolling in. There are several factors, I think, that contributed to my success. One of them is a piece of good advice that was given to me by a dear friend who is a well-known proctologist. Very early in the game, he said to me, "Whatever you do, Burton, remember that you should never hurt your patients when you examine them." Now, this fellow was working in the lower end, doing rectal exams and putting scopes and tubes and so forth in those areas. He treated me once as a patient. He had a metal instrument up my rear, and he was so gentle and so kind about the use of this instrument that I couldn't even believe it. Well, the same way, when you examine ear, nose, and throat, you can do it in a mild manner or you can do it roughly. Sometimes there are things that you have to do which will hurt the patient, and then I'll anesthetize the area. I'll even do that for a routine examination. It's particularly important for children, but it's also true for adults, who aren't much different from children when it comes to going to the doctor.

You have to be decisive at all times, and give very definite opinions, because the patients don't want to hear an answer of "maybe." It can be onerous, but it's exciting. People believe in me. My wife could pick up the phone and say, "Take two aspirin and you're going to be okay." But when I say the same words, the patients get better.

And that's why people are shaped in a special way by working in this field. A lot of people come into medicine with their own hangups or immaturity, but the responsibilities are so real that they have to change. We are forced to make decisions that involve life and limb of an individual. I don't have it quite as much in my specialty, but even in my situation I can't avoid it. I get really important questions, like "Doctor, am I going to live to see my daughter's wedding, or will I live to do such and such? Can I travel under these circumstances?" and so forth. You have to give an answer, and you can't have a playful attitude to another person's life. So medicine begins to mold the doctor into a more solid kind of individual.

That doesn't mean you can please the patients every single time. I spend more time with some patients than I should, so I keep others waiting, and then I come into the examining room and I can feel the hostility. When I face that kind of situation, it's like a game with me. I know I have to turn the patient around from being angry and hostile to walking out on cloud nine. Usually I can do it. I don't really know where that skill came from. Maybe God's been kind to me in that way. I use what skills I have, as a physician and as a person, to get the patients to feel that I really do care and I want them to get well. I may not be the greatest doctor, but my patients think I am, and they really do get well.

Ear, nose, and throat is a surgical subspecialty, and I do surgery at least three mornings a week. I always operate at Memorial, because its facilities are probably the best in the area. I do tonsils, nasal surgery, laryngeal surgery. I love doing ear surgery, but these days a lot of it tends to go to specialty groups.

I don't see a lot of fatal diseases. I've picked up a few cancers, but even cancer of the vocal cords is ninety-nine percent curable. I have no doubt I picked doing tonsils, doing nasal surgery, because they're curable situations. The most frustrating circumstance that I encounter in my field is bleeding that I have trouble controlling. There are some doctors that deal in huge amounts of blood. Guys in Ob-Gyn, for instance. They'll say, "I had a great surgery today, only lost 700 cc's of blood." They've got blood all over the table and the floor, and so forth. They're just used to a lot of bleeding. But for me, the loss of blood is something to be avoided. Having to give the patient extra units of blood is something that is personally very upsetting. Somehow or other, I feel I'm losing part of my patient's life if I'm losing blood, and I do all that I can to control it.

But even when I'm very tense, very concerned, I manage to suppress it. My patients would never know. They'll greet me and say, "Oh, you're so calm, you're so even-tempered." That's the image. Of course it's an emotional drain to put that across, but I think I've gotten used to it. In fact, I think it's therapy for me. There are days when I get out of bed and I'm exhausted from the previous day, and I'll wish that I didn't have to go in to the office. But I get there, and I see that first patient, and I'm alive! In some respects they do more for me than I do for them.

I try to pay some of that back with all my activities in medical organizations. Sometimes it's three or four nights a week with one meeting or another. Maybe I'm trying to take on too much. I'm very active in the local PSRO, the Peer Standards Review Organization that tries to weed out or discipline doctors who aren't up to the standards of the profession. In addition to that, there's our major medical fraternity, which is Phi Delta Epsilon. We try to aid medical students, interns, residents, and so forth. And I just completed a term as president of the local group and now I'm one of the regional officers.

My biggest commitment is to the County Medical Association. I've been very much involved for the last twenty years, and I've served six terms as president. When I think about the time that goes into it I sometimes wonder if I'm crazy. I'm not quite sure why I do it. Part of it is that I have a lot of difficulty saying no. And because I do a good job, I tend to get a lot of other jobs pushed on me.

One of the consequences of all this activity is that I have a lot of doctors who come to me as patients. I'd have to say they are very difficult. Most doctors never think of themselves as sick. They divide the world into the sick people and the doctors. We're vertical and they're horizontal. You comfort them. It's more difficult for a physician to be ill and to get effective treatment because he is aware of all the little tricks that he uses as a physician that are now being used on him.

The other place I meet a lot of doctors is on the golf course. It's a great way to unwind, and a lot of us really love to play. It gives you the chance to concentrate on something as simple as hitting a ball. I just focus on that little ball and I totally relax. I don't even wear a beeper when I play, because I really don't want to be disturbed.

I play twice a month, but I like to spend most of my free time with my family. Our two kids are grown up now, but I still like to get together with them. Barry is twenty-six and Laura is twenty-four. He used to be a musician, piano and drums, and so forth, but now he's back in school. He's going to try to finish a B.A. and then he's interested in engineering. Laura is working for a rock-and-roll TV production company, and she's also thinking of going back to school.

I don't think I have a real warm relationship with them. I don't think they're the kind of people who want a warm relationship. I don't know if it has anything to do with medicine, because it would probably be the same if I was a businessman or a professor at school. But sometimes I do blame myself and feel like I should blame my work. As I look back, when the kids were young, I guess I didn't spend enough time with them. I was busy running around to various meetings, or being on call when I was a resident. I regret it now. They weren't unhappy as kids, because they had a very strong mother at home, but I certainly could have done a better job.

I've very proud of my marriage. It's been thirty-two years now. And it gets better—the last ten years were better than the first twenty, and those first twenty were good. But now there's more a sense of working together and just the feeling of comfort, companionship. Fran works in my office, she does all the bookkeeping and so forth. We eat lunch together every day. I have things with her that just wouldn't be possible to have with another person. I have my children, but they're distant, and my parents are gone, her parents are gone. I don't have many close friends. And my wife is that friend to me.

I've always had Fran as my number-one priority, and I think I've avoided exaggerating my own importance as a physician. I think a good doctor recognizes that he's just helping along what are the natural body recuperative processes. I'm constantly amazed at the recuperative powers of the body. And they do work, the body repairs.

I remember a young man, a young black man, who came in with a terrible sore throat, very red; it looked like a typical strep throat which should be sensitive to penicillin. So I gave him a prescription for penicillin and I told him to take it and come back in a week.

I'm really not sure why he did come back, but there he was the following week and I looked at the throat and it was no longer red and the glands had gone down and he was much improved. So I was sort of silently patting myself on the back, and I said to him, "I guess the medicine really worked." He was very embarrassed and sort of looked down at the floor and then pulled out of his pocket the crumpled prescription I had given him the week before. And he said, "I really didn't have enough money to buy that medicine." He got well without it, and I had absolutely nothing to do with it.

It just goes to show how most of the people who we think we cure would probably be cured just as well without us. Maybe the most important thing we can do is to give them that psychological boost that's going to help them heal themselves. That's why I'm very concerned that the technical aspects of medicine have sort of taken over some of the human aspects. What really bothers me is the way we try to make our patients cling to life with all of this mechanical gadgetry right until the very end.

When you think about death you have to come back to the conclusion that it really is out of our hands. When the body is working, it's a beautifully integrated mechanism, with bones, muscles, nerves, hormones, and all of the perfect little receptors. But if it begins to falter, all the systems start to fail. I've become very attuned when I'm working with a patient as to whether I'm dealing with a local systemic phenomenon. Is the patient bleeding because they cut a little blood vessel in the nose or has the whole mechanism of blood clotting somehow gone awry? When the systemic problems start to crop up, then all that beautiful balance begins to fall apart, and it's terrible to watch. That's why I could never be a cancer doctor like Brody or Ferraro. For them, the battle's over before they even start to fight.

When I do have to deal with tragedy, I let my religious feelings come into it. Not religious in any formal, organized sense, but my strong feelings about God and nature and the way it all works. For

154

me, there's no question that working as a doctor has made me more religious. You have to acknowledge how remarkably well the body's put together, with all of its subtle restorative powers. I really do believe that all this is the work of some other Hand and I'm just there to help. After thirty years in this field, I have no doubt that God is a major factor. He helps me. And I help Him.

DEATH'S
ASSISTANT

DR. EDWARD FERRARO
Medical Oncologist

DR. BURTON WEBBER, Ear, Nose, and Throat

Eddie and I went to school together. He always got better grades than I did, and he never let me forget it. Today, he's an excellent physician. Keeps up with all the latest developments in his field and cares about his patients to an outstanding degree. In his personal life, I'd say he was a little bit on the loose side. He's been married several times and he has a reputation as a bohemian type. He's kind of an offbeat person, but in terms of medicine he's a very devoted, very dedicated guy.

DR. STEVEN EBERSOLL, Radiologist

You look at him and you know he's unhappy. It's interesting that he's into oncology, which is really a grim specialty, a real bitch. It seems to me that he bears a cross, he likes to suffer.

PEGGY HAGERTY, Head Nurse, Delivery Room

Eddie is multidimensional. He's interested in things that most doctors don't even know about. Politically, we share a common background in the antiwar movement and the feminist movement. He started out as more of a conventional doctor, but he evolved into someone very special.

DR. ARNOLD BRODY, Director of Medical Oncology

Eddie is definitely a good doc, yeah, he's damn good. He can't work nearly as hard as I do, but he still gives it all he's got. I just wish he'd dress up more as a doc and not try so hard to be avant-garde. I think the patients would appreciate it. That's another problem with Eddie: He doesn't know how to treat people nicely on a personal level. He's very insensitive, like a lot of my liberal friends. I'd rather live next door to a Reagan Republican. They're better neighbors than these guys who are always wanting to do things for the masses. To hell with the masses, man, be nice to your next-door neighbor! Be considerate. In medical school, Eddie could be really mean. He would make the most cutting, biting, nasty remarks. I have a tongue too, so I'd give it back and we'd end up cutting each other to ribbons.

Our relationship has always had that competitive edge—especially since we wound up in exactly the same subspecialty, directly competing for patients. We're still basically friendly. We have the best conversations when we're alone, just the two of us. But you get us in a crowd where there are women around and he goes absolutely bananas. So it's kept us from being closer friends than we are. And in my book, that's too bad.

A quiet Sunday morning proved to be the perfect time to interview Dr. Edward Ferraro. His live-in girlfriend was spending the weekend with friends in Los Angeles; Ferraro felt lonely without her and welcomed the opportunity to talk. We sat down over coffee in the family room of his rambling Victorian home. Ferraro is a small man, no more than five feet four inches tall, with a shining bald pate, bushy black beard, and wire-rim glasses. He wore faded jeans, an oversize Hawaiian shirt, and rubber thongs.

Before we could begin we were interrupted by Laurie, the fifteen-year-old daughter of Ferraro's housemate, who came in wearing her pajamas. Ferraro explained that I was there to interview him for a book. Laurie scratched her head incredulously. "A book? About you?"

"You see?" Ferraro answered her. "Not everybody thinks I'm boring."

Settling down to business after she left, we began with the obvious question of why he had chosen to enter a field as morbid as oncology.

I NEVER MADE a conscious choice. I kind of drifted into it, and one day I looked around and I was a cancer doctor.

Most of my life has been like that. I was thinking about it at two-thirty this morning. Judy, the woman I live with, is out of town, and I was supposed to take care of her daughter. Laurie was supposed to let me know where she was going to be and to leave a phone number, but she didn't do it. So I got very parental and I stayed up waiting for her and watching TV. I watched the movie *Same Time, Next Year.* Laurie finally showed up at one-fifteen, but by that time I couldn't go to sleep so I finished watching the movie. I poured myself a large glass of brandy, and this morning woke up hung over. Right now I feel kind of weird, hazy, hung over. And I spent a big part of the time thinking about the discontinuity in my life. I think it was precipitated by that movie. It's about two people who have an affair, and they keep seeing each other just once a year for the next twenty-six years. The woman talks about how she can never leave her husband because of the experiences that they've had together. I wish that I had something like that in my life. That I had twenty-six years of experience with one woman. I haven't.

You see, I'm different from the other doctors you'll talk to.

158

Medicine isn't the most important thing in my life. Relationships are. And I've made a mess of my relationships.

I was born in San Francisco and I grew up in North Beach, which was—and still is—an Italian neighborhood. My parents were immigrants. My father was a sewing-machine operator in a factory. My mother was a housewife, but she also worked part-time as a saleslady. Today she is seventy-nine years old, and since '66 she's worked in my office. She is our insurance clerk. My sister works for me too. She never got married, and she's worked for me for twelve years. She's our bookkeeper and office manager.

When I was a kid I was crazy for books. I used to hang around the public library. One of my favorite books was *Microbe Hunters* by Paul DeKruif. It told the story of past heroes in the fight against disease. Then I saw the movie *Louis Pasteur*. By that time I had decided that's what I wanted to be. My romantic image was that I was going to be a medical researcher. I think I also knew at that time that I was going to have a beard, like Paul Muni in the movie.

I got a full scholarship to the University of California, and I was premed from the beginning. I worked hard, because I felt like I had something to prove. My parents never even graduated from grade school, and when I got into medical school, my mother framed my letter of acceptance. For my first year, I kept on living at home, but then I got married.

When I look back on it, I have no idea how that happened. At that point in my life I had no experience dating. Really none. Then at the end of my first year of medical school I was introduced to someone by one of my classmates. She was three years older than me and had just separated from her husband. She was, I think, physically attractive—or at least interesting-looking. She sang professionally before I met her and had a good voice and an interesting jazz style. Emotionally, she was very fragile, and that was part of her attractiveness to me.

Her name was Judy. My second wife was also Judy, and the woman I live with now is another Judy. So if I wake up in the middle of the night whispering somebody's name, I don't have to worry. They're all Judy. It's one of those strange things.

Judy Number One was my first sexual experience. She was very buxom and very aggressive. On our second date we made love. After that we became intensely involved. She was working as a receptionist, but she started spending all her extra time transcribing my notes from class. Most of the things she did revolved around my activities. Almost like she had no real identity.

My mother was appalled when I announced that we were getting married. This woman was divorced. She wasn't Italian. She wasn't even Catholic. However, my mother is an accommodater. She accommodated to it, and she still has a relationship with Judy. More of a relationship than I have.

I became, in a lot of ways, a different person with Judy. I was an unsophisticated kid from North Beach, and she opened up the world of theater, the arts, of traveling. She also worked to put me through medical school, and made it possible for me to live away from my parents' home. She was a lovely, gentle, tentative kind of person. But also a big pain in the ass.

We were married for eight years. By the time I finished medical school she had a variety of symptoms that were unexplained, including fever and fatigue. She found it more and more difficult to go out in the world. She became mildly phobic in a lot of ways; for example, she wasn't able to go marketing without being accompanied.

I guess some of this was gratifying to me. Here was this person who had nothing in the world except me. But it became an enormous price to pay. I was wearing handcuffs in a lot of ways. I can recall when I finished my residency, and I was about to go into a job that involved a year of research. We did not have a lot of money, but Judy and I planned a party where we were going to invite a number of my new bosses. She was not working at the time, but the preparation became an overwhelming kind of thing to her and she wanted to have the party catered. We had an enormous quarrel, and she took off her ring and threw it on the floor and said she didn't want to be married to me anymore.

I guess it was kind of a relief. I had the fantasy many times during our marriage that she was killed in an accident or something so that I wouldn't be responsible for ending the relationship. But when she threw the ring down, I saw an opportunity and moved out.

Then we got divorced, and I thought I was going to start feeling better. Instead I got very depressed, despondent. I felt like my world had ended and there was no possibility of ever having a relationship again. I ended up going into analysis for two years, and to support that I had to get a couple of extra jobs. I was already doing research, and I started working in an emergency room and doing a couple of hours a week with a group of general practitioners. I learned something very interesting—that I felt shitty all the time except when I was engaged in doctoring. So I finally gave up my romantic kind of boyhood idea about doing medical research. I got a job at the VA hospital working on a special project with a group of patients with hematologic blood disorders. And that's how I first got my background and my reputation as a cancer doctor.

As I started working more and more with patients, I discovered something very interesting about myself.

Patients, for some reason, like to unburden themselves with me. I'm always astounded at what comes out, but I was even more astounded when the same thing started happening outside of medicine. I would meet women and they would immediately want to confide in me and become intimate with me. All of a sudden, lots of women became available to me in a way that I could never conceive of a few years before. I was going out all the time.

But sexually it was a disaster. There are different kinds of impotence, and I had all varieties. Sometimes I couldn't get an erection, sometimes I was unable to sustain an erection. Sometimes I ejaculated prematurely and sometimes I ejaculated without any real sensation. Now, when I was seeing so many women, it was just horrible. I'd be so embarrassed that it was rare that I dated somebody more than a time or two.

Then one night I made a housecall. The patient was an attractive young lady who had a respiratory-tract infection. I examined her, prescribed for her, and left. Then the next day she called in the middle of the afternoon and said, "Do you believe in Freud?"

It was a provocative question, and I said, "Yeah, I think I do."

She said, "Well, you left your stethoscope at my house last night."

I stopped by to pick it up, on my way home, and I found myself angry at her. She was a smart-ass, gratuitously psychoanalyzing. I didn't like her, and I wanted to punish her by fucking her, showing her she was no big deal. And later that night we ended up in bed and I was sexually super. We had an incredible physical relationship. I was everything I'd ever fantasized myself to be. I could fuck her ten times and it was wonderful and she came lots of times. After that, my impotence problems just went away. I continued seeing this lady for a while, but it was a very stormy relationship.

My career was still kind of pathetic. I was working as an assistant for an established internist. He had an enormous practice, and most of his patients were very wealthy, very spoiled people. One expression that they used was "I use Dr. So-and-So," like he was a bar of soap or toilet paper. I really hated it.

I was already thinking about going into some different aspect of medicine when I met Judy Number Two, my second wife. We met at a party given by two homosexuals who I was treating at the time. These two guys said, "She's the perfect person for you. The only problem is that she's married, but that won't last." Physically, she was very attractive. Very petite, with a wonderful figure, and a big smile and dark eyes. There was a stylishness about her that made her stand out. She was an accomplished violinist, and she probably could have had a concert career if she wanted it.

The first night I found her just terrific. She told me she had just left her husband and she hoped that she would see me again. The very next day I got a call from her that she was ill, her regular doctor was unavailable, would I see her. She came into the office with a low-grade infection and a little fever. I did an examination and she undressed. While I was examining this beautiful body, she asked me to come to dinner at her house. Of course I accepted. She obviously had put a lot of effort into making a gourmet dinner. We had some wine, and ended up going to bed together that night. It was an exciting night.

We decided to get married right away, but we had to strike a couple of deals first. Judy had to agree that we were going to have a family. I didn't want to get married again unless I was going to have children. But she wanted to continue with her music, studying and giving lessons, so we were going to get full-time help. Both of us were thirty-three at the time. Both of us felt like we were approaching being over the hill. Getting married was an attempt on both our parts to settle down and be normal.

I realized I had to get my practice together. Up to this time I was very unsuccessful. It had been seven years since I finished residency, and I had never made more than fifteen thousand dollars in one year. For a doctor, that is absolutely pathetic. I was working for other people, or doing research jobs, or trying to start my own practice in internal medicine. My first year in practice by myself, my income above expenses was four thousand dollars. The normal mechanisms for building up a practice were just not available to me. I didn't belong to a medical fraternity. I didn't socialize with any doctors. I got no referrals. I had no special talents that I could present to the medical community. I had an office, but no mechanism for attracting patients.

Judy had the idea that I should step forward as a cancer doctor. This was the early sixties, and the whole idea of oncology as a separate specialty was just getting started. There were only two other people in the orbit of Memorial practicing cancer medicine. Both of them were unacceptable choices to a lot of people. One of them was an older man who overprescribed medications to hurry the process of death, and he was more or less known for poisoning his patients. The other one was Arnold Brody, who is a friend of mine and a good doctor, but a very aggressive, difficult personality. He was like a salesman about his practice, trying to pack in as many patients as he could and not giving the kind of time and attention that a lot of people wanted. So there was room for me. I offered an alternative that was attractive to a lot of people. I was unaggressive. I was relaxed. I didn't poison people. I had lots of time, I loved to spend time with them. And I started getting referrals for all the difficult patients, who were having real emotional problems associated with their cancer.

Around this time we bought a house in Berkeley and got involved with the whole intellectual and political community that was developing in the mid-sixties. Judy was very much part of that, and she kind of brought me along. I stopped wearing a suit and tie, and started coming to the hospital in turtlenecks or sweaters. I also grew a beard, and I was the only guy on the entire staff at Memorial who had a beard at that time. I really took some heat from the other doctors, but a lot of patients liked it. They liked the fact that I had a different style, that I was a little unconventional. When people are dying of cancer a lot of times they want somebody who's not your typical efficient, uptight doctor.

In 1964, shortly after we were married, we were invited by a friend of Judy's to listen to a Quaker who had just come back from Vietnam. As we walked out of that experience Judy said, "My kid is never going to go to war." She was pregnant at that time, and the issue of Vietnam suddenly became important to her.

The next week she called together fourteen, fifteen of our friends and neighbors and started organizing a group of middle-class women to oppose the war. She was involved in some of the first teach-ins, and then in every step of the antiwar movement after that. She got very involved in the peace effort and became sort of a celebrity in the movement. She gave up her music to devote herself totally to the cause.

Right at the beginning of this phase our son was born. That was really a good time for me. It was so delicious, here we were in our late thirties with this wonderful little boy at home. We talked about having another child right away, and I really wanted it, but Judy wasn't so sure. She was out of the house every day with her movement work, and sometimes traveling around the country. Then one day she came home from a meeting in Chicago and she walked in the door and announced that we weren't going to have any more children. That was it. No discussion. She never recognized that there was another human being with needs and desires who had to be consulted.

Things were okay while Joey was a little boy and the peace movement was going on. But in the seventies the movement started winding down, and she started getting depressed. She talked about getting back to her music, but she started transferring her energy from the peace movement to Berkeley politics, working to get a radical slate on the city council. I didn't like the people who were doing that, and I thought she should be spending more time with Joey. The problem was that Judy didn't really feel good about herself. We became less intimate, less friendly. It was a marriage where I think I would have bailed out lots of times except for the fact that we had a kid.

There were a series of angry exchanges, and one night I came home from work and there was a political meeting in our living room, as there frequently was. After the people left, we quarreled. I told her I needed a home, not a meeting hall, and I told her to get her own place. Within a week she came up to me while I was reading the paper and she had a big smile on her face and she said, "I'm getting my own place. I'm moving out."

She left Joey with me, and I maintained a household with him. And that part of my life became very satisfying to me. There was something wonderful about Joey and me being together and not having another person with needs and demands to contend with. It was a very nice time.

Then I met my present lady—Judy Number Three. When I told Judy Number Two that this new woman was going to move in with us, that's when it all blew up. All of a sudden she wanted to take Joey away from me and she wouldn't agree to joint custody. It was like *Kramer vs. Kramer*—she had walked out on her son but then she changed her mind and wanted him back.

It ended up in court. It went on for ten months and it cost about five grand in legal fees. We were in court for more than a week, and they put Joey on the stand and he started crying and everybody thought it was because he was so unhappy living with me. Judy asked for sole custody and she got her way. She also poisoned my son's mind against me.

That was a difficult thing to go through, but I did what I did after my first divorce: I fell back on medicine. By this time I was really happy in medicine, I had a practice that made a real contribution. It's an unusual practice. And I think that my partners and I are unusual people. My income is maybe one-third of what most people would make in this specialty, because we spend enormous time with out patients. Most people deal with cancer as a technological exercise. But we're different. We deal with psychosocial support.

One of the conscious decisions I've made is that I'm not going to be real busy, because when I'm really pushed, working long hours and moving rapidly from one thing to another, I feel terrible. And I get depressed. That's why my two associates and I share all our patients. There are times when I'll say "I can't stand it" or "I can't make this decision about this patient, and you do it" or "Talk to me and hold my hand." We give each other lots of emotional support. That's important, because if I'm relatively happy, I'm well rested and I feel good, then I deal with my patients in a warm, friendly, concerned personal way. If I'm tired or depressed or pushed I can be angry, unavailable.

There's another thing I like about oncology. When I was in a general practice, I spent lots of time working with trivial kinds of decisions. The decision as to whether to tell somebody to gargle with salt or hydrogen peroxide, or whether to take Librium or a Valium. Now almost all the decisions I make are critical. And that feels good. I know that I'm never wasting my time.

In our practice, we average one death certificate every week. Very frequently the death of one of our patients is a relief. But sometimes there is an involvement with a patient that makes the whole process very sad. Naturally I pay an emotional price for what I do, but there's also an emotional dividend. Sometimes that comes from prolonging life, and sometimes it comes from shortening it. I know that there are things that I do that most people are unable or unwilling to do.

A lot of times I'm willing to step in and do things that make the situation easier for everybody. I'll cut short the suffering. There's no dramatic, climactic episode. I won't give them a lethal dose of anything. But maybe I'll give them enough morphine to make them unaware of their dilemma, physically and emotionally. It reduces the pain they're going to feel, but it definitely shortens their life. That's what we call "snowing" a patient. Helping them let go of life more quickly and quietly.

Sometimes a patient will ask for that kind of help, but other times she may be incapable. There are times when a patient is in the hospital and I decide it's not in her best interest to prolong existence. We just had a case like that—a woman in her early sixties, no family, never married. And she was just skin and bones and riddled with cancer, lying in her bed crying all the time. In my judgment, she didn't have the capability of participating in decisions about her treatment. She was afraid of dying but she also didn't want to end up in a convalescent hospital. And if we prolonged her existence she would have to leave the hospital and she would end up in the convalescent home, which would be a terrible experience for her. So I made the decision and increased her dosage of morphine. She died relatively peacefully about two weeks ago.

I know there are people who say I have no right to make decisions like that, but they've never been in situations like I see every day. I'm something more than a personal servant with technological training. It's not my job to do everything exactly as the patient wants it. I'm a physician, and I'm supposed to act in the best interests of the patient. Sometimes that means shortening a life.

Sure, it makes me sad. A lot of times I'll feel tearful. Sometimes I bring my emotions home with me and it takes me about an hour to settle down. My present lady is very good about that. She knows when I come home from the hospital she has to wait about an hour or so before she can start treating me like a normal human being. We've lived together three years now, and she knows me. She's thirty-nine, fifteen years younger than me, and she looks younger than that. She's a fashion designer and she makes a good living at it. She's Jewish, and the first night we met we got into a big argu-

166

ment about Israel. Maybe there's something about me that puts anger and hostility very close to love.

A lot of people ask me, "Why don't you get married?" I remember the last time I saw Arnold Brody, he said, "You know, Eddie, you can't be a middle-aged hippie all your life. What kind of a statement are you trying to make by living with this woman and not getting married?" I'm not trying to make any kind of statement. We live very married. Our financial arrangement, everything, is married. But neither of us needs to go through a ceremony. For one thing, there's a religious difference that would be upsetting to our parents, and besides that, there is something I like about handling this relationship in a different way. If Judy wanted to get married, I would get married to her. But I would only do it under the condition that she would accept my last name. And so far she refuses to be the third Judy Ferraro.

But she is definitely an important part of my life, and a lot of things have changed because of her. I'm more concerned with money than ever before. Up till two years ago, I never saved a dime. But then I had to go in for a hip operation and it didn't turn out to be a complete success. I don't have a serious handicap, but I can't ride a bicycle anymore, or jog, or do anything like that. I'm much more intensely aware of my own mortality, and I realize that a time may come when I won't be earning money at this level and providing for Judy and her kids the way I do now. I'm trying to build up an estate so it'll take care of them no matter what happens. I also want to have enough so that my own kid, Joey, can get a really good start in life. I'm trying to start saving, to manage my money. It's a little late, but I think it'll work out.

I've been thinking about death more and more the last couple of months. I've already had cancer several times in my life—I mean in my fantasy. There have been several times where I had symptoms and there was a reasonable suspicion that I had cancer, but it never turned out to be anything. I've rehearsed my death and dying several thousand times. Usually it's not a painful thing to think about. I tend to make it romantic. Because of all my experience, I think I could handle it well and let it bring me closer to people.

But I still want to stick around for a while and watch Joey grow up. If he chose to be a doctor that would be very nice for me, but I don't think there's a shot in the world that that's going to happen. He's fifteen now, and he's entranced with the theater.

I want him to be happy, but more than that I want him to be useful. If he turns out to be happy and a used-car salesman, that's not okay with me. That shows you how I feel about my life. For all my troubles, for all my failures, I think I've done a good job. And it's not just the fact I'm a doctor, but the kind of doctor I chose to be. There are whole fields in medicine where people are just mechanics. They might as well be working on computers. Like radiology, where most of those guys don't even know the patients. It's a big difference from what I do. And if you want to see the opposite extreme, go talk to Steve Ebersoll. He's a radiologist and he's bored. The rumor is he's getting ready to chuck the whole thing.

THE ESCAPE
ARTIST

DR. STEVEN EBERSOLL
Radiologist

DR. JACK BUCKMAN, Director of Emergency Medicine

I'm not sure he's a person of integrity. I would not want him doing a procedure on me, let me put it that way. We were residents together, and he's not up there on what I would call a level of super competence. In addition to which, I don't think he gives a flying fuck about medicine.

DR. HARRISON O'NEILL, Gastroenterologist

Steve used to be a friend of mine, but I've seen him change. When he came out of medical school he was your basic hotshot young doctor. He was very interested in medical politics and he was going to used Memorial as a power base. But he got a reputation for double dealing, and he turned around and started putting down all the other docs in town. Started acting like a rebel and getting heavily involved in smoking grass. I don't know if Steve does other drugs, but I wouldn't be surprised.

DR. MILTON TESSLER, Cardiologist

I've worked with him several times, and he gives the impression of a highly capable radiologist. His specialty is angiography. That's where you take a little tube—a catheter—and you insert it through an artery and inject a special dye into the body. Whenever I'm watching it with one of my patients, I always get nervous. But Dr. Ebersoll is totally relaxed about it. I've seen him whistling or telling jokes when he's doing his work. He has sort of an oddball sense of humor and he likes to make off-color remarks about the nurses.

DR. ARNOLD BRODY, Director of Medical Oncology

His whole attitude is totally flip. He comes in and he does his supersophisticated technical procedures and then he walks out. Nobody likes him, but everybody works with him because he's established himself at the hospital. There's something slimy about him. It's a good thing he's a radiologist, where the patients don't have to respond to his personality. If he had to depend on direct patient contact, this guy would probably starve.

Dr. Ebersoll and his wife lived on board a yacht called Independence, *which was docked at a marina more than an hour's drive from Memorial Medical Center. On the evening of our meeting, they sat on deck enjoying the sunset with a pitcher of martinis.*

Ebersoll wore a silk shirt unbuttoned over his tanned chest; his straight blond hair fell to his shoulders and a number of gold chains encircled his neck. His wife, Annelise, spoke with a heavy German accent and wore a flashy yellow jump suit. Her hair had been bleached a harsh white and razor-cut to a length much shorter than her husband's. They were both understandably proud of the Independence, *which was the largest and most elegant craft in the little harbor. After showing me the spacious accommodations below decks, Annelise went to her cabin to watch TV, and*

Ebersoll seated himself at the galley table to discuss his pride and joy.

SHE'S THE ULTIMATE, I think, in a cruising boat. She's a sixty-one-foot rigged ketch, with fiberglass hold, all-teak interior, and an eighty-foot mast. And she just sails like a bloody demon. We've done things to her to just make her perfect. And we've done everything to prepare ourselves for a long voyage. We may write a book about going to sea in a boat like this, doing what we're doing, and why we're doing it.

I'm taking a leave of absence from Memorial. We're going to be gone at least two years, maybe more, sailing around Mexico and South America. The name *Independence* is very important, because that's what she represents. We've already been living on the boat for eight months, getting her ready. Living on the boat is fabulous. You sit here and eat your dinner and look out the porthole and see the water. You listen to the buoys. We have a little community of people here who live on their boats. And it's like being away from civilization. It's another world.

I usually get up early in the mornings, around six o'clock. I'm studying Morse Code, so I do that or I run or work about. I'm at the hospital at ten o'clock; I work hard, but I'm usually done by four. I do two or three angiograms every day. I try to get most of the angios done in the morning so I can have a few hours in the afternoon for looking at film and consultations with doctors and dealing with the body scanner and a lot of paperwork.

An angiogram usually takes about an hour and a half. A lot of times it's neuro-angiography, which means we go into the brain. The catheter goes in through the groin and up into the arteries and the neck, up into the head. We push it right up there. It's a little device about the size of a pencil lead, and it goes in about four feet. We can do an angiogram of the heart, or the kidneys, whatever we want, to diagnose tumors or vascular disease. The patient has a local anesthetic and we premedicate them with some narcotic so they're kind of twilighty, but we don't want them out. They've got to be awake. We want them to tell us if something goes wrong.

171

You tell them what to expect and if there's anything strange you'd like to know about it.

After the catheter is in place, we inject contrasts—dyes—sometimes very fast. We have a power injector on the machine and it makes kind of a whine. I've been doing angios for fifteen years but I still feel myself wincing when the injector whines. You've got to get just the right amount of dye. If you don't get enough, the picture won't turn out. But if you inject too much you can kill the patient.

There's a limit to what an artery can take, and sometimes you pass it. I've been on that borderline sometimes. That's the really touchy time, when you don't know whether to go forward with that one injection that will give you the diagnosis, but it might also kill 'em. I've lost a few on that one, but I don't blame myself because they were very sick people. I don't think I ever hurt somebody. Most of the time I feel good about getting into an artery or a vein that nobody else can get into. And the other doctor, the surgeon or the internist or whatever, says, "You'll never get in there, Steve, without hurting the patient." And I say, "Yes I will. I'll bet you a bottle of wine." And every time that's happened and we made a bet, I've ended up with the bottle. But most of the time it's relatively routine. You go in there and you do the catheterizing that you need and you take the pictures, bam, bam, bam.

I always liked the scientific aspects of medicine. When I was an intern, the diseases interested me more than the patients. I felt that if I went into radiology I could deal more with diseases and diagnosis. I could also deal with smarter people—that is, the doctors. I'm not forced into a relationship with the patients. I don't have to be nice to them so they'll come back to me. I'm really good with my hands, and the angiography allows me to play with the surgical thrill. It also allows me to make about two hundred and fifty grand a year, more money than most internists or other people. And I can leave the hospital at four in the afternoon.

My father was a dentist, an excellent dentist, and he worked harder than I do. I grew up in Portland, Oregon, and he was very much beloved in the community. I was an only child and I guess I was a bad boy. I ran with the wrong people and I was an underachiever. I had some trouble getting through high school, passing Spanish and things like that.

I always gave my dad a rough time. I thought dentistry was a pain in the ass. Digging little holes in little mouths—nothing very interesting about that. But the body is terrific. A lot of interesting stuff in there. I just took it for granted I was going to be a doctor. I was flunking out, but I knew I was going to be a doctor.

I went to the University of Oregon, but I became sort of a bridge bum and I flunked out my second year. My father wouldn't even talk to me. I came down to San Francisco and sold vacuum cleaners and encyclopedias door to door. After a while I had people working for me and I was making a lot of money. I was living with a lady who was four or five years my senior.

It was fun for a while but then it got boring. I came back home and started school all over again. I went to a junior college and got all A's so I could get into the University of California. I worked really hard and I went right through medical school. I was on a hot streak and I was doing real well.

The only problem was that I got married right in the middle of that little episode. I was twenty-three, my wife was twenty-one, and we had two kids thereafter. We also had an absolutely miserable life for the next thirteen years. We were poor. I was in school, and my dad didn't help me at all, because he thought I should be able to take care of myself. He wanted to teach me a lesson, I guess. Maybe he was right, I don't know.

My father didn't approve of anything I did. We were never really able to get together. And it's a damn shame, 'cause my dad was a super guy. I really loved him. Finally, after I finished medical school, he started to accept the fact that I was really going to be something. I hadn't seen him for two years, but we were kind of getting back together. I was on the road, on my way home from medical school, when he died of a heart attack. It's just a damn shame.

After that I felt like I was really stuck with my wife, who was a manipulating little dummy. She was little and cute and I needed somebody to darn my socks, but it was terrible from the beginning. All she wanted was a home in the suburbs and the prestige of being married to a doctor. She kept talking about moving back to Pittsburgh and us getting a house right next to her parents. All along, I knew I was going to get a divorce. It was just a question of getting out into practice so I could afford it. I needed money because I had to provide for my kids because she could never take care of them and nobody would ever marry her again. So I hung on through medical school and residency, but as soon as I went into practice I just left.

And my kids turned out to be a disaster story. My daughter is eighteen. She lives with my ex, but she runs away all the time. She was gone for about a year, and we didn't know where she was. She goes to her mother when she needs help. A few months ago she was in an automobile accident when she was drunk and she got badly hurt. So she's living with her mother now, but I know she'll leave again. I spent thousands of dollars on psychiatry for her, but it doesn't do any good.

And my son is sixteen and he's in boarding school and maybe he'll be okay. He's very pushy and selfish and manipulative. But very smart. He's been arrested a couple of times for shoplifting, but otherwise he's okay. He says he hates me, but maybe that's typical for his age. Potentially he's a terrific kid, and we could have had a great relationship, but we lost it and now it's too late. I may not like him, but he's going to do well.

My divorce came through in '72, and there was a lot or turmoil with my ex and my kids. But I wouldn't let it interfere with my work. I think my career was enhanced, frankly, because I worked harder than I would if I had a happier life. I got very involved with things politically and got very involved with the hospital and all that kind of stuff. So I overachieved as a compensation.

It wasn't till I met Annelise that I started to mellow out. We've been together now for about five years and we got married two years ago. She was born in Germany right after the war, and her family was very poor. She came to America and opened a beauty shop, but she sold it last year so she could spend more time working on the boat. She's been married a couple of times, but she never had any kids. We met one night in a bar. I just got lucky. She's very earthy, very physical, and the most honest, down-to-earth person I've ever known. When I get home at night we just take it easy. We've been withdrawing from social commitments more and more. We've been working on the boat, reading, planning. A lot of times we'll smoke dope before we go to bed. I'd say we get high about three times a week and it really feels good. It takes the edge off. It gives me a sense of perspective.

One of the things we've talked about is whether we're going to have kids. Annelise is thirty-five, so we'd still have a shot at it. But I am selfish enough to want to go do my thing with Annelise and she is selfish enough to want to do her thing with me—just the two of us. My experience with kids hasn't been great, so we're not going to take the risk.

The big thing right now is the cruise. We're going to head for South America. We're going to catch what we eat along the way. The ocean passage really becomes a routine of schedules and watches and chores. But then another part of it will be when we dock and go into town and meet people. Getting to know the countryside. I really want to see the world. And I don't want to do it with the ugly Americans by TWA and Hilton Hotels. I want to do it by seeing the people and spending as much time as I want. And maybe when we're on shore I can do a little doctoring. Barter my services for shrimp and vegetables and that kind of thing. That's one good thing about medicine—they need doctors everywhere.

I won't miss the hospital. I've gotten to the point where there are a lot of things I don't want to do anymore. I've done radiology—it's not exciting anymore. And things have changed, so it's gotten worse in the last few years. One of the reasons that I went into medicine was because it was respected in the community. Now people look at us as a bunch of wealthy guys who flake off and won't make housecalls. Who play golf every Wednesday and screw all the nurses.

There's a whole different attitude toward doctors, a kind of hostility. Part of it is from the attorneys and the malpractice thing. It's becoming a bigger and bigger pain in the ass, and I think it's going to disenchant more and more guys. The attorneys are really dishonest, immoral people who drive their clients to make a lot of nuisance suits.

Who needs that? There's enough trouble in medicine without it. The whole atmosphere at the hospital is something I want to get away from. I see guys all the time who are suffering right along with their patients. I see what they go through when they know they're losing control. Maybe they joke about it, and it's kind of strange, you know, when someone is telling me that he can't handle the patient's metastases or the chemotherapy he's using isn't working. Or this brain tumor's coming back and he can't go in again. He'll just shrug and say, "I guess that's another one for the coroner," or "He's circling the drain." Of course that levity is a kind of defense.

They try to hide it but sometimes they're just crushed. There's so much depression and there's so much anxiety. When doctors are going over the films with me and the word gets to them that they're not going to win, they get really upset. It cuts them up, every time. It takes its toll. People get divorced, people get drunk, people get stoned. After ten or twenty years they're not the same people they were when they went in. There's a lot of madmen at Memorial, and everyone feels sorry for them because maybe they started off as good docs but then they went downhill. They couldn't handle it, but nobody told them to stop.

I'm getting out before I go crazy, before I get sloppy. A lot of other guys ought to do the same thing, but they won't. They stick around, and maybe they hurt the patients, maybe they hurt themselves.

KILLERS AT LARGE

DR. STEVEN EBERSOLL, *Radiologist*

About ten percent of the guys around Memorial shouldn't be practicing, but it's a real bitch to do something about it. We had a gastroenterology guy, a black guy, who was killing people, and everybody knew it. But we had a hell of a time getting rid of him, and then he just moved to another hospital. It was more difficult because he was black, and now we've got that same problem with this guy Lockwood who's screwing up in the delivery room. With this other guy, he sued us through the NAACP and made a big stink. It was awful!

JOE RIVERA, *Emergency Care Technician*

There are a few guys in particular who just don't care. I've had a lot of run-ins with one guy in OB-GYN. Some of his patients come into the ER and they're aborting, they're losing their babies. Rather than go up to the OR where it's more sterile, his attitude is that he'll handle them down here. He just scrubs 'em down with Betadine, which is a surgical solution that kills bacteria. I told him,

Betadine isn't gonna kill all those germs. If the patient gets infected, she can get really sick and die. But he doesn't care, he doesn't want to bother to go up to the OR. And it's becoming a well-known fact. This guy's trouble. His name is Garland Lockwood, and people on the staff know about him, but they don't do anything. And I see patients come in from simple C-sections, and they're all messed up. It's put down that he accidentally cut the colon! How can you have an accident on something like that? You're talking about something you can see.

But it's a very cliquish society, and they stick together. If you know somebody who's doing something wrong, and you voice your opinion too loud, then you're going to be hung up to dry. Because everybody makes mistakes, and then they're all gonna come down on you when you do something wrong. Nobody's gonna back you up.

DR. CARL GORMAN, Neurosurgeon

A couple of years ago we had a neurosurgeon, a very talented guy, who was an alcoholic. As a resident, I worked with him a couple of times when he did brain surgery, six, eight hours in the OR, when he was drunk as a lord. He still managed okay, and I don't think he hurt anybody. In fact, if he hadn't picked up a bunch of lawsuits, I think he'd still be here. Now he's at one of the big hospitals in New York City, and he's back in business.

DR. HARRISON O'NEILL, Gastroenterology

There was a case recently where a doctor's wife called my committee of the County Medical Association and asked for help. It's a committee set up to handle the problems of the alcoholic physician. This man was sixty-two, in family practice, and he had already gotten in trouble with the PSRO, the peer-review-organization, where they discovered gross malpractice and restricted his privileges. We met with him a couple of times. My job is to get through his denial. I am alcoholic, and having been there I can tell him, hey, look, it's possible to recover from this.

He finally accepted treatment and was hospitalized for four

weeks and got clean and sober. But the workup showed that he'd had a lot of cerebral damage from his disease. When he got out of the hospital he didn't return to drinking, but he started taking drugs. It's unfortunate but it's not unusual to see a man stop one addiction and start up with another.

He is still practicing medicine. He is seeing patients, and committing malpractice daily. His speech is slurred, he staggers, but he doesn't smell like he used to when he was drinking because now he's just a drug addict. So the patients don't know. They still come to him. There are a lot of guys like that, still out there, seeing the patients. Actually, I'd rather not count them.

DR. BARNETT GOLDSTEIN, Plastic Surgeon

It's so damn hard to get rid of these assholes that most people don't even try. But I see it differently. If I can't screw 'em the normal way, then I'll find some other way. When I was in the emergency room, I used to work with an orthopedic surgeon who didn't know his ass from a hole in the ground. I remember a lady whose finger was crushed in a door. This orthopedic surgeon put in some deep sutures and then went off on a fishing trip. He left his nurse to take care of the post-op care. Well, the finger got darker and darker until it got black and dry—it became gangrenous. The nurse said, "Oh, there's nothing wrong, the doctor will be back soon." And the lady got very suspicious so she came to the emergency room. When she told me the name of the doctor, I knew right away he had screwed up. By that time she had dry gangrene, and when I moved her finger around just a little, it came right off. Fortunately, she wasn't looking when it fell off. I covered her whole hand with bandages and said, "Lady, you need immediate amputation of that finger."

We took her back to surgery, because I saw I had a chance to get this guy. We put the lady to sleep, and we put a few sutures in the bottom of the finger and put it back on, so we could get pictures of it intact. It looked gangrenous and it looked terrible. Then after we got the pictures we took it off again, and we did a graft to fix the stump. I went to a lot of extra trouble to get that son of a bitch, and finally the hospital canceled his privileges. Then he moved out of California and the last I heard he went to Phoenix and kept right on practicing.

DR. ALLEN BARSAMIAN, Staff Psychiatrist

During my wife's illness, we never paid for anything, everything was courtesy, because I was a doctor. If we'd been paying for it we would have done what most people do—we would have gotten care and pursued it, no matter how many visits or how many phone calls it took. But since it was all courtesy, Vera was careful not to bother her doctors.

I believed in the magic of this place—we used to call Memorial "Mecca." I took it for granted that if we went in through these doors she'd be well taken care of. I wasn't an intelligent consumer of medical care. And you know, they relied on me. They kept saying, "Well, what do you think?" And after that experience I will no longer take any responsibility for family members. I refuse to take care of my daughter even when she has the most minimal problem. I take her to a doctor and I insist on paying for it. I won't take professional courtesy because that care is notoriously poor.

The care my wife received was obviously deficient. She shouldn't have died. I'm sure I could sue them and make a lot of money. But I wanted to go on practicing in this community, so I couldn't sue. I was so angry that I wrote to the obstetrician and I suggested that he make a substantial contribution to the charity fund we set up in Vera's name. He was probably so worried that I would sue him that he came through with the contribution right away.

JEFF CARDEN, Critical Care Nurse

I've seen more deaths than most people at this hospital. More than most nurses, more than most doctors. I've seen hundreds. I may have killed a couple myself.

One time I went in to suction a patient. He had a tracheotomy and the respirator was hooked on to the hole in his throat. I suctioned him out, then put the hose back over his trachea. After that, I went to check on some other patients and then I came back. I looked down at the monitor and saw his heart rate slowing down. I thought, "Oh, shit!" So immediately I checked on the hose and it was off. It wasn't in there the way it was supposed to be. Could be that I didn't put it back on. Or maybe it fell off. He might have coughed in such a way that it came off. I don't know. By the time I noticed it was too late. The patient died. I couldn't bring him back.

This thing has always haunted me. If I didn't put it back on, then it was an error, and it could happen again anytime. Even the minutest little thing I try to double-check, double-check, double-check—check it as many times as possible to prevent that sort of thing. I really fear it.

DR. CHARLOTTE KIRKHAM, Hematology Fellow

Just the other day we killed a kid. He got medicine injected into his back that should have gone into his vein. It's a kid that we all knew, a cancer kid who was in remission. He was getting chemotherapy, but one of the interns wasn't trained in terms of knowing the colors of the medication. It's a mistake that an experienced oncologist or hematologist probably wouldn't have made.

We tried to save the kid. Everybody knew him and everybody got involved, but he died right there. I had to step out into the hall because I felt like I was going to cry and I didn't want anybody to see it. But I didn't cry; I just stood there for two minutes. Then I went back to work and concentrated on what I was doing. I don't think anybody noticed that anything was wrong.

DR. DAVID ANZAK, Obstetrician-Gynecologist

I recently had direct experience with two instances of gross medical incompetence. One is an elderly obstetrician, a man in his late sixties, whose son is a world-famous professor of obstetrics. The old man is senile, but the son contacts people to "assist" his father so he can continue practicing. What it means is you have to stand there and prevent him from hurting the patient. I don't know if this man was ever any good, but now he is just terrible. I saw it with my own eyes, or I wouldn't believe it. I was asked by the son to assist his father with a C-section. And this fellow didn't have the first idea what was going on. There is no way he could have handled the situation if I hadn't been there to guide his hand.

The other case was a new doctor who had just finished her residency. This was absolutely shocking because someone who's just gone through a training program and gotten approved ought to be okay—otherwise what's the point of the whole residency? But there's a lot of political pressure to bring more women into our field, so nobody cracks down on a potential female gynecologist.

Fortunately, at Memorial we have a policy that when new physicians are attempting major surgery or other procedures during their first six months, a senior member of the department has to check on them. I was the one assigned to check on this young woman. She had already put a patient under general anesthetic and she was going in to remove an ovarian tumor. I looked over her shoulder, so to speak, and there was no tumor on this patient! Nothing! Nothing had to be removed. I stopped the surgery right there and started shouting. I wanted to see the charts and see the tests, and sure enough there was nothing abnormal. A second-year medical student could have told you that. This patient didn't need surgery, she didn't need general anesthetic, she should have been home.

These are specific cases, but there's also a general problem here at Memorial. We're supposed to have one of the best obstetrics departments in the country, but the cesarean section rate is more than twenty-five percent, which is absolutely outrageous. My section rate is about ten percent, and that means that somebody else out there has to be doing thirty-five percent or more. I talked to the head of the OB clinic and he told me there are some people who section fifty percent of their patients! That's either incompetent, or unethical, or both. Part of the reason is financial. You can charge a lot more for doing a cesarean than for doing a normal delivery. And part of it is convenience. Instead of waiting around for the women to do it naturally, you just go in there and start cutting and the whole job's done in a couple of hours. Either way, it's outrageous. I later found which people are doing it, and of course, Garland Lockwood is on that list. He is definitely bad news. I've made a lot of enemies, trying to get him out of this hospital. He's a disgrace to this department. Sure, I feel sorry for him, but mostly I feel sorry for his patients.

THE TROUBLED SUPERMAN

DR. GARLAND LOCKWOOD
Obstetrics-Gynecology

DR. BURTON WEBBER, Ear, Nose, and Throat

When Lockwood first arrived here we looked on him as a superman. Here was this very tall, very handsome young man who had been an All-American football player at the University of Missouri. A Rhodes Scholar. Harvard Medical School. What more could you ask?

Then right away he started getting into trouble. There were lawsuits and controversy and it's still going on. I am particularly sensitive about the whole thing because in the past, I've referred a number of patients to Dr. Lockwood. I like him personally, but I have no idea of how competent he is as a physician. It's important to understand that most doctors don't know the doctoring ability of their colleagues. They know them socially, maybe they play golf together or go out as drinking buddies. But you never know what other people are doing in the operating room, in the treatment rooms with the patients.

JOE RIVERA, Emergency Care Technician

He's a black guy who acts real high and mighty because he's made it to be a doctor, but everybody around here knows what kind of doctor he really is. He makes mistakes all the time. He's so bad that we don't send him patients. He's on the referral list for us, but I always send patients to somebody else. You just know he's going to screw up.

PEGGY HAGERTY, Head Nurse, Delivery Room

Garland is basically a good doctor, but he's kind of insecure. As a resident he was one of the best we had. He was very empathetic to his patients. Sometimes too much so—they could manipulate him. Now, all of a sudden, he's not sure he wants to be in medicine. He's had a tough time, with lawsuits and things, but I don't think he deserves it.

DR. JACK BUCKMAN, Director of Emergency Medicine

He's smart and he's slick. A very smart guy. But the bottom line is he lost two patients this year, two mothers in the delivery room. In his specialty, you don't lose patients like that. In that whole department nobody else lost a patient. If I were in obstetrics and I lost two patients in a year, I'd go out and shoot myself. If Lockwood wants to take care of it, I'll go and buy the bullets.

———————

Garland Lockwood's home is a designer's showcase full of contemporary Italian furniture, with huge abstract canvases covering the walls. He identified the artists as some of the leading modern masters, including Richard Diebenkorn, Sam Francis, and Ellsworth Kelly. He had bought the paintings through a girlfriend who owned a gallery, and he explained that another girlfriend had been responsible for the interior decoration. "I don't care about that stuff," he shrugged. "But she wanted to do it and she spent months and months and lots of her own money. When you're a doctor, people want to take care of you. Especially if you're divorced. I've got another woman who I see socially and she takes care of my finances. She works for a stockbroker and she handles my money. Right now I'm supposed to be doing pretty well."

In addition to the striking collection of paintings and furniture, Lockwood's living room contains a neon sculpture of a stork with a baby in a blanket dangling from its beak, and a doctor's bag under one wing. Below the bird, illuminated red letters proclaim: "DR. LOCKWOOD DELIVERS." Near this work hangs a huge framed photograph nearly four feet wide, showing Lockwood in his surgical greens, reaching between the spread and sweaty thighs of one of his patients, in the act of delivering a child. With the baby's head resting on his rubber-gloved hand, the doctor wears a look of pride and self-confidence. The face in the photograph, like Lockwood's face in person, is clean-cut, handsome, and surprisingly boyish for a man of thirty-seven.

THAT PICTURE WAS a gift from one of my patients. Her husband took it in the delivery room and then they had it blown up and gave it to me to say thank you. That's one of the good parts of medicine, when the patients show appreciation. I used to think it was because you did a good job, but now I know it's more to do with personality. Patients like or dislike doctors because of personality traits. The main thing is making the patient feel comfortable. That's very important in my specialty, because ninety percent of what we do is very, very routine.

But maybe I shouldn't say that, because I've had some really bad cases lately. And suddenly, routine doesn't seem so bad! I had a pregnant woman die about a month ago, one of my patients. A couple of months before that I was involved with another OB patient who died, but she wasn't my patient. I was covering for a friend of mine, and I didn't know the woman at all so I didn't have much of an emotional involvement. But it was still pretty horrible, because it was a C-section delivery and there was a problem with the colon and it got pretty bloody. But it was the other death, the one a month ago, that really hit me hard.

I'd known this patient for four years. She was a young girl, twenty-two years old, who was a waitress in a Denny's restaurant. She was Catholic, but when she got pregnant once before, she had an abortion. She felt a lot of guilt from that, so when she got pregnant again, about a year later, she and her boyfriend decided to keep the baby. They got married when she was four months pregnant.

It was a normal pregnancy and she was a very healthy girl. But when she came in to deliver the baby, she was not progressing well in labor and I decided to do a C-section. I really think that was the right thing to do. It's a lot safer that way for the baby. We really worry about damaging babies these days, and with a C-section that's not going to happen. I do C-sections maybe one-third of the time, see, but there are guys in this department who do more than half. You can shorten your time in the hospital by about five hours per delivery, you can charge more money and people will think you're a hero, so why take the chance that you might damage the baby? But when I see myself doing two C-sections every week, I start building up a lot of doubts, and I say to myself, "I shouldn't be doing this." But in this case, she was having trouble with labor and I know it was the right thing to do.

So I did the section and everything was fine. I walked out of the room to tell her husband he had a baby girl. Then a nurse came out and said to me, "We're having trouble waking her up." The anesthesiologist had tried to take the tube out, but she didn't start breathing on her own so he put the tube back in. We thought that perhaps she had an allergy to the anesthetic, which we sometimes see, and that means the anesthetic takes several hours to wear off. As long as you have the tube in and you're breathing for the patient that's not a problem, so we were sitting there waiting and watching her. Everything was really stable and all of a sudden her pulse started going down, down, down. Just like you see in a movie. Then the pulse rate just went flat.

We proceeded to do the resuscitation. I started working on her, but in about five minutes we had a whole resuscitation team in there with cardiologists and technicians and residents. I was still the doctor of record, but there wasn't anything I could do. So I went out to talk to her husband and her parents. I didn't tell them she had a cardiac arrest but I told them we had a tough time waking her up. I said everything was going to be okay, this happened all the time. The husband showed a lot of concern, but he's not that intelligent, so I couldn't sit down and explain the situation to him. He just took my word that everything was going to be fine.

I went back into the room and they were working on her. They worked on her for about two hours, but I had nothing to do with it. I just watched, and I kept thinking how these people, this resuscitation team, was so insensitive to death. They come in and they see the patient and she's a dead person already. They're trying to bring her back to life. But in my specialty we're dealing with life all the time, and we're not used to death. I couldn't believe what was happening. I kept thinking she was going to wake up, but I know that the longer someone goes without coming back, the worse it's going to be. When they gave up on her and pulled the sheet up over her face, I said to myself, I don't believe this! My patients aren't supposed to die and this is the second one who died this year! Really, it was like a joke. I had to explain it to the husband, but he wouldn't understand, because I didn't understand, and I felt like I was just walking around in a bad dream. I went to the nursery where he was looking at the baby and I told him that we tried for two hours, but it didn't work and she was gone. He didn't scream or cry. He just kind of blinked, see, and he said we've got to tell the rest of the family in the waiting room. As we were walking down the hallway I put my arm around him because I wanted to help, and I told him there was nothing anyone could do, it just happened. Then we came to the waiting room and there were about twenty people from the family who were there because they were worried there was something going wrong. I saw their faces and then something bad happened. I burst into tears. I just sat there crying in front of all those people and I couldn't talk. The husband had to console me. He had to bend down and put his arm on me and get me to stop crying. It was terrible.

It was about six in the evening and I got up and checked myself out and went home. I got a friend to cover for me. The anesthesiologist who worked on this patient came over to my place and we tried to talk about it. And we got drunk, pissing drunk. We couldn't figure it out, but to be honest, I don't think he handled the case as best he could. I'm taking responsibility, and yet I know in my mind it wasn't my fault. But I've had these other bad times, and now I've got a bad self-image, and a bad image with everybody else.

I've had bad luck. I really think it's bad luck, but maybe I'm a bad doctor. Who knows? Right now I've got seven lawsuits that have to be settled. I can't get malpractice insurance anymore, so I practice without it. I didn't have insurance when this last case happened. Three of these cases I didn't have insurance, so I have to fight them on my own. It costs a fortune—sometimes the legal bills are five thousand dollars a month. I have to kill myself in my practice to pay for that. And none of these lawsuits, in my opinion, has any substance in terms of real malpractice.

There's one woman who is suing because of a problem with the sponges. I did a C-section, and everything turned out fine. We use sponges during surgery to soak up the blood, and we have to take them out before we close up. And before we finished the case I asked the nurse to count the sponges and she said they were all out, but she was wrong. We closed up the patient and then we counted the sponges again—we always do another count just to make sure— but this time it didn't turn out. So we had to go back in and look for that sponge. It's no big thing, really. All we did was reopen this incision and I went in there and looked around. You've got to look hard, because the sponge can get lost between the intestines. But this one wasn't hard to find and the whole thing took maybe fifteen, twenty minutes extra. She probably wouldn't even have known about it except that I told her. I went into her room afterwards and I said, "Well, we had this little problem but everything turned out fine." See, I'm a little too naive and a little too honest. The patient smiled and said, "Thank you, doctor," and then five days later she sued me.

And there's another case where they're suing me for a million dollars. That's for a baby I delivered three years ago. It was a very difficult case. The mother had a problem in the second stage of labor, where she tried to push the baby down through the birth canal. It was taking longer than usual and there was a problem with the fetal heart count, so I had to go in there and deliver that baby as soon as I could. I decided to use the forceps, and what happened was the baby's head delivered easily but then we encountered difficulty with the shoulders. The baby had shoulder dystocia, which is one of the worst things that happens in obstetrics. Usually, the head is the largest part, so once the head is delivered the rest of the baby comes quickly and easily. But with shoulder dystocia the head is smaller than the shoulders and the baby gets sort of stuck. Once the baby is partially delivered, there's a time limit involved. You can't just sit there and wait indefinitely, because the umbilical cord isn't functioning anymore. Eight minutes is the maximum you can wait if the baby is going to survive. If it's more than four minutes the baby will definitely have some damage. So you've got to make a split-second decision. You can't do a C-section because the baby's already partially delivered. But you can use the forceps to rotate the baby and take it out diagonally. In that situation there's a good chance of injury. Sometimes the baby will break a bone or have brain damage or spinal damage or damage to the eye. This particular baby had some residual damage to his left arm. It's pretty minimal, actually—what some people call a "floppy arm." It's kind of twisted, see, and it's a little weak, but the baby is three years old now, and he can do most things. But they're still suing me for one million dollars.

Maybe I'll win the case, and maybe I'll lose. But I keep asking myself, "Did I do anything wrong?" Maybe I did, maybe I didn't. Three of the leading guys in this field in the whole United States are ready to testify for me. They say, "Gee, I think you handled the case pretty well." On the other hand, there are other people who try to second-guess me and say, "Well, you shouldn't have done it that way. You should have done a C-section in the first place." I could lose the lawsuit when it goes to the jury because here are these nice, white working-class parents with a baby that has something wrong. And here's a rich physician, who also happens to be black. And they'll bring up some expert who'll say, "If I encountered this problem I wouldn't have done this kind of delivery, I never would use a forceps." There are certain people who are always ready to do this kind of testimony, always ready to prostitute themselves. I have plenty of enemies here in the hospital. Maybe they'll use this opportunity to get even with me. I don't know. I just know if I lose this case, when it comes up in a year or two, I don't have a million dollars to pay the family. I don't have insurance. So if it goes against me I'll just declare bankruptcy and go off to Tahiti and take it easy for a while. But meanwhile I've got to keep practicing. I've got to pay my legal bills. I'm doing fine with my ongoing patients. I get along with them, and they have confidence in me.

And some of the people on the staff here have a certain sympathy for me. The head of the department of obstetrics is very sympathetic. I was his first resident when he came to Memorial ten years ago, and we've always felt sort of an affinity. So I get a lot of support, from the doctors, from nurses, from the women I see socially. I get more support than I used to get during all the time I was married.

We've been separated three years now. That marriage was never any good. I met my wife when I was in second year of medical school. She was nineteen, from a very rich family. Her father was a federal court judge and one of the highest-ranking black judges in the United States. They were very impressed by me because I was a Rhodes Scholar and Harvard Medical School, even though my family had no money. My dad was a schoolteacher in St. Louis; he died when I was twelve. He never had to push me to do well in school, because I always did great without even trying. I didn't really worry about the studying, and I spent most of my energy on athletics. All through school I was a pretty happy-go-lucky guy, and when I had the chance to go to England, I went over and studied philosophy. I still wasn't thinking about medicine, but when I came back it just seemed like the thing to do.

I didn't know what I was getting into! My first year of med school I started freaking out. I started going to therapy at the student health service and I couldn't handle the demands. The studying was just unreal. I was feeling very insecure and unhappy and thinking maybe I didn't want to be a doctor.

That's when I met my wife. She was pretty and she was smart, and I thought, why not? Maybe if I got married it would help me to survive med school. That's why so many people get married in medical school—everybody is so into medicine they just want to find someone and settle down and get on with their lives. That's what I did, anyway.

We were married for thirteen years. And what happened to me is typical of a lot of people, a typical sort of midlife crisis. When I started making it in medicine I stopped worrying about my career and started thinking about my marriage. Then I realized I shouldn't be married to this person I'd been married to.

But it wasn't easy to get out. We actually got along fine during all the years we were married. We had common interests and two kids who really turned out nice. But over the last five or six years our general views on life, our general opinion of friends, started moving in different directions. My wife is a little rigid in some of her ideas, and I'm maybe a little too liberal, a little too giving in certain areas. I remember when I was still in medical school and one summer we took a vacation to California. We went to Haight-Ashbury and that was still the time there were a lot of hippies there. My wife hated it, but I loved it. I thought it was very brave to experiment with drugs. And since we came out here to live I've gotten into drugs a little bit myself. I smoke a lot of grass. I occasionally take Quāaludes. I use cocaine fairly regularly. I have taken mescaline. I don't have a drug problem, because I'm not addicted, but because of my specialty, because I'm called into the hospital at unpredictable times, I do have to go in sometimes when I'm stoned. The recreational drugs never got in my way, but they did cause problems in my marriage. My wife is very nice and sweet, but she didn't understand what I was going through. I was just feeling very upset about medicine, very bored.

That's about the time I discovered Maui. Some friends of mine have a place up in the hills of the unsettled part of the island. I had a medical meeting in Honolulu, see, and they asked me to come spend a few days with them. My wife didn't want to go, because of the kids and because she never liked these people. So I went by myself. It was the first time I was on my own in ten years. I was with people I liked in a beautiful place, and I did use a fair amount of drugs, cocaine, drinking, whatever. We took off our clothes and sat in the sun and went to the beach. And I came up with all sorts of ideas about changing my life and things I wanted to do. I felt like I was fighting for my life. I decided I wanted to get out of medicine and come back to Maui and start a business there.

I was really serious about these things, so I went back home and discussed it with my wife, but she thought I was crazy. I was talking about starting a nightclub or a restaurant, and I wouldn't give up and two weeks later I went back to the islands with some of my friends. Three beautiful women and one other guy. They were just sort of free spirits—rock singers and professional dancers. We had a great time. I remember we were all lying on the beach and kind of playing around and making out together, and I started thinking more and more, "Gee, what the fuck do I need my wife for?" And coming back from this trip I was a day late, we missed our flight. I didn't show up at my office and a lot of patients had to be canceled. My wife was really freaked out. She went down to my office to straighten things out and went into my desk and found some love letters from one of my patients. When I came home the next day she was ranting and raving and said, "Why don't you just leave the house!" So I said okay. And I woke up the kids and I talked to them and then I packed a suitcase and I left.

I stayed with some really weird people during the next couple of weeks. Some people from the drug world, from the world of rock and roll. It took me a while to settle down and get my own place, because I kept thinking about Maui and setting up this nightclub. I didn't mind being separated. It felt great. But then something happened that ruined the whole thing.

It was another lawsuit, actually. All of the lawsuits are ridiculous, but this one was absolutely unbelievable. A patient sued me for going out with her. In this case I was just a poor innocent guy with a crazy woman who took advantage of him.

It was a patient who was recently divorced who got the idea she wanted to have an affair with me. She used to call my office three, four times a day. She'd leave word with my service in the middle of the night. I always said no, I didn't want to see her. But finally I said, "All right, I'll make a deal. I'll have lunch with you one time if you promise to stop calling me." So we met one afternoon at Golden Gate Park. She brought a picnic basket with champagne and caviar and she spread out a tablecloth. But then it started to rain, and we were getting soaked, so she said, "This is ridiculous. Why don't we go eat this food in my apartment?" We went back there, and, lo and behold, we ended up in bed. I saw her once after that, but that was it. Two times, total. She kept calling and sending telegrams, and she flipped out when I said I wouldn't see her anymore.

The next thing I know she sued me for medical malpractice. She said in the suit that I abused my position as a doctor to take advantage of somebody in an emotionally unstable situation. I probably could have won if we took it to court, but I couldn't do that because of the publicity. This is a very sensitive area, particularly in gynecology. I already had problems with lost patients when husbands met me and found out I was a good-looking black guy. They want their women to go to some fat little Jewish doctor with glasses. The funny part is that it's actually the unattractive doctors who use their position to get dates with patients. See, I never had any trouble meeting women; I don't have to wear a white coat to feel attractive.

I had to settle this one case out of court or else it would really hurt my practice. I had to pay her twenty-five thousand dollars, at a time when money was starting to feel tight anyway. It really ticked me off. Some of my colleagues found out, and one of them, David Anzak, started making a stink. He found out about the various lawsuits, and one of my former patients came to him and ran me down. Anzak wrote letters to the chairman of the department and the board of directors at Memorial; he wanted to stop me from practicing medicine. I think he's jealous. He's having a rough time with his own practice and he thinks he's going to pick up a lot of my patients. But I've still got more patients than I can handle. Maybe it's because I'm a little more loose, a little more tolerant, than a lot of the people in this field.

During the last year with all of the controversy I had to give up the dream of going to Maui. Anzak, and the other people who were trying to screw me, kept saying I didn't have my mind on medicine. So I had to settle down and concentrate and stop talking about doing something else. Maybe I *will* quit medicine someday, but it has to be my choice, not theirs. I don't want to go because I was forced out.

I still think I'm giving my patients a hundred percent. I am able to block out my divorce, or the lawsuits, or whatever's happening. That's the challenge of being a doctor. And it's one thing I'm good at. I honestly feel that in obstetrics, gynecology, most of what we do is pretty mindless. I could even be stoned out of my mind and still do a good pap smear. I could do a good pelvic exam and make the patient feel comfortable and listen to her problems and bullshit with her for a few minutes. That's basically all you have to do, and I really know the basics of what I'm doing. Surgery is the hard part, and when I do surgery, I'm really thinking about surgery.

But lately I'm more cynical about the whole thing. Some people have faith in religion, have faith in God. I don't. And everybody has faith in medicine and doctors. I don't. I see what's going on. I see the way they all turn against you out of jealousy or prejudice or whatever. My wife is against me, and she's trying to get to the

194

kids. She tells people I'm a drug addict, and I'd be a liar if I said it doesn't hurt. I'm a sensitive person, and I think I'm a good doctor. But when these lawsuits keep coming up, year after year, and even the trivial ones drag on and on, I start thinking, maybe I'm not such a good doc. But at least I'm a good human being, and that's more than I can say for the people who attack me.

THE STRAIGHT
ARROW

DR. DAVID ANZAK
Obstetrician-Gynecologist

NANCY PROCTOR, Nurse

He's a very controlled, disciplined type person. Maybe he has
a constipation problem. When he got involved with Charlotte
Kirkham nobody could figure it out. I used to call them the Odd
Couple. They had a very torrid romance before they got married,
then they got divorced right away.

DR. CHARLOTTE KIRKHAM, Hematology Fellow

I'm not surprised at the way he's fighting with Garland
Lockwood. David has always been narrow-minded and judgmental. He is the most judgmental person I ever have met. He
has opinions about everything. When we were married he used
to tell me how to dress. He's very conservative and very traditional; he has his own ideas and nobody's going to change his
mind.

Maybe that's what attracted me in the first place. I had lost my
father a few months before and it could be that David served as a

replacement. He certainly treated me like a child; he treats all women like children.

He was always trying to get me to improve myself. He gave me books to read and classical records to listen to and kept pushing me to work harder in medical school. I didn't want to be David's version of me, I wanted to be myself.

DR. HARVEY FREDMAN, Professor of Gastroenterology

He was a brilliant student, one of the best, and it's a shame he didn't go into research. He is completely dedicated and he's exhausted from working too hard. He's made a lot of enemies because he's uncompromising about medical standards. He's not afraid to criticize the other people in his department, and that takes a lot of courage for a young doctor who's just starting out.

PEGGY HAGERTY, Head Nurse, Delivery Room

David doesn't know how to turn on the charm and he doesn't have a sense of humor. I don't think I've ever seen him smile. I'd have to say he's a straight arrow who is totally involved in medicine. But there's a sweetness about him that most people don't see. He really loves his patients and he'd bend over backwards to take care of them.

———————

David Anzak canceled our scheduled appointments twice when emergencies kept him at the hospital. He apologized but insisted that these sudden disruptions offered a more forceful illustration of the frustrations of his life than he could possibly provide in an interview.

When we finally met, Anzak arrived twenty minutes late, pulling up in front of his two-story townhouse in a yellow Ferrari, which seemed totally at odds with his sober, no-nonsense image. Anzak took quiet pride in this "most expensive toy." The car included a $4,000 sound system on which he played his favorite works of Bach and Mozart.

197

Dour, lantern-jawed, with a long ascetic face and thinning blond hair, Anzak spoke in a tense high-pitched voice. He pronounced his words with unusual precision and formality, which led me to ask whether he or his parents had been born abroad.

WE CAME OVER from Czechoslovakia in 1956 when I was nine. When we first arrived my father worked as a dishwasher. Then for a few years he drove a truck, and then he put together enough money to buy a grocery store. I grew up in the apartment over that store. We all worked, my father and my mother and my two sisters and me. We saved our money and my father bought a trailer park and got involved in some other businesses. He was just starting to do well when he died in 1967. Heart attack, unexpected. He never had a chance to enjoy any of the money.

I was a sophomore in college at that time. I was at Yale, full scholarship. I felt very much at home there. Freshman year I was on the fencing team and I spent a lot of time on the *Yale Daily News.* My senior year I spent the whole year in bed with a girl. Didn't study, didn't do anything. Buy my junior year I sat down and I studied and I really learned a lot. That was the year right after my father died.

He always wanted me to be a doctor, and we had a lot of struggles about it. In the end he won, though I think if he had lived I would have continued to resist him. I was thinking about going into the foreign service, or about being a journalist or a lawyer. Medicine was way down the list. But after he died I felt a very strong compulsion to fulfill my father's ambitions. That was when I started taking premed courses.

One of the happiest and saddest days of my life was the day I graduated from medical school. I was the valedictorian, and afterwards I went to the cemetery. I sat there for a couple of hours. It was like I was saying, "Look at me, Dad. I did it."

I came back to California to go to medical school because of my problems with my family. My sisters were falling apart, and my mother is not a strong person. For my youngest sister in particular, it was essential that I be there. I really sat on her for a whole year, cracking the whip, making sure that she got into the University of California system. If I hadn't come home, she would have gone to a junior college and dropped out after a year and gotten more and more involved with drugs. I had to provide the strength to keep my family together.

Medical school was never that difficult for me, but I did have some upsetting experiences. When I was a fourth-year student, I was on the pediatric service at Memorial and we had a three-year-old child who had been burned. Her parents had left her with a baby-sitter and the baby-sitter pushed her into a tub of scalding water. The child was losing all the skin on her arms and legs and she was getting skin grafts. Every time I went into her room she would scream, because I meant pain. And the kid was right, I did mean pain.

The worst part of it was that we really didn't have burn specialists to take care of her. The resident I was working with wanted to transfer her to a hospital with a special burn unit, but the chairman of the department said we could take care of it. It was a pride thing. The truth is that the skin grafts were never completely successful. I was only a medical student, so there was nothing I could do. But I promised myself that once I was established, I would always speak up if I saw something like that.

I met Charlotte when I was a senior resident and she was a third-year medical student. She was assigned to my service. I couldn't believe it. Here was this very attractive, very intelligent girl who just happened to walk into my life. I really went after her. I pursued her like the holy grail.

I didn't know then that she had a consuming ego, she just burns people up. She has a great need to do things the way she wants, and she's extremely intolerant of other people's way of doing things, other points of view. If a social scientist were to observe her, he'd have to describe her as an extraordinarily selfish person. She is manipulative. She has very little regard for the welfare of other people. Even, ultimately, not too much regard for the welfare of patients.

As a physician, she's the bottom of the barrel. She's had trouble all along. She's one of the few people I know who ever flunked a course in medical school. She's very bright, but she's completely undisciplined. She's made it through by kissing asses. As an intern, she had about a dozen complaints against her. Now she's got a fellowship, but when you get down to brass tacks she doesn't know very much medicine. She is reluctant to consult with other physicians when she's in over her head, so I'd never trust her with a patient.

It's all very clear to me now, but I didn't see it when we met. I proposed to her on the second date. Oh boy, I was hot. I was twenty-nine years old and I wanted to start a family. In every superficial way she was the perfect woman. Except for one thing. I overlooked the fact that she was basically not a good, kind person.

We had a gorgeous wedding. Big hotel. Everybody's delighted. You know, first marriage for both. They're both doctors. We went to Hawaii on our honeymoon and stayed at a very posh resort. And one afternoon we were lying on the beach, looking up at the sun. And suddenly Charlotte sits up and starts fuming. She goes, "Grr! Did you see that girl?" "What girl? Where?" "The girl walking by on the beach. Well, that's the kind of fancy women you're going to be seeing every day in your practice." She got up, stomped off, and went to the room. This was one of the big themes for the whole year we were married, that there's something slimy and evil about my being a gynecologist. That I get some kind of weird sexual satisfaction from my work. That I enjoy lording it over women, that I'm reenacting my relationship with my sisters in my gynecological practice. The corollary to all this was that I should immediately quit gynecology, go back and do another residency and start all over again.

All this came pouring out after we got married. She really expected me to go back, after my four blood-letting years doing residency at Memorial. She would repeat this demand every single day. And her mother began to support this idea. She would call from Illinois and say, "If you want to save your marriage, then you've got to change you specialty." I couldn't believe this was really going on.

The basic problem is that Charlotte is an insanely jealous and competitive person. When she found out my practice was succeeding beyond all expectations, it drove her crazy. If we went to a party and somebody took me aside and asked me a medical question, she'd get insulted. Why didn't they ask her? God forbid a woman should take me aside, then it was already a sexual overture being made to me!

I lost my temper with her several times. Once we were driving on the freeway, and Charlotte got pissed off over some male chauvinist thing and opened the door and almost jumped out. I grabbed her arm, got off the freeway, stopped the car, and started hitting her. I hit her on the arm, the shoulder, on the back. I didn't touch her face, but I think she got the idea.

Another time I came home from a meeting of the alumni group for OB-GYN residents. I'd had a few drinks, which Charlotte didn't like, so she started to walk out of the house. When I tried to stop her, she physically assaulted me. You know, nails, fist, kicking, everything. I tried to restrain her but it didn't work. I had to slam her against the wall a couple of times before she calmed down.

It was an absolute nightmare, and the sexual side of the relationship also started to change. We still had sex, but it was like hostile sex. I remember having intercourse with her and then leaving the room because I didn't want to be in the same room with her.

The idea of divorce was inconceivable to me. When I finally realized I had to do it, I was held back by embarrassment. How could I do such a dumb thing as to get married and get divorced after ten months? I kept hoping that after another six months a shrink would cure her. Or that she wouldn't be so unsettled when she finished medical school. I kept waiting, but finally I just couldn't take it anymore.

At first she tried to get me to stay. When I finally left there were phone calls from her mother to get me to come back. It was tense for a while, but eventually they gave up. I heard from third parties recently that she's been disseminating the story that for months she wanted me to leave and I kept hanging on to her. Well, that's amazing! It's like calling the sky a tangerine.

During the whole time we were married I was miserable every day. I would immediately get depressed at the thought of being home. I loved leaving the house and going to the office or going to the hospital. In a way, I became a better doctor, because medicine began to mean so much to me. I got a lot of good feedback from my patients, and I was so busy with my practice that the whole experience of the divorce wasn't as difficult as I thought it would be.

I usually work between sixty-five and seventy hours a week. In a normal week, there will be three mornings in surgery. Hysterectomy, vaginal repairs for urinary incontinence, tubal repairs for infertility, ovarian tumors, D and C's. The rest of the time I'm in the office, seeing patients. Some are prenatal patients for regular visits, some are routine checkups. A lot of vaginal infections, irregular bleeding, missed periods, infertility, pain. On the average, I'll deliver two or three babies in a week. And then there are abortions. Last year there were more than one hundred and seventy abortions. It's not a happy thing to do but the alternative is worse, having a child that nobody wants.

In the course of a year, I'll see two hundred and fifty to three hundred different patients. I don't get to know most of them very well. Sometimes I can't remember names. I'll meet a patient at a shopping center; they greet me like a long-lost cousin and I have no idea who the hell they are. There's a basic inequality. When they come to see the doctor, it's a big event for them, but it's not a big event for me.

Last year I earned about one hundred and twenty thousand dollars. It's going up every year. Well-established people in my field have an average income around two hundred and fifty thousand. A guy like Lockwood, who cuts every corner, will earn around three hundred and fifty thousand. OB-GYN is probably the best-paid specialty outside of surgery; you can make an incredible amount of money.

But there are other rewards that are more important. It's a great experience to assist at the birth of a baby. Sometimes you can touch people very deeply. I had one patient, for instance, who had fevers, pain in the pelvis, a lot of difficulties, and she was seen by any number of consultants. This was going on for years, and she was in and out of the hospital, and all this time she couldn't get pregnant. I did the usual infertility evaluation and didn't find anything wrong. Finally I suggested to her that her husband use condoms for six months, just on the chance that she had a sperm allergy, even though the test was negative for that. It was a very remote, far-out chance. They used condoms for six months, and then stopped using them and right away she got pregnant. The kid was a boy and they named the kid after me. It made me feel great. In fact, the kid is going to have a second birthday on Sunday and I'm going to the birthday party.

I really care for most of my patients. I like women in general, despite what some people—including my ex-wife—might say. There is a stereotype of gynecologists who feel contempt for their patients and who use this specialty to take out their hostilities against women. I think that is just absurd. Gynecologists as a general rule like women more than the average man does. We certainly are more comfortable with women. And the idea that a man can't do as good a job as a female gynecologist is just ridiculous. A comparable line of argument would be that you can't be a good cardiologist unless you've had a heart attack. That's just ridiculous on the face of it.

Naturally there are people in this field, and in all fields of medicine, who exploit their position to have sex with their patients. My problem is the opposite, having patients who are running after me. Out of the hundreds of patients that I see, I'm sure there are about a dozen that have *constant* fantasies about me. Then there are any number who have occasional fantasies about me. Just because of my position. Not in any way a credit to me at all.

Some of these women are very attractive, but I've made an absolute rule to never go out with a patient. I don't go out much anyway, because I don't have time. I should go out more than I do, because I want to get married again.

I have some fairly clear ideas about my next wife. For one thing, she's not going to be another doctor. I recognize now that a marriage between two doctors can never be an optimal marriage. A woman physician has to have a strong ego or she would never have made it to be a doctor. Even if she's willing to compromise and concentrate on her family, that ego is still there, and there will be inevitable conflicts between careers. I don't think that men and women are the same. I don't want to live with somebody whose life experience is essentially the same as mine. I want to be with somebody who complements me, who has a different way of interacting with the world.

A lot of my patients are professional women, attorneys, businesswomen, and a lot of them have personal problems. It leads me to conclude that these women are pursuing the same false gods as men. They believe that happiness is going to come from a career, from earning a lot of money. But they're wrong. I think happiness is a good marriage and children—and it's true for both men and women. I'm in a profession that is probably the most rewarding that society has to offer, but it isn't enough. At the moment, I don't consider myself a happy person.

I worry a lot about my health. My father died of a heart attack when he was fifty-four. My grandfather died of a heart attack when he was fifty-one. And I see that as my fate.

I know very well what it means that my basal pulse in the morning is about eighty-four. It's not healthy. And I know what it means that my triglycerides are over one hundred and fifty, and that I have a fairly tense and rigorous life, and of course I ought to do something about it. For a while I was jogging, but somehow it just got lost in the schedule. I could try to make my schedule more reasonable, but it's difficult. And it seems to get worse instead of better.

I'm still accepting new patients all the time. It's not that I need the money. I don't. But if I turn them away, who knows where they'd end up? If I say no to a patient, she could go to someone like Lockwood. Or, God forbid, to a doctor like my ex-wife.

THE GYPSY
PRINCESS

DR. CHARLOTTE KIRKHAM
Hematology Fellow

NANCY PROCTOR, Nurse

She was a terrible doctor when she was an intern. I went out on transport with her once. We went out in an ambulance to pick up a guy who almost drowned. It's our job to keep him alive until he gets to the hospital, but Charlotte would have killed him if I hadn't been there. After that, I told the head nurse I would not go out on transport with her, and most of the other nurses said they wouldn't go either. We weren't going to go out with an incompetent intern who could screw everything up.

BECKY KRIEGER, Nurse

I think she's a good doctor. For one thing, she's not afraid to go up against the big guns. If one of the doctors in the community wants to put somebody in the hospital and Charlotte doesn't think they belong there, she'll say, "We can't do this. It isn't right." I respect somebody who will make that kind of a stand.

Everything she does is unconventional. She doesn't follow the usual dress code, and that upsets a lot of people. She's got waist-length red hair that's always kind of flowing free. She usually wears something fairly slinky and slit up to the hip, and heels that are about eight inches high. She never wears a bra and she's always kind of falling out on top. She has a very overtly sexual look, which throws a lot of people off.

DR. STANLEY RUCKERT, Intern

She's super-sexy on the wards, but she doesn't use her attractiveness except to put people in their place occasionally. I think she really knows her stuff and she's a good physician. I like her a lot. She'll walk up to me and say, "Hey, shithead," and I'll say, "What do you want, turkey?" You can't push her around, but she's a really great person. I think we could use about ten more like her. She is also a fox. I mean, when you've been on the wards for twenty-four hours and you're kind of dragging your rear end, it helps to see Charlotte Kirkham walking down the hall.

DR. HARVEY FREDMAN, Professor of Gastroenterology

She dresses like a gypsy, and that doesn't inspire a lot of confidence in the patients. Sometimes she wears so much jewelry that she jangles—you can hear her coming when she's going on rounds. Another problem is the way she talks. She swears like a truck driver. None of the male physicians feel the need to talk that way. She talks crudely about her sex life and her affairs and all the details of her divorce.

She had a rough time in her internship because of that divorce and because of other things that happened to her. In fact, she almost knocked off a patient of mine. She wrote an order for sodium replacement solution for this patient who had diarrhea. The order was for four times the concentration of what it should be, and the pharmacy, unfortunately, never picked up the mistake. The next morning, the patient looked a little funny, and I checked the solution. Then I looked at her orders and I really came down on her. She almost killed this kid through her carelessness! She was contrite, but later in the year she blew it again. She did a sloppy, incompetent diagnosis on a kid with diarrhea, and when I bawled her out she had the attitude that it didn't really matter, mistakes were inevitable.

So I filed a complaint. And there were three or four other complaints already in her file. I spoke to the dean, and he said if he got one more report she'd be out of the program. She got warned more than once, and finally she started to shape up.

This year she's doing a fellowship in hematology, and I understand she's much improved. She is a very bright woman; there's no reason she shouldn't do a good job. But she still has big problems as a doctor. Just the way she talks in front of the patients. The other day I saw her doing a procedure with a patient who was in a coma. She was saying, "So what are we going to be today? Are we a carrot or are we a rutabaga? Are we a radish or are we a green pepper?" It was supposed to be funny, because the patient was a vegetable. But it was also supposed to give the impression that she was very tough and nothing bothered her. And maybe that's true, but what kind of doctor is this woman going to make?

———————

Charlotte Kirkham's high-energy charisma would keep any male visitor at the edge of his chair; she delivered even the most banal information in a warm, husky voice that suggested precious intimacies. With her wild red hair, electric green eyes, glistening lipstick, and black silk blouse unbuttoned most of the way down her chest, she looked more like a cabaret singer than a hardworking physician specializing in blood diseases. She clearly enjoyed the incongruity between her appearance and her position, and accentuated her languorous and sensual poses almost to the point of caricature. Chain-smoking as we talked, she blew smoke rings in the air above her head to express her contempt for medical colleagues who found her difficult to handle.

WOMEN IN MEDICINE are screwed from the word go. The only chance is if you're so ugly that they forget you're female. Well, I don't fit into that. So what happens is, if I use my femininity and

I'm nice to people, then I'm prostituting myself. But if I'm professional and businesslike, then I'm a bitch.

It was the same thing in my marriage. If I wanted attention from my husband, or I saw our personal life as more important than his career, then I was an incompetent woman who couldn't hack it in the real world. But if I worked hard and tried to be a success, I was competitive and emasculating. I couldn't win. David's attitude is totally fucked up. I don't think he could be with any woman who had a mind of her own or wanted a career.

My parents didn't raise me to be a housewife. My father was an investment banker in Chicago. He died right when I started medical school. My mother is your basic suburban clubwoman, but she's very smart. She's active in all of the charities and she's head of the volunteers at one of the local hospitals. She always wanted me to be a doctor. I was the only child, so they both had high expectations for me.

I went to Cornell in the late sixties, right in the middle of the whole social upheaval. Everybody I knew was getting stoned and saving the world. I was raised with the expectation of working in a helping profession, but I thought that the doctors I knew were uptight and conservative. So I went to medical school with the idea of going into psychiatry. But the more I thought about psychiatry the more I thought it was bullshit; by that time I was already doing the rotation and I just got into it. I also met David, who was very big on scientific medicine, and that definitely had an influence. I was a third-year student when I met him. Up to then my social life in medical school just absolutely sucked. At Cornell, I went around with some interesting people. Poets, radicals, student activists. Then I came to California and I was stuck in medical school about sixty hours a week. All of the men I met were these one-dimensional jerks who liked to play with themselves and study gross anatomy and that was about it. I had one-night stands but nothing exciting. After that dry spell David looked pretty good. He was interested in music and politics, and he was very well read. He was cocksure about everything. He was also sure he wanted me, so I sort of went along.

That was the biggest mistake of my life. David felt about me the same way he felt about his car—I was a big toy he could show off to all his friends. Sexually he was very sick. He was basically a voyeur, and maybe that's why he went into gynecology. He only got

208

turned on when he was really pissed off at me. A couple of times he beat me up and that was the biggest turn-on he ever had. Like most of the male gynecologists, he actually hates women, and when I talked about doing gynecology myself, he acted like I was cutting his balls off.

When he finally moved out it was a big relief, because I was already seeing a couple of other people. But David wasn't through with me, not by a long shot. He told everyone I was an incompetent doctor, I was a dilettante and an idiot. So I had a really bad internship year, lots of trouble, lots of complaints.

A lot of the trouble came from a nurse named Nancy Proctor, who was interested in David. I don't know if she ever got to fuck him, but she certainly tried. It was a whole bunch of little incidents that people were throwing up at me. One time I was working on an arrest with one of the attendings and I let him run it because I obviously had no experience. This got written up as another incident, because he said I should have done more as an intern. Well, it turned out later he was a friend of David's. And all these things were coming down where I felt if other people had done the same things there wouldn't have even been a question.

It took me a while to carve out a place for myself, but right now I'm happy where I am. I'm doing a fellowship in pediatric hematology, which is mainly blood diseases and malignancies in kids. I always liked working with children. Probably sixty percent of the patients have some form of leukemia. It's fascinating from a scientific standpoint, and you don't experience the disease the way a lay person would.

My reaction to death is different each time, depending on the kid. If the kid, if the family, is bright, upwardly mobile, if the parents seem to understand what I'm talking about, then I'm more likely to be upset if that kid dies than with people where they don't know what the hell I'm talking about. I've got this one kid right now who's three years old. The parents are crazy, they're older. They're just bizarre and stupid. The kid is a retard, basically, and he has ALL, that's acute lymphoblastic leukemia. He's probably going to do fairly well, but there's no way in the world I would cry if this kid dies.

I'd like to think that I'd be just as thorough with this kid as any other, but maybe I wouldn't be. Maybe my feelings do have an effect on the degree of extra concern that I'm willing to show. If the parents are hostile and suspicious it has to make a difference.

There was one case recently with a mother of a newborn where the baby was about four months premature. Most people couldn't see keeping him alive to begin with, but we hung on to him for about a year. What made it bad was that the mother was tremendously demanding and unreasonable and hating all our guts and saying so. And I remember being senior resident on the ward last year and having her curse me out and slam drawers. Well, I just wanted that mother out of my life. I didn't have time for her and I don't care that much about her kid.

Sometimes it's the kids themselves who get pissed. They start screaming and calling you names and biting and scratching. I can deal with that. With the older kids it helps that I'm a pretty woman. Most people respond to that when I want them to. When I was a house officer and I needed a surgical consult, I could call up and say, "Hey, would you come down here and say hello and look at this kid at the same time, pretty please?" and I'd get a response where other people wouldn't. The attendings get a kick out of coming on to me—"Oh, I don't believe you're a doctor, you're too sexy for that." I know it's bullshit to a certain extent, but I enjoy it.

I always get hustled, and it didn't stop when I was married. It used to happen so much that I thought that when I got divorced my social life would just go crazy. But it hasn't. These men aren't serious. And a lot of people look at me and think I have a lot more exciting life than I actually do. Part of the problem is that the only people I meet are the doctors I see at work.

It's getting frustrating, because I want to get married again. I want to have kids. I just turned thirty, and I'm feeling the biologic time clock now. I want more than one child, and I'd like them to come out with a normal number of chromosomes. But I don't want to compromise, and I think the longer you stay single, the less likely you are to bend. I'm much more picky now than I was before David. I'm looking for someone whose background and values are very similar to mine. Someone who will view children the way I do and will share responsibility in an equal way. Someone who is family-oriented but is also extremely successful at what he does. It's a tall order, and maybe it's unrealistic.

I'm basically a romantic. I'm a dreamer, and I have a lot of mystical ideas. Sometimes I look at a kid, one that has leukemia or a malignancy, and I know whether or not they're going to die. It sounds very bizarre and presumptuous but it is honestly a feeling I have, a sixth sense.

I am fatalistic about everything, basically. I think that most things are predetermined. Things happen because they're meant to happen. I believe that you come into this world more than once, that you live more than once. That means that as a physician, all I can do is essentially carry out what's going to happen inevitably. It doesn't mean you're not going to try your damnedest, but if a kid dies, I feel that kid was supposed to die. I know it's a shitty thing to say, but that's what I believe.

So I don't get depressed, but I do get nostalgic. I'm surrounded by all this sickness and terrible stuff, and I miss the days when I was at Cornell. I enjoyed myself a lot more in those days. I smoked dope, I did acid, I did mescaline. I was thinking a couple of months ago that I'd like to try it again, but I'd want to do it with somebody.

Maybe everybody feels this way in their late twenties, early thirties, but I look back on my life when I was in college and I think it was a lot more adventurous, a lot more broadening than it is now. Now it's an everyday grind. I go to work, I come home, I go to the gym, I'm with friends. I get laid. I'm just in this little niche. I feel burnt-out at times and I feel like shit. I'm tired of medicine and I'm tired of doing this every goddam day. What I'd really like right now is to take a year off. I want to get away from this place and travel around the world, but I know I'm not going to do it. I feel like I should finish my fellowship and get started in practice. But the main thing is there's nobody to travel with right now. If I had someone to do it with and we could swing it, I'd probably take off.

It's very difficult to separate frustrations about my own life from frustrations about my field. If I'm sick of my life, it's very easy for me to say, "Oh, it's medicine," but I really don't think it is. I want to be married and settled and getting started with kids. It was terrible with David, but when I look back, I miss being married. It's not very liberated to say that, but I can't help the way I feel. There's a big empty place in my life and I don't know what I'm going to do.

I just know I have to be back at the hospital at seven o'clock tomorrow morning and I know I'm going to hate it. It's pretty grim, basically. If I didn't have a sense of humor I don't think I'd make it.

211

HOSPITAL HUMOR

JOE RIVERA, Emergency Care Technician

When you're working, you've got to laugh. You may stick a needle in somebody and it may bend or come loose and you're screwing up but there's nothing you can do because the patient's there. But as soon as you get out of the room you're gonna fall out laughing. You may sew somebody's suture and maybe the needle will fall in the wrong place. Or you may drop something and the patient says, "What's that?" And you say, "It's just nothing," but it's really something important, but you can't tell 'em. So maybe that strikes you as funny.

Or sometimes you'll go for a practical joke. When I worked at the VA hospital, we had a guy with a total body cast on him. He'd been there for months. We used to get bored with the young intern ordering vital signs every fifteen minutes, 'cause we'd have to get in there and take a rectal temperature on this guy who was just completely gone. Then one Sunday we had a visitor who brought him some flowers, and after the visitor left, we took the flowers and stuck 'em in his butt like it was a thermometer. The guy was just lying there and he didn't know the difference. But you'd watch the response of other people who'd go by, looking at this guy in a total body cast, with carnations sticking out of his butt.

DR. DAVID ANZAK, Obstetrician-Gynecologist

The only humor in this job is the patients and what they expect of you. For example, when I was a resident and I was working the emergency room, a woman came in with her teenaged daughter. The girl was about thirteen and she had just given birth to a baby. They came in with the baby still attached to the umbilical cord and they were carrying her in a cake pan. The mother was enraged, the girl who's just given birth was sort of whimpering, and the baby was just howling. The mother demanded to know how this could have happened because she was dead sure that the daughter had never slept with anybody in her life. When I told her there was only one way people could make babies, she started shouting and throwing things and trying to hit me, while I was trying to get this baby out of the cake pan. It was so unbelievable that we had to laugh.

DR. ARNOLD BRODY, Director of Medical Oncology

When I was an intern, I was reviewing a lot of records as part of my training. I came across one chart for this sixteen-year-old gal who had been admitted with an attack of acute rheumatic fever. The resident, in the course of his evaluation, had written, "Heart: great; lungs: clear; breasts: very nice." It was right there on the chart. I was hysterical when I saw it.

BECKY KRIEGER, Nurse

The best practical joke that ever happened at Memorial was from Nancy Proctor, naturally. She was working in the neonatal unit, and she took a Baby Ruth candy bar, chewed it up, and spit it out into a diaper. Then she took it to the resident and she looked all concerned and started talking about this kid who was having a lot of trouble. He'd been having these very peculiar stools and she wanted the residents to look at it. She had this lump of Baby Ruth sitting right there in the diaper. And the resident looked at it and said, "Oh no! There must really be something wrong!" Nancy said that she had to find out what it was right away and she picked up some of the stuff out of the diaper, put it into her mouth, and started sampling it. The resident turned white and almost passed out. Then she laughed and told him what was going on. About five minutes later he was trying the same trick on someone else.

NANCY PROCTOR, Nurse

When I was working with old people, some of the patients were very confused, which is why I hated taking care of them. There was one man in particular who we just couldn't figure out. He never had a BM. No stool, ever. One night we went in there and the smell from the closet was overpowering. So we opened the door and took a look. He'd been shitting in his briefcase for over a week. Nice man.

DR. STANLEY RUCKERT, Intern

When I was on neurosurgery this old man came in. He was eighty-seven years old and he was complaining because he kept falling off his bicycle. We did a brain scan, and it turns out he's got a benign tumor up there as big as a softball. We took out the tumor and this little old guy was doing okay, but he's sort of zoning in and out of things. He also has this charming habit that when the nurses would be trying to put him in the bed, he'd grab their asses or grab their boobs. So he became sort of a popular favorite, and they used to sit him out in the hall so he could watch people as they walked by.

One day he's sitting out there when two nurses come up and they're talking about another patient. They're saying, "We have to get him into the chair every day so he doesn't get bedsores. You know, he's paralyzed. So we have to get him out of bed." The one nurse says to the other. "Yeah, we've got to get him up." So this old guy hears that and he shouts out to them, "Get it up? Get it up? I ain't got it up for thirty years!"

There are a lot of jokes about "crocks," because we get plenty of crocks at this hospital, and that's a term that is sort of medical shorthand for "crock of shit." A crock is somebody who's not really sick but who wants to get attention so they come into the hospital. They have a problem with hypochondriasis or they're just crazy. When a crock comes in, we have a special test for him. We run a test to check for "serum *porcelain* level"—in other words, to see how much of a crock he really is. You'll say that seriously in front of the patient to another doctor. You'll say, "Doctor, I think we may have to get a serum porcelain count on this one." That's just another way of saying that the patient is a crock.

Then there is also a lot of humor about GOMERs. The word GOMER is an acronym for "Get Out of My Emergency Room." GOMERs are old pathetic patients, and in any decent, life-respecting society, they'd be allowed to die gracefully. The GOMERs are so sick, their lives are so miserable, that we're not doing them any favors by keeping them alive. You can go into a place like the VA hospital where there are hundreds of thousands of dollars being spent every day taking care of these old GOMER guys who would have been dead months ago except for technological medicine. But they're alive, and you have a number of things to describe people like that because it's so outrageous.

You can say, "Well, how's Mr. So-and-So doing today?" And the answer would be, "This morning he showed a positive O sign." An O sign is where the patient is just lying there comatose with his mouth open in the shape of an O. That's bad, but it's not as bad as a Q sign. That's when a patient has his mouth open with his tongue hanging out to one side. The worst sign of all is the dotted Q. That's when a fly came down and perched at the edge of the tongue. If a patient is really at the end of the road, we'll just say, "He showed the dotted Q sign this morning," and everybody knows what you mean.

Then we also talk about the triple P syndrome. They'll even say in front of people, "This patient has triple P syndrome." That stands for "Piss-Poor Protoplasm." That's just a person where millions of things have gone wrong and you're holding them together with a bunch of Scotch Tape. Society forces you to take care of them, but it can't stop you from talking honestly and finding the humor in the situation.

DR. MILTON TESSLER, Cardiologist

The other day a resident was presenting a case to me and he said, "At twelve-oh-three last night I admitted this eighty-two-year-old SHPOS. . . ." So I let him get all the way through his presentation and then I made him come back. I said, "I know all about GO-MERs, but what's this SHPOS business you're talking about?" He looked really surprised and he said, "You've never heard of that? SHPOS stands for 'Sub-Human Piece of Shit.' " And he just shrugged and said, you know, everybody uses it, everybody does it. And a few days later, I saw that another resident had written down the word, "SHPOS" right on a patient's chart. In my opinion, that's carrying humor a little bit too far.

DR. BARNETT GOLDSTEIN, Plastic Surgeon

When I used to work emergency rooms, the best part was all the weirdos who used to come in. We had this one guy, a queer, who couldn't get an erection so he fixed himself by taking the filler from a ballpoint pen and putting it in his penis. He was having sex with another guy, and he just went at it until the ballpoint filler went through the posterior portion of the other fellow's urethra and right into the bladder. We had to cut open the bladder to take it out. And I decided to save the ballpoint filler as a souvenir. I put it up on the bulletin board with a big sign, "If you can't come, write."

Then another time they brought in this guy that had rectal bleeding. I did an examination with my finger and it felt hard and rough in there. So I got a little scope and I looked up there with the light and it looked like a piece of wood. So I got a pair of tongs for grasping things, and I put it in and pulled and pulled and finally got a piece of wood about six or eight inches long. I said, "You had a piece of broomstick stuck up your ass!'' He just sort of scratched his head and said, "Mmmm! I wonder how that got there!''

And with gynecological cases we sometimes got the same kind of thing. One time I'm examining this big fat lady, with fat drooping down her legs and her arms, and I feel a mass. She spreads her legs and the whole place all of a sudden smells terrible. I never smelled such a stink. I'm kind of holding my nose and trying to reach up there to see what's going on. Then I felt something, and it was really funny, it was hard, and round, and I said to myself, "Poor gal! She's got a giant tumor mass. No wonder it smells so bad!'' So finally I put my speculum in and it starts to come right out. I took it out, and you know what it was? A sprouting, rotten potato. I pulled it out, and I said to her, "Hey, how did that get in there?'' She said, "I must have sat on it one time and didn't know.''

That's the kind of thing that always used to happen. It kept us laughing. I look back now and I kind of miss it.

THE HAPPIEST MILLIONAIRE

DR. BARNETT GOLDSTEIN
Plastic Surgeon

DR. ARNOLD BRODY, Director of Medical Oncology

With that thick New York accent and his big black cigar, he's like a character out of Damon Runyon. He's also about as rich as God, which is something he'll tell you within two minutes after you meet him. It makes me a little uneasy the way he talks about his money because it fits so perfectly with all the anti-Semitic stereotypes. I heard another surgeon, a non-Jew, who said, "I can just imagine Goldstein, sitting down with his patients and haggling over the price of a nose job!" That made me uncomfortable, but if Barney heard it he probably wouldn't care. He may be *nouveau riche,* but he's not a social climber, and he won't kiss ass.

DR. BURTON WEBBER, Ear, Nose, and Throat

Dr. Goldstein is sort of a clown. Just the way he dresses, for one thing. I ran into him today and I could hardly believe it. Green-checked pants and a pink shirt with ruffles down the front! I don't know how he keeps attracting patients. He doesn't have a lot of friends within the medical community. He's supposed to be very competent at what he does, but his personal style is abrasive. Maybe if you're a plastic surgeon, you're expected to be a little offbeat and eccentric.

DR. HARRISON O'NEILL, Gastroenterologist

In a place like Memorial a lot of physicians are very pretentious, very impressed with their own importance. Not Barney. He's a down-to-earth, hang-loose kind of person. Kind of unspoiled. He's my patient and my friend. One of the best people I know. He has a tremendous sense of humor, a tremendous interest in people, and he's a very creative plastic surgeon. I recommend him to anyone who wants plastic surgery. If they go to Barney, they not only get a good job, but they get free entertainment along with it.

————————

Barnett Goldstein's recently remodeled mansion seemed more suited to a Hollywood back lot than to the dignified, old-money San Francisco suburb of Hillsborough. The immaculate white columns in front, the Greek statuary and gently lapping fountain in the entry rotunda, the dramatically curving staircase in the main hall, all suggested an elaborate movie set. As if reading my mind, Dr. Goldstein declared, "Kind of reminds you of Tara, doesn't it?" It did indeed, though Goldstein's appearance left the impression that Tony Curtis had been cast in the role of Rhett Butler. He wore blue monogrammed slippers and a maroon smoking jacket fitted elegantly over his broad shoulders. His features, dark and ruggedly handsome, were partially obscured behind an enormous handlebar moustache with heavily waxed points. He gestured at everything

*with the dead stump of a cigar. As his wife came into the study with
a tray of sliced fruit, he grabbed her finely sculpted chin in one
hand and used that cigar to point out the various items of surgical
reconstruction he had achieved over the years. "I've done everything. I've done her nose, her face, her eyes twice. I've done a
tummy tuck and a boob job. She looks great, doesn't she? She's
in her late forties and she's still a great-looking gal. I've done my
whole family. I've done my brother's face and nose, I've done
my cousins, I've done my daughters. Everybody asks me why I do
my own family. I always tell 'em it's because I don't know anybody
better than me. If I knew somebody better, I'd send them to him."*

MY REAL NAME was Baruch. In Hebrew, that means "blessed."
But when I started school, my mother wanted something more
classy, more American. She came up with Barnett, but my friends
always called me Barney.

I grew up in Brownsville, which is part of Brooklyn. Greatest
neighborhood in the world. Home of all the big Jewish gangsters.
Murder Incorporated. Louis Lepke, Bugsy Siegel. I was a very
tough kid, and those guys were my heroes. My nickname was the
Bone Crusher. I hit one guy and broke his jaw. Another guy, I
broke his arm over my knee. Never thought of being a doctor. I just
thought I was the toughest guy in the world.

My father was born in Russia. As a little kid he ran away and
shipped out on a Russian freighter. He spent time in many countries and spoke a lot of different languages. Never educated, but a
very bright man. He came to New York and started selling fruit
from a wagon. Then he opened a fruit store. He made a lot of business contacts and they started taking numbers in the back room.
Then they started taking book on horse races. My father got into
that, and first think you know he was a very trusted man.

When I was a kid, the police came to the house, looking for my
father. My mother had us in the bed, my father was hiding under
the bed. She started screaming at the cops, "Don't wake the kids!"
We had bunks. My younger brother and I slept on the bottom bunk,
my older brother slept on the top bunk, and my mother and father

slept together in a separate bed. All in one room. We had no bathroom. In fact, I can remember when they put a bathroom in the house. That was the year the *Hindenburg* flew over. And I remember my mother going out to the street and she was holding my little brother by his hand and she looked at him and said, "Bubeleh, is the *Hindenburg*. That's Lindy." You know, they used to think everything that flew was Lindy. Because what did they know?

During Prohibition, my father was in and out of jail. He owned two speakeasies, and he was always in some kind of trouble. My mother used to dress us in rags and take us down to the jail. We would cry and scream until they let him out. That usually worked, but there were other problems. One time he went out to start the car and the car blew up. He was in the hospital for two weeks, and after that he took all our savings and bought life insurance. He was scared, and we all felt it. One day when I was seven years old he went out to a business meeting and he never came back. We waited all week but we never heard from him. He just disappeared. They probably put him in a concrete vest and dumped him into the East River. When my mother finally tried to collect the insurance, they wouldn't pay. They never found his body, so we got nothing.

We'd never had any money, but after he was gone we were really poor. I worked as a delivery boy in a market, and so did my brothers. As we got older we became clerks. I must have had sixteen, seventeen jobs when I was a kid. My big dream was that someday I'd make a hundred bucks a week.

In high school I won all kinds of scholarships and prizes, so I could have gone away to college. But my mom hated it when I went away, even for a weekend. So I stayed and worked, and went to City College. But when I got my degree I wanted to get away from home. Unbeknownst to her, I wrote a letter to my draft board asking them to draft me. This was the time of the Korean War.

I did basic training at Fort Dix, and they gave me a choice of medical corps or chemical corps, because my aptitude was high. A guy I knew from Brownsville was already a corporal and he says to me, "Barney, you ought to be a medic." I said, "I don't know anything about medicine." He said, "You don't have to know anything. All you have to do is stay in Japan and screw all the nurses." I said, "Get me the job."

The next week they called out my assignment with the medical corps, and I went up and said, "What part of Japan is that, sarge?"

He said, "Japan, hell! You're on the front lines!" Within twenty-four hours I was on the front. If I could have found my friend, I would have killed him.

So the first thing you know I'm up there on the Yalu River and the Chinese are overrunning everything and our boys are getting slaughtered. Five minutes after I got off the truck this guy hands me this emergency bag and tells me to get going. I say, "What's all this shit? I don't know what I'm supposed to do." He looks at my name plate and says, "Goldstein, huh? That's the trouble with you fucking Jews. You don't want to fight." I hit him so hard that after that he tried to get me killed. If we were out on patrol and somebody had to go out under enemy fire and pick up a wounded GI, Private Goldstein got nominated every time. I was lucky I made it. I got wounded three times. I got a bullet through my hand, a bullet in my shoulder, and shrapnel in my left leg. I had to spent some time in the hospital and they came around and pinned on a Purple Heart. Big deal.

Then later I got the Silver Star. I was in a combat zone and the Chinese were coming down and we were evacuating. We were under heavy fire and a big black guy was hurt. He fell and cried out, "Somebody help me!" There was blood coming out of his mouth, and I said, "Where're you hit?" He said, "I don't know. I just feel terrible." There was nothing visible, it was probably all internal. So I picked him up and I carried him over a mountain. It must have been four or five miles, through an area where nobody else was moving. All I wanted was to get him over that mountain, but I was stupid. I should have looked to see how he was doing, because when I got to the first-aid station he was dead. They gave me a medal, but it didn't make any sense. I probably contributed to his death, because he had internal bleeding; it would have been better to just leave him there.

I was in Korea from 1950 to '52, and believe it or not, I liked being in the service. I am very patriotic. I'm a flag boy. If it paid off financially, I'd be in the service right now. I like what it stands for. I like the power that you have. I'm a good guy under stress. My thoughts are clean and clear and I can act, I don't get ruffled. That's been a big help in medicine. It also got me through Korea in good shape.

My last six months in the army I got reassigned to the 12th General Dispensary. We didn't do much except test people for VD, so there was a lot of free time. With a buddy of mine, I got some money together and we opened up a whorehouse in Pusan. Then we started a dance hall and a funeral parlor. We also started doing black market. We made a lot of money—sixty thousand dollars in just a couple of months. So when I came back to the States, I could give ten grand to my mother and still have plenty left over to go through medical school.

The medical schools were very impressed with my record as a medic. A war hero. I got in everywhere, but I always wanted to live in California. After the first few weeks I never wanted to leave. This was the place for me. In some ways medical school was like the service. I worked as a clerk at County Hospital all the way through, and you got to see a very weird side of humanity.

There was this one old lady who really liked me. Every time I worked the emergency room she managed to come in. She used to call the fire department and say she was bleeding and she'd come in with a blanket stuffed between her legs. We'd put her up on the table, and she'd spread her legs and laugh. I'd say, "Where's the bleeding?" She said, "Well, it *was* bleeding!" But there was no blood on the blanket or anywhere else. She just loved me to look at her.

Another time I was working late when a guy comes in with blood all over his hands and his clothes. He walks up and slaps something down onto the counter and says, "Here! Look! I got even with my girlfriend!" I looked at what he put down on the counter. It was a testicle. He had cut both his testicles off. I said, "You're right, you got even with your girlfriend!" We had to rush him to surgery or he would have bled to death.

Then there was another wild one, a woman who came in with the paramedics on emergency call. She had her son with her, a three-year-old kid. She was a religious fanatic. No smile, no makeup, straight hair, print dress. No style, no class. A big metal cross hanging around her neck. She read in the Bible about circumcision and she decided to do it herself. Except she didn't really know what circumcision was, so she took her three-year-old and cut off his penis. The whole thing. The poor kid was in shock, and he bled to death. We couldn't save him.

There were lots of things like that. County Hospital was the worst. They used to have a couple of hundred people in what they called the holding ward. The beds were so close you could hardly get in between them. I used to say, "Nobody falls out of bed at County Hospital. They fall onto the next bed." You would walk through there and all the patients would go, "Doctor? Doctor? Are you my doctor?" And every night we used to have people die in there.

After the service, and after working at County, I had enough of blood and guts. I wanted a specialty where you didn't have to see people who were always sick or crazy. Plastic surgery appealed to me. I'm an artistic guy. Art was always my favorite subject in school, and I did a painting when I was ten years old that got hung in a children's show at the Brooklyn Museum. Plastic surgery is creative, it's artistic. So I got a surgical residency and then a preceptorship in plastic surgery. I got it because nobody else wanted it. In the mid-fifties it wasn't a popular field—there were only five guys doing it in the whole Bay Area.

I had a tough time getting started in practice. I would do anything I could to get work for myself. I used to cover all the emergency rooms and run around. People came in from traffic accidents and I'd fix 'em up. Half those things I never got paid for. I would just make myself available, let them know I was there. My first nose job I did on a lady who was a good friend of mine. I kept telling her she'd be a gorgeous gal if she'd just let me fix that nose. Finally she let me give it a try. I'm sorry to say, it wasn't the greatest nose job. But she loved it, and to this day she still sends me patients.

In the beginning I wasn't very good. I did lots of jobs that were bad or mediocre by my standards now. But I was learning and I needed the practice. A good operator is not a guy who gets an occasional good result, but a guy who's consistent. You can bank on him, like the sun coming up in the morning. Today I'm known as a good operator.

Most of my practice is nose jobs and boobs. What we do with a nose job is to take the tissue that's there and try to rearrange it. As time has progressed we take smaller and smaller amounts of tissue out of the nose. In fact, sometimes we put it back. We even take part of the ear sometimes and put it in there. What we are really doing is creating an acceptable form of mutilation. Like circumcision has been done for years. We mutilate to create a more pleasant reality. By whose standards? By our society's standards, by the patient's standards. It's all a matter of opinion.

I believe in what I'm doing. I've had my own nose done *twice*, that's how much I believe in it. The first time was a bad job, by my standards, so I had them do it again. I wish I could have figured out a way to do a nose job on myself.

As for my wife's surgery, she insisted. I thought she was fine the way she was, but after she saw the results I was getting, she wanted me to try it on her. I did her nose about ten years after we got married. I first met her when I was in medical school and she was going to school to be a pharmacist. She was a Phi Beta Kappa, she's bright. She dropped out of school and helped to run a clothing store to help us get started. She's a tough business lady, and she's also a devoted mother. She would kill for her kids.

But now we don't have to struggle anymore because my practice is very well set up. I charge more than most of the other guys, and that helps people realize I'm better. The average cost of surgery I do is around twenty-five hundred dollars, ranging up to five thousand. I operate twenty to twenty-five times a week, which makes me the busiest plastic surgeon in town. I clear at least twenty thousand dollars every week. That's net, after all my expenses. It comes to a million a year, you can figure it out. It's like I have a license to rob banks. Sometimes I wish my dad could see what's going on. I'm fifty-three years old, and my net worth is about fifteen million dollars.

I get all kinds of interesting people in my practice. A lot of wealthy people, jet-set-type people. A lot of middle-aged women who want to get their husbands excited again. I also do prostitutes, mostly high-class call girls. They're very big on boob jobs, cosmetic surgery on their rear ends. There are also Mafia people—a lot of underworld guys and their girlfriends. They are just about my best patients. In addition to paying you in cash a lot of the time, they usually give you a big gift. Watches, bracelets, oriental rugs. They like me because I'm a regular kind of guy. They know they can talk to me. There's one guy where I just did a face lift, an older Mafia guy. He's giving his wife seven million dollars for a divorce, but she's not happy with it. He told me, "She may be the mother of my kids, but if she keeps it up, she could disappear from this earth."

Most of the time I operate in my office. Most plastic surgery is being done that way. You have to have equipment for respiratory problems and cardiac arrest, so you're set up to do almost anything a hospital can do except maintain a patient over a long period of time.

I still have to work at Memorial about one day a week, because there are some insurance companies that won't pay for office surgery. It's a big waste of money, but I go along with it.

There are other types of surgery where I insist that we go to the hospital. If the amount of anesthetic you need is going to be really high, I want to be over there. Or if you need blood transfusions, like in reduction mammoplasty. That's where you're taking some large breasts and reducing them in size. I get a lot of them. Two days ago I did this one girl, who was seventeen. At age nine she had a 34D, at age eleven she was a 36 double D. Here she is at seventeen, with long hanging breasts that look like cantaloupes at the bottom. She can't participate in any sports in school. And she has difficulty wearing clothes. She's very self-conscious, and she has a lot of neck and back pain. So I cut 'em down for her and it makes a big difference in her life.

I've been sued for malpractice about a dozen times, but nothing really serious. People know I make a lot of money, so I'm a good target. I've been sued a couple of times for keloidal scars after a face lift. They are scars that are thickened and raised—tumors of the dermal layer. The face lift may look fine for a while, then it becomes keloidal. Some people are just prone to that kind of thing. My wife gets keloid scars, it's no big deal. Then there was another woman who sued me because she came back different colors from a skin peel. That's very common. It's when you burn the outer layers of skin with acid to take away small wrinkles. When people sue me I always settle out of court. I give them a couple of grand and that's it. The largest settlement I've had was for twenty thousand dollars, and that was a suit we would have won. It's a nuisance more than anything else.

A lot of times people complain without any justification. They don't realize there's a lot of art in plastic surgery and when I make a nose they don't like, it doesn't mean it's bad. You never know what's in a person's head. I have people that want me to make monsters out of them. They want real turned-up noses or something like that, and they don't know their ass from a hole in the ground. They don't understand that you're limited by the material you're working with. You can't just throw it out and start over again. There are definite limitations. We can't perform miracles.

Most of my patients are delighted by the way they come out. I certainly don't have the problems of some other guys in this field. I know two plastic surgeons who have actually been shot at by crazy patients. Maybe they promised results they couldn't deliver. What people have to understand is that we're doing psychological surgery. We're not curing people, we may actually be hurting them. The most we can do is make them feel better. We meet a need that people have right now. Rejuvenation, perpetual youth, all that kind of stuff. Maybe twenty years from now people will have a different attitude and I'll make a lot less money. But nobody says you have to go to a plastic surgeon. If you don't want to go, you don't have to.

There's other stuff that I do that has nothing to do with vanity. I do get a certain amount of patients who have real problems. Burns, accidents, that kind of thing. And then this summer I'm going to New Guinea with a Catholic missionary society. A kid from Brownsville going with all these priests! I'll do plastic surgery. The natives have a lot of cancer of the jaw from chewing betel nuts. They have a lot of cleft palates that have never been operated on. I'll be there for a month and I'll enjoy myself. I'll be at an exotic place I really want to see.

I've been around the world four times, and that's something I really enjoy. I had a few adventures along the way, because I can be an emotional kind of person. Last year we were in China and we had a problem in a restaurant. It was sort of family-style and they put us down at a table with a couple of fat German tourists. We started eating and they asked us what part of Europe we were from. I said, "I'm not from Europe. I'm from the United States." Then he said, "Oh, but you speak English with a very strange accent." I said, "There's nothing strange about my accent. I'm from New York." Then this fat German sits back and with this sickening smile says, "Oh, you're one of *those* people!" And I said, "Yeah, I'm one of those people, and I'm gonna get out of this goddam chair and hit you in the fucking mouth!" I got a pretty good swing at him, but my wife tried to pull me away. Then the waiters came over and threw us out.

But that's the kind of guy I am. I think the people who saw it would be surprised I'm a doctor, a plastic surgeon. Maybe they thought I was a truckdriver, a longshoreman. I definitely have a violent streak. I like fighting and I'm good at it. I'm not a great arguer, and if I'm talking with a guy and arguing he'll chop me to pieces. But if I stand around long enough to get mad, I'll take a swing at him. I'm an easygoing guy, but when I get violent I don't care what happens.

But basically I like people. I like people a great deal. I don't mind poor people. I'm not embarrassed by being with them. I don't think I'm better than they are just because I'm a doctor. Sure, people trust me and tell me their troubles, but they also talk to beauty-shop operators. Too many doctors think they're hot stuff, but I'm just an ordinary guy. I'm just a technician, and I could teach anybody to do what I do. You need a little judgment, that's all, and some experience. Everybody says, "Oh, there's all this training that goes into medicine," but that's a bunch of bullshit.

There's a lot of other people who work in this hospital. Not just doctors. I know nurses and orderlies and maids and maintenance men. I talk to all of them. They see the same things we do and they've got feelings about it. And if you want to see the picture from another side, you've got to hear what they have to say.

THE LORD'S HELPER

WILLIE MAE PARKER
Custodian

GEORGIANNA HARLAN, Ward Clerk, Translator

The orderlies come and go. They don't have much contact with the rest of the staff. But Mrs. Parker has been here forever, and everybody knows her. She just stands out. She's always doing something extra. She used to work on our floor and everybody loved her. If they had an emergency and they needed the room cleaned right away, she wouldn't wait for housekeeping to send somebody. She'd do it herself, even if it wasn't her job. She really cared about the patients, and it was like she was part of the medical team.

BECKY KRIEGER, Nurse

She is a wonderful person. Absolutely wonderful! She's an older black woman who is always smiling and loves to talk. She's sort of a granny for all of the nurses and the patients. She brings us cakes and cookies that she bakes at home. When she worked on pediatrics she made dolls and games for the kids.

She used to work nights, and I would always be working late so we got to know each other. She's interesting in her philosophy because she's very religious. Once I was on the wards and I went to check on a patient. Mrs. Parker was sitting there and reading out loud from the Bible. I said, "You're not supposed to do that. You know there are rules against using religious propaganda with the patients." She said, "I'm just making her feel better." I saw that the patient agreed with her. So what was I supposed to do? I walked out of the room and left them alone.

———————

Despite her plump and diminutive stature, Willie Mae Parker was a commanding presence as she sat back in a thronelike leather chair in her living room. Her high cheekbones, leathery mocha skin, and intense brown eyes gave an impression of great strength and unshakable conviction. She lives in a tiny, tidy apartment located in a rather dreary lower-middle-class neighborhood not far from Memorial Medical Center.

WE USED TO have a cute little house, but we got this place when my babies left home. No call for all that room! I'm a mother of six, grandmother of four. They are my pride and joy, those kids. They went to private school, every one of 'em. Regular schools were never any good, so they went to parochial. I never was Catholic but I want the best. It paid off, because now every one of 'em has a college degree after his name. And their mama didn't even make it through high school!

I was born in Montgomery, Alabama, in 1923. Been in California for thirty-six years. Came out with my first husband right after the war. He was a carpenter, made a good living. I never had to work. Stayed home with my babies. Then he got sick, he got cancer. He couldn't work anymore and I had to make some money. Went to work at a department store and stayed there two years. Then a friend was hired at Memorial and she thought I would be interested in coming along. I've been there ever since—twenty-one years now. The money is good. I get twelve hundred a month and I get a month's vacation. I work forty hours a week but I'm a hospital volunteer part of the time when I'm not working. That's eight hours a week.

I love my job. I get along real well. I love the people. The patients especially. They can be ever so ill, but I'll walk into the room and they'll say, "Oh, it's so nice to see a smiling face like yours!" That does something to me. Because I'm there not only for the domestic part, but also for the mental part of the patients.

I come in every morning at 7:30. I'm wearing my uniform. It's pale blue, trimmed with white, and white shoes. I get my barrel, and I go into all the rooms and pick the trash up. Then I start the regular cleaning. You do the baseboards, you put in the soap, you put in the paper towels. You see that the bathroom is clean, that the tub is clean. Do the dusting, pick up dirty things, tidy up the whole room.

I talk to the patients when I go in. If you're in the room cleaning that doesn't stop you from talking. I never open myself up to them unless they open up to me. If they want to talk, then I respond back to them. A lot of the time they know their condition and they're feared and they don't want to talk about it. They keep their curtain drawn so you just go in and do what you have to do and come out. But the next room you can't even get out of there because you're so busy holding a conversation. It's different types, different ones, all the time.

I have quite a few souvenirs from the patients. Like that vase over there. One of those fashion models from New York gave it to me. It's a crystal vase which is very expensive. She was visiting and she got sick with some stomach trouble. We just got to know each other. She used to kid me about my lovely face, like I'm the one who ought to be a model.

A lot of times a patient leaves their address with me and they want to keep in touch with me. Especially now that I'm on oncology floor. We have a lot of terminal cancer patients and plenty of times they're lonesome. I will go in and sit and talk and we get to know one another. They ask me to do things that are not my job, but I don't mind doing it. If the patient needs water, I do that. If she wants the channel changed on the TV I do that. If I can assist her getting to the bathroom I take care of it. That's on my own initiative and that's how I have made quite a few friends there.

You can become really attached to some of the patients. I've got a little old lady who's got no family. There's nobody but herself. And nobody tells you to do it, but maybe she wants to go for a walk down the corridor and I walk her down the corridor and we laugh and talk and I feel like I'm helping somebody. A good laugh is a good cure, that's what I always say.

The doctors are also nice and we get along real well. They send me little notes at Christmastime. One of the young doctors who moved away just wrote to me and said how he was thinking of me and how I was really an asset to him. How I used to read the *Daily Word* to him and how it helped him when he found out I was a Christian.

Whenever I can, I like to talk to people about the Bible. I feel my way into that. A lot of people are not religious-inclined, so you hint around to see if it's a suitable subject.

It was amazing what happened with one of the ladies who was there three months. She was nothing but tumors and IVs. She had cancer and was down to seventy-five pounds. When I came in every Monday she said to me, "Willie Mae, did you pray for me this Sunday?" At church we have a prayer list that we give to the pastor and he reads the name off, and I kept her name on the list. I'm a founding member of my church—the Mount Hope Baptist Church—and I've been active there for twenty-five years. One Sunday I was praying for this lady and I started crying because she was so sick and I didn't have much hope. But the next day there she was, walking down the corridor. I was ready to shout because this was really a miracle and I said, "Well, praise the Lord, this calls for a celebration!" We both thanked God and I kept telling her not to give up. I said, just pray, just hold on. And she left the hospital after six months and she went home to her children and grandchildren. It was truly a blessing. Prayers do get answered and you never know what you can do. A maid's job is to help somebody and I'll help 'em any way I can.

When I was working on pediatrics floor, we had a little boy

about three years old who never left the hospital. Since he was born he was really sick and he just had everything wrong with him. Everybody loved him, and he was just a little bony boy who was still the size of a baby. He couldn't control his stool, so it was a hard task to clean his room. We had to wash him off and clean him up all the time. I used to take his clothes and wash them at home so he'd have clean clothes and we could dress him up. He was a sweet little boy and we called him John-John. Sure enough, he got better, thanks to Dr. Fredman, who's a wonderful man and one of my good friends. For his fourth birthday, he was ready to go home. We were all happy but we were sorry to see him go. We gave him a special birthday party and we got his mother a washing machine. They were poor people and she needed to clean him up all the time since he still had this problem. We all went in together on this washing machine and she was so grateful she just cried. Everybody gave in money, all the housekeeping and custodial and everybody.

They are congenial people, the ones who work here. Most of the women stay a long time because the pay is good and it's a good atmosphere. You feel like you're doing something important, not just mopping floors. My husband, my second husband, he's also in the custodial department. That's where we met, fifteen years ago, after my first husband died.

That was a hard time for me because I had six kids to raise and I had big tuition bills for the parochial schools. Somehow or other we just got by. And I had a friend who works with me and she said, "You know, that guy over there, he likes you." I said, "I'm not interested." Then a year later, she says, "He's still waiting." I said, "That's his problem." She said, "Willie Mae, he's a nice guy. I know how you love your kids and all, but he's what you need right now. I know he's not much to look at. . . ." And I say, "You don't have to tell me that! Why do you want to push him off on me?" And she said, "His financial status will probably help you meet some of your requirements." Well, I just flared up and said, "Don't look down on me like that! I'm working, you know!" She finally gave up.

And it just passed until one day I was done with work and I was waiting for the bus. And it was raining just fierce, and he pulls up to the bus stop and says, "I'll give you a ride home." I said, "I don't need a ride from anybody!" He went away but then he came back in about five minutes and I was getting wet. He says, "Don't be silly, let me give you a ride." So he did and we started talking and then he came in to meet my kids.

Finally we started dating and we got married. It's been fourteen years and we're very happy. My kids just adore him. He's a good man and he works two jobs. He works at the hospital and he's also got a dairy where he has a franchise with another man, a friend from the church. He wasn't a Christian before, my husband, but he became a real active Christian and he's been wonderful to my kids. We both look forward to when we're going to retire. I've got four years to go, and my husband's got six. Then we'll have some money saved up and maybe we can travel around the country.

But I'll still come back to the hospital as a volunteer. I really enjoy it, even though sometimes I get real upset when I see what the Lord is doing to some of the people. I start to cry, but I never let the patients see me cry. I go into the washroom and I don't come out till I'm better. I try not to bring it home, and my kids never let me do it. They say, "Mama, leave it there. We don't want to hear about the hospital." And my husband does that too, he says, "Honey, I'm at the same place eight hours a day. You get too carried away over those patients."

Sometimes I get upset over the way a doctor acts with one of the patients. I'm not medical-inclined but I know when they're doing something wrong. Take an example where the doctors are standing outside a patient's room discussing her case, and she yells outside, "I can hear you discussing me in front of everybody." If they had something that had to be discussed they should go inside and discuss it to her face.

There are all kinds who work at the hospital. We get new doctors every so often and some of 'em aren't what they should be. They don't show any interest, and they don't care how they speak to you.

We had one doctor who threw up in the sink in the treatment room and he said, "Mrs. Parker, you come in here and clean this up!" My head nurse told me, "Willie Mae, don't you do that. He has to do it himself." So I gave him everything to clean it up and I showed him what to do and I said I hoped he was feeling better. Then I didn't pay him any attention for the next week until one day he walked up and said, ''Willie Mae, thank you for your kindness.'' We became good friends after that.

Doctors have problems just like everybody. There are happy ones and sad ones. Sometimes they have a drinking problem. Dr. O'Neill used to be a drinking man and now he's helping the other ones. The doctors have that problem like everybody else but with them it's got to be more serious.

THE REPENTANT SINNER

DR. HARRISON O'NEILL
Gastroenterologist

DR. ARNOLD BRODY, Director of Medical Oncology

O'Neill is a brilliant guy, and the problem is he knows it. Man, he could have had an amazing career except his personal problems held him back.

DR. BURTON WEBBER, Ear, Nose, and Throat

He's been active in the County Medical Association, particularly with our committee on alcoholism. There is something sour about his personality, something self-righteous. He is absolutely evangelical on the subject of the impaired physician, and he's offended a lot of people with some of his statements.

Harry and I were very close at one time and now we've become enemies because he's become very bizarre. His *modus operandi* for accomplishing anything between the GI department and the radiology department is to attack, to go around behind people's backs and talk. It's just a shame. That guy could have been one of the giants of gastroenterology, except he convinced so many people he was out of his mind.

A couple of years ago I ran into him at a Christmas party. I'm standing there talking and I'm drinking an eggnog. Harry comes up and says, "Steve, when are you gonna do something about your alcoholism?" I said, "I'm not an alcoholic. I don't know what you're talking about." And he says, "That's what they all say. Why don't you come with me to a meeting of AA?" Other people are hearing this and they're very uncomfortable. They thought Harry was kidding around, but the sad part is he was serious.

He loves to talk about alcoholism, like he's the biggest expert in the world. But when you get down to it, I don't even believe he was alcoholic. That's just a convenient way to explain his problems. It's a lot easier to say "I was a alcoholic and now I'm sober" than to have to admit that you're a psychopath, and you're never going to change.

———————

On a balmy Sunday afternoon, Dr. Harrison O'Neill sat under a sycamore tree in his backyard, enjoying a cup of coffee. He wore a tattered blue terry-cloth bathrobe that kept slipping off his knees, exposing a pair of pale, hairless legs. Bald, moon-faced, with a fringe of graying hair and a neatly trimmed goatee, he spoke in slow mellifluous tones and apologized for the noise from the living room, where his twelve-year-old son was watching a baseball game with two of his friends. Dr. O'Neill also warned that our interview might have to be cut short in order to return the boy to his mother by four o'clock. After their bitter divorce battle, O'Neill's ex-wife became hysterical if the boy's scheduled visits were extended by even a few minutes. The doctor lit a cigarette and leaned back on his lawn chair. He preferred talking about his practice, he said, to entering a lengthy discussion of his marriage and divorce.

I SPECIALIZE IN stomachs. Every kind of digestive problem, you name it. A lot of it is psychosomatic. GI symptoms are often the equivalent of psychiatric symptoms that the patient can't face and can't deal with. One typical profile would be a nervous old lady with functional complaints. Another would be the alcoholic patient.

Probably forty percent of the patients I see are alcoholics. That's typical for a GI practice. Alcoholism is the most common underlying problem. I see them because of the physical problems that go along with it, like liver disease or pancreatitis or gastritis or diarrhea.

It's easy for me to recognize what's going on. I am alcoholic. I'm active in AA. But even with that special insight I sometimes miss it because the patient denial is so strong. Alcoholism is a disease of denial.

My patients don't know that I had the problem myself. A couple of times I've let people know, when it seemed that it'd do them some good, if they were alcoholics who were recovering from alcoholism or trying to. But ordinarily, it would just lead to confusion or to more trouble, because people have all kinds of preconceived notions, a lot of which are pretty crazy.

Alcoholism is a genetically determined adverse drug reaction. My great-grandfather was an alcoholic. He was a farmer who emigrated from Ireland. And going back, he's the index case, so to speak. My father and grandfather didn't drink. Very strict Roman Catholics. My grandfather was the mayor of the town, a little town in Ohio, and later he was a state senator. My father was a lawyer who made a lot of money and ended up as a judge. Growing up, I was aware of our high social status. The highest in town. That felt okay. I had a good childhood. I was an athletic kid. I was active in sports. I was a good student. And there was religion. Lots of religion. The Catholic church was okay as far as I was concerned until I started drinking.

That was my first year in college. I went to Notre Dame and hated it. It wasn't a very good school. The premedical course was easy and dull. I started drinking because I was bored. I drank beer, just like a normal college student, but it did something different to me. It caused a lot of anxiety and a lot of fear. I was afraid of failure. My goal at the time was to get grades that were high enough to get into medical school. I was on top of my class, but that didn't do it. I was still afraid. So I got psychiatric help, but it made me feel worse and I didn't pursue it.

Then I went to medical school at the University of Michigan. Right away, life got better. I rarely drank when I was there. I was feeling good and I was enjoying myself, but I didn't make any connection with the fact that I wasn't drinking.

On graduation day we had a little cocktail party before the ceremony, and I had a couple of drinks. Then we drove up to the graduation. I was the speaker, because I graduated first in my class. But I have no recollection of giving the speech. So the next day I was feeling depressed and I said to my mother, "It's too bad I missed graduation." She said, "What? I heard you speak and you were wonderful!" I'd had a complete blackout. As far as anyone could tell I was functioning normally, but I couldn't even remember that I was there.

After that, I went to Chicago for my internship year and then did my residency in California. I did several fellowships here at Memorial, because I really enjoyed academic medicine. I also met my wife in that period, so it was a lovely time for me. She was a nurse at the hospital. She had just arrived from New York and she was very wide-eyed about everything. She was pretty and vivacious and very adoring toward me. It made me feel good to have her around, and during the whole four years we were going out, I didn't drink.

Then we got married and gradually I began to realize she had a problem with alcohol. She had terrible behavior after she drank a little bit too much. My mechanism for dealing with my wife's problem was to join her. And I became almost instantly addicted to alcohol and I was a far worse alcoholic than she was. I developed the same fear that I had in college, and I still couldn't figure out what I was afraid of. Again, I didn't connect it with alcohol. It was a bad time, because I had to make some major decisions. I wanted to go into gastroenterology research at the university, but I didn't

239

have the self-respect or the confidence to do it. I went into clinical medicine instead.

My practice was okay, but I don't think I was very good for my patients. Every evening I drank the equivalent of five, six ounces of Scotch. Or maybe I'd drink beer. I never drank in the morning or during the day. But alcohol greatly impacted on my abilities to perform. It limited my scope and it limited my imagination. I thought I was developing a schizo-affected disorder because I couldn't think as clearly as I could before. I had rapidly changing moods I couldn't understand.

The thing is, I never learned anything about alcoholism in school or residency training. Just like the guys today learn nothing about it. It's a tragedy. Knowledge of alcoholism would have saved me an awful lot of suffering.

The symptoms got progressively worse. Slowly, subtly. We had a son in the middle of this period and for a while that was very joyful. But alcoholism blunts the feeling of joy. In the last five years that I drank I didn't know what joy was. I felt increasing anger toward my wife but none of it was ever expressed. It just stayed and smoldered and built up. We became strangers to each other.

And it went on like that until a peculiar series of things happened. A girl named Terry came to work at Memorial as an electron microscopy technician. She was active in AA; she was a recovering alcoholic. One day she was sharing her experience with one of the girls who worked in my lab. I stood there listening while I was pretending to do something else. It was like a window opening up in my mind. I asked her out for coffee the next day and I began to share with her. I still didn't make the diagnosis of alcoholism, but from that point I stopped drinking. Pretty soon I felt better, and the emotional things began to clear up.

Then about a year later I went to a party one night in Mill Valley. It was a nice party, full of my old buddies. I felt good and I had a couple of drinks. Then I felt a compulsion to have another drink. It was overwhelming. I kept drinking, but rather than getting happy, I got anxious.

I had six or eight drinks. After a year of not having anything at all. And I left the party because I began to feel like I was getting drunk, getting crazy. On the way home I smashed my car into a tree. I wasn't badly hurt, but during the next couple of days I had really horrible feelings. Delusional ideas, suicidal ideas. I was sure

I was going to kill myself. I figured out how to do it. I'd inject stuff intravenously to stop the heart.

I took time off because I was too crazy to see patients. It was a big, decisive experience. And it finally dawned on me that this all happened after drinking alcohol. I had to face the fact that I had a problem with alcohol. I went through a whole series of denials. "I don't drink that much. I'm too smart. I'm too well educated." The usual kind of garbage. But the thing is I got drunk at a party and smashed up my car, and had to deal with these massive feelings of remorse and worthlessness.

I got in touch with Terry and said I wanted to go to an AA meeting. That meeting was a real turning point.

I heard a man describe the symptoms of alcoholism. He described his depression and lack of self-worth and a couple of suicide attempts. As he described the disease I realized that's what I had. All those years when I wondered what was wrong, and I never responded to medication or psychiatric treatment, I was clearly alcoholic. That's what the diagnosis was, and that's what it had been all the time.

After that first meeting I never had another drink. That's not at all unusual. Half of the people who go to *one* AA meeting, regardless of the reason they go there, never take another drink.

Alcohol is not one of the strongest addictions. It's harder to stop smoking, physiologically speaking, than it is to stop drinking. But alcoholism is a subtle disease. It affects the whole of one's being, and recovery is very slow. But that recovery, when it takes place, is unbelievably beautiful. There's a sense of euphoria, or rebirth. Year after year, the sober alcoholic keeps feeling better, calmer, saner, healthier.

The problem was that my wife couldn't share what was going on with me. She didn't want any part of AA. She didn't think I was alcoholic. She was drinking at the time too, and she continued to drink. It became a major issue.

She was pretty sick then and she still is. She became delusional and she thought that I was trying to injure our son. She ran away and hid him for a while. I think that her paranoid behavior was caused by her own alcoholism. When she came back, I got her into psychiatric care. Things were up and down for a while. Then she went to her sister who lives in Minnesota and told her a very plausible story of how I was beating her and beating the kid. I didn't realize how sick she was or how delusional she was until we got to court.

There were a lot of problems in our marriage. In our sex life she became frigid. Common symptom of alcoholism. She couldn't stand to have sexual relations unless she was drunk, and I didn't want to touch her when she'd been drinking. One of her delusional ideas was that she wasn't heterosexual, she was gay. A lot of psychopathology developed, and it increased. Part of it, I think, was my fault. I was depressed, I was quiet. And angry. Sort of seething, underlying negative feeling. Living with an alcoholic will destroy one's self-image, and that's what happened with her. She let herself go physically—overweight, sloppy, started wearing just jeans and a T-shirt. She stopped going out to medical dinners, retreated. Wouldn't buy new clothes. Lack of self-worth. All the money in the world and wouldn't spend it.

It climaxed when she decided to get a divorce. With my Catholic background I couldn't initiate it, but I was glad when it came. The unfortunate part was the custody battle. She got into the hands of a famous women's-lib attorney, who makes her living by being a man-hater. My wife didn't want to just split. She wanted blood. I asked for joint custody, but she wanted to exclude me. So we had a messy court case and it was gross just to watch the way this man-hating attorney preyed on a very sick lady. When the decision came down I won. We got joint custody. Our son lives with her, but I see him every weekend.

During the time I was married I never got involved with another woman. In retrospect, I think it probably would have been a good thing. It would have taken pressure off the marriage. But I didn't. I'm a puritanical kind of guy, really.

I wish that I had screwed around more when I was younger. I spent all that time working. It's one of my biggest regrets. And that's why I'm not ready now to settle down with somebody else. I need a broader exposure to life.

I go out about once a week. Different women. One thing you find out after you get divorced is that everybody wants to marry a doctor. I've gone out with ladies who are absolutely gorgeous, but I don't do that anymore. When I go out with somebody who's twenty-three years old and a perfect physical specimen, sometimes I feel inadequate. I have performance anxiety. So I feel more comfortable with somebody who's not totally gorgeous.

If I do get married again I want to pull back from my work a little bit. Coming from a rather wealthy family, I've never had to worry about money. But when I was married, I had this compulsion to acquire more and more. It came from the alcoholism, the anxiety and the fear, and I could never get enough. When we got divorced, my wife took about a million in assets and I had another million left over. My practice brings in more than enough and I don't have to worry about it.

People are always surprised when I talk about money, because they have this distorted image of an alcoholic physician. They think of a pathetic old rummy who's the dregs of the medical profession. But that's not true. There was a study in New York by a sociologist who found that the majority of alcoholic physicians graduated in the upper third of their medical school class. They earned a lot more than the average physician. Nobody knew they were alcoholic.

There's a conspiracy of silence, because the medical profession doesn't want to face the problem. When I first got sober it really bugged me. There are more than two hundred doctors in the Bay Area who are involved in AA. Those are the lucky ones, but there are hundreds more who don't face the problem. The attitude is that alcoholism is some kind of moral weakness. And the thing is that physicians are supposed to be morally superior.

There's an internist I know who's maybe the best diagnostician in town. He's alcoholic and he's deteriorating. He's not anywhere as good as what he used to be but he's still superb. One night I got together a bunch of guys and we tried to confront him. We had a poker party and we talked to him, but we didn't get through. He didn't even remember the conversation the next morning because he had a couple of drinks and he was in a blackout.

Talking about blackouts, there's a neurosurgeon here in town who had an unbelievable experience. One morning he came in a little bit hung over, and he said, "Where's Mrs. Gottlieb? I'm supposed to do a craniotomy this morning." The nurse said, "Mrs. Gottlieb is back in her room recovering from the operation." The neurosurgeon blew his stack because he assumed someone else had operated on his patient. But the nurse said, "What do you mean? You came in last night and did the operation. It was a good job and she's fine." The guy had been drunk and he had no recollection of it. He opened her skull and he functioned on a high level but he

243

didn't really know what he was doing. This guy has been in AA for about a year and right now he's sober. In my opinion, he hasn't recovered enough to do neurosurgery. But that doesn't stop him. He's still operating every day.

The County Medical Association now has a committee to deal with the impaired physician. That's a euphemism for the alcoholic doctor. We advertise in the bulletin of the County Medical Association. We have a hot line, but usually it's the friends or family who call, not the doctor himself. When we get a call we'll go talk to the guy, try to get him to face the problem.

The committee doesn't have a punitive function. We don't try to take people out of practice. If somebody's so sick that they've gotten into real trouble, the state's set up to deal with that. Most of the time it's not a question of medical competence. The technical expertise is still there, but the alcoholism does another kind of damage. You get totally self-obsessed. You don't have anything to give to your patients. You start developing an attitude that's hostile. After my accident, when I was thinking about suicide, I'd be listening to my patients and at least half of them weren't really sick. They came to me with gas, constipation, bloating and none of it seemed very important. I started hating my patients for taking up my time. It doesn't matter if you're alcoholic or not—if you hate your patients, you're not giving them what they need. It's a problem in medicine right across the board.

THE PATIENT AS THE ENEMY

DR. HARRISON O'NEILL, Gastroenterologist

I get rid of patients I don't like. It's better for me and it's better for them. I usually react badly to people who have destructive characteristics that are part of my own personality. The ones I dislike the most are the alcoholic people who could get well, but choose not to. Who choose to hang on to their disease, who choose to suffer. And I, in turn, choose not to suffer with them.

DR. STANLEY RUCKERT, Intern

The type of people who really get me are those who are suspicious of everything. They say, "What are you doing now? Why are you doing it?" They're really saying, "Are you sure you're not screwing up?" They start off with a negative viewpoint, and it really bothers me. It's still my job to take care of them, but there's not going to be much warmth in the care. If you're afraid to walk into the room because you know they're going to yell or complain, there's going to be something missing.

DR. MILTON TESSLER, Cardiologist

One afternoon I was putting a temporary pacemaker in a lady who was about seventy. I had given her a local anesthetic, but of course she was uncomfortable and she kept nagging me to hurry up and finish the procedure. I said, "Look, it's only going to take a couple of minutes," but she kept on complaining. Finally she shouted at me, "Stop this minute! If you don't stop I'm going to sue you for malpractice."

So I looked up at her and said, "Lady, you just said the magic word!" I called the nurse and I said, "Let's go. Let's take her back." And I started walking away with this procedure half completed. The lady really panicked. She said, "No, wait! I was just kidding! Come on back."

For the rest of the procedure she didn't say a word. But it still bothered me, and it's typical of a common problem. Part of the ego gratification of being a physician is the feeling that you're appreciated by patients. I like being thought of as a good guy, and I get miffed when I'm doing something that's good for the patient and they keep bitching and moaning and telling me it's terrible.

DR. ARNOLD BRODY, Director of Medical Oncology

I'm a controller. And when a patient bucks my control it pisses me off, because I know better than they do. I listen to what they have to say, but when someone starts giving me a bunch of crap, questioning me every step of the way, I get pissed.

I'll give you an example. There was a gal I'd been taking care of for a year and a half who would come in wide-eyed, dry-mouthed, saying, "What's this? I think I've got something." And I would feel and feel and feel. "Jeez, I can't feel anything." Then she says, "Here it is." And you finally feel some little pinpoint of nothing. Now I could go to another part of her body and feel around long enough and come up with the same thing. Admittedly this gal is terrified. She had breast cancer. She's lost her breast, she's lost her husband. She wasn't good-looking before the mastectomy. Her breasts were the best-looking part of her. And she

246

lost half of that. I mean, there's a whole laundry list of things that explain this woman's behavior. But that behavior is still neurotic and she's still a pain in the ass. Now she's gone to another doctor. She was just somebody that wanted too much from me.

There's a worse kind of patient, even though they don't want anything at all. That's the GOMER, an old decrepit bastard who's just a shell of his former self. Not a person. These poor hulks should be laid to rest somehow and not messed with. Some of the crap that goes on with the young docs and their GOMERs is just sickening. They get these poor people out of the nursing homes and they use 'em as pathology museums. Four or five or six doctors working on these derelicts, sending the fees to Medicare. For the docs it's sort of enjoyable. You don't even have to spend a lot of time talking to them, because there's nothing to talk to.

DR. DAVID ANZAK, Obstetrician-Gynecologist

I like patients who are intelligent, responsible people and I hate patients who are irresponsible slobs. The Medi-Cal patients—the people on welfare—are the worst of the bunch. Since the government is paying for it, they just don't care about what's going on. They don't show up for appointments, and they never call to tell you. They don't take their medicine. They call you Saturday night, three in the morning, with a problem that could have been taken care of on Wednesday afternoon.

On top of that they have very unrealistic expectations. People who are well educated are a little more realistic about what a doctor can do. But often the uneducated, welfare-type patients have wild ideas about what medicine can accomplish. They come in thinking that the doctor waves his magic wand and you get cured. They don't understand our limitations and they don't take responsibility for their own health. Half of the problems these people have could have been avoided by just minimal precautions. Abortions, infections, venereal diseases and all their complications. It's irritating to have to take care of people when they don't make the slightest effort to take care of themselves.

DR. MONICA WILKINSON, *Chief Resident, Pediatrics*

I cannot deal with anorexics. Maybe this shows a racist bias, but they are always white, upper-middle-class adolescent females. I cannot take their concept of not eating. In poor countries, or among poor people in this country, this is a disease that never crops up.

The problem with the anorexic patients is they don't really see anything wrong with what's happening to them. They feel they're fat, and they don't understand they're wasting away—it's like somebody from a concentration camp, or in Biafra or something. These fourteen-, fifteen-year-old girls who are just past skinny. They shouldn't be brought up to pediatrics. The psychiatric ward is the place for them.

DR. EDWARD FERRARO, *Medical Oncologist*

The alcoholic patients are the worst. I used to see quite a few of them when I was just starting out and I worked for this internist in town. I used to go on housecalls. There was this one couple I remember very well. He was a famous jazz musician and he and his wife used to have terrible quarrels at night. He was a drunk and she was a drunk and they used to call in the middle of the night. What they wanted was a referee. They used me, and I felt lousy. I felt obligated to go and I hated it. The whole experience was degrading. That's the trouble with patients who are alcoholics—they tend to drag you down into their world.

JOE RIVERA, *Emergency Care Technician*

The patients I really hate are the gypsies. There are a whole lot of them in this area, so they come in maybe once a week. And they are just the worst, the absolute worst. Their whole culture is based on lying, stealing, cheating. Anything to survive. In the ER you don't have time to deal with all their problems. I mean, you're talking about people who still believe in obesity, who think it's beautiful. I don't know how often they take baths, but they all come in with terrible body odor. And you have to deal with the ignorance of the whole family. If one of 'em comes in you'll have twenty-five in the waiting room, and each one of those twenty-five will get up and ask you what's going on. It drives you nuts.

DR. JACK BUCKMAN, Director of Emergency Medicine

All patients are pretty much the same to me, but I don't like the crybabies and complainers. You have to deal with them like you'd handle an immature child. Sometimes we get a lot of that type in the emergency room—faggots in particular.

It's hard for me to understand them, and what they do to themselves. I mean, talk about a bizarre social aberration! I'm convinced that faggotism is a result of the breakdown and failure of the whole society. You ought to see see what these guys do to themselves, all the stuff they shove up their assholes. They perforate their colons, they do all kinds of damage, then they come in here and we have to fix 'em up. The other day we took out a big rubber fist about two feet long, a black latex fist. We've also had table legs, light bulbs, jars of Alka-Seltzer, dildos, pool balls. This is what they do for fun! As far as I'm concerned, that's pretty much on the raggedy end.

But I feel more out-and-out disgust for the rich suburban ladies who come into my emergency room demanding that you instantly make their sore throats better. Whatever they have, they'll demand the maximum amount of attention, and it has to be cured instantly. They should suffer no pain, no inconvenience. They should be able to make their bridge game or whatever else is on their mind. So unrealistic compared to the rest of the world! Who says you have a right to feel healthy every minute of every day? Whoever says it hasn't spent time in the emergency room. Let 'em come sometime and take a look.

MR. MACHO

DR. JACK BUCKMAN
Director of Emergency Medicine

NANCY PROCTOR, Nurse

He's Mr. Macho. He comes in with hiking boots all the time. And he thinks he's just wonderful; he's just consumed with himself.

DR. BURTON WEBBER, Ear, Nose, and Throat

Jack Buckman runs a very tight ship in the emergency department and it's considered to be one of the best in the country. But there are rumors that he's impossible to work with. He's always firing people, and making some kind of noise. At one time, his lack of diplomacy cost him his position. He was gone for about six months but things fell apart so they brought him back again. Most people still hate his guts, but now he's untouchable.

DR. LANNY BUCKMAN, Pediatric Resident

Jack is an outstanding physician. When we were married I was very proud of him, very happy to see his success. I was probably living vicariously through his work.

As a person he's very aggressive, very dominating. He is determined to get exactly what he wants, no matter how he gets it. He pays very little attention to people's feelings. He trained as a surgeon and in many ways he has a typical surgeon's personality. I don't think that medicine made him the way he is. He was that way from the very first day I met him in the first year of medical school. But his type of aggressiveness is more acceptable in medicine than anywhere else.

JOE RIVERA, Emergency Care Technician

If you screw up, Dr. Buckman lets you know it. He can be a shitkicker when he has to. I've seen him pick up a resident and throw him across the room. The resident wanted to do some test on a patient. And Dr. Buckman knew he was wrong, but he didn't want to make a fuss in front of the patient. So he asked him, "Will you step aside here because I have to talk to you." The resident sort of ignored him, and wouldn't leave the patient. Finally Jack lost his temper. He grabbed this guy under the armpits and tossed him across the room. The resident landed on his ass and then got up and walked away looking real upset. By that afternoon he was gone. Dr. Buckman told them upstairs that this guy was fired from the ER.

Another time I saw him punch a guy out. It was Friday afternoon and a patient came in with an injured finger. He needed a hand specialist or he was going to lose that finger. The patient had no money and it would take about two hours for an ambulance to pick him up and take him to the specialist. Jack was off-duty but he decided to take him in his own car. Then the ambulance guy came down and started screaming, "You can't do that! You can't drive him! It's against union rules." Jack said, "Fuck you! You're a flaming asshole!" The ambulance guy tried to hold him back, but

Jack slammed into him and knocked him down. Then he got in the car and took the patient crosstown. He did all that for one poor guy on welfare who didn't even know what was going down.

Even with a substantial lift from the heels of his boots Jack Buckman stood no more than five feet eight inches tall. His broad shoulders and muscular torso reflected fifteen years of body-building—and conveyed the impression of a much larger man. With his jeans, broad belt, Pendleton shirt, and craggy, weather-beaten face he looked more like a lumberjack than a physician. He propped his feet on his desk in the office adjoining the emergency room, lit a series of slim black cigars, and spoke with a trace of a sweet mountain drawl.

I GREW UP in Tennessee, but you couldn't really call me a country boy. Knoxville is a big city. My father is a surgeon and I started out in surgery myself—I'm a boarded general surgeon but I don't do that anymore. I just do emergency medicine. Surgeons as a group are not happy people, because they lead very structured lives. When you've got sick people to operate on, you've got to follow them so closely that it regiments your life-style. In emergency medicine, we have set hours. You come in and cover at certain specific times. When you're here, you work your tail off. But when you're off, you're off. It's a lot more interesting, more variety, than surgery.

I got started with this job because nobody else wanted it. I was fresh out of residency and putting together my practice in general surgery, and I was also working part-time in the ER. They needed an acting director, and I volunteered. At that time the department was seeing fifty thousand patients a year, and I was the only faculty person assigned to ER full-time. Even being a man of unusual energy and skill, I couldn't keep up with that. I made recommendations that they should have eight full-time faculty to keep an eye on the place around the clock, and they should start a special residency training program in emergency medicine. They wouldn't do it, so I quit. Then they offered me more money but I said, "Fuck you." There's no way I was going to make myself crazy because some fool administrator didn't see they had a problem.

About the same time my marriage was breaking up, so I took a job in Phoenix, Arizona, as head of emergency services in one of the city hospitals. They gave me a free hand to rebuild that department. But a couple of months later they called me from Memorial and said, "We surrender. Come back and we'll give you whatever you want." The only problem was that I had a commitment to Phoenix and I couldn't just walk out. There were a lot of negotiations, and for a while I did both jobs. I spent a lot of time in the air, going back and forth. Sometimes I'd wake up and not know where I was. You forget which city you're in, whose bedroom you're in. I was real glad when that was over and I could spend all of my time at Memorial.

I'm good at emergency medicine, because I think fast. You have to be intuitive, because if you think strictly on the A plus B equals C level, you're going to go down the drain. You have to hold yourself open to every patient and absorb all the information within a couple of minutes and come to a decision. You've got to trust that intuitive response. It's almost like "Let the Force be with you."

I may be the director, but I work out there in the trenches like everybody else. The people who work with me are the best in the business. They're hand-picked and specially trained. Before I let them work on their own, they spend six months buddied with somebody who's experienced in this department. I won't allow anybody to screw up, because we practice in a fishbowl. All our work is reviewed by physicians afterwards, because if it's serious, the patient gets extended treatment in the hospital. When they check over the records they can't believe how well we do, given the pressure we have to face.

We rarely lose a patient. Sometimes they're dead when they get here. But if they get through that door alive, we'll get 'em out of here alive. What happens to 'em two days later, or two months later, that's out of our control. But if it ever happens that somebody comes into the emergency department alive and awake and fifteen minutes later he's dead, the physician taking care of him better have a goddam good reason why it happened. Otherwise, I'll have his ass.

The stress level is always high, but there's an *esprit de corps*, and a sense of teamwork. You develop a family-type feeling when you work together side by side, day after day. Everybody's integrated into it—the doctors, the nurses, the technicians, the X-ray guys, the laboratory support.

Most of the time, emergencies are easy to treat once you make the diagnosis. The complex job is trying to sort out the neurotics from the people who are really sick. Only twenty percent of our patients are actually admitted to the hospital. There are a lot of people who have cuts that need to be sewn up, or they have a urinary infection and they need antibiotics, or they have a sore throat and they need medication for that. We deal with it right here and then send them home. But a lot of patients—maybe fifty percent—don't need to be seen at all. If they waited at home for a day or two, whatever is bothering them would just go away. They don't need a doctor to intervene, and they certainly don't need emergency medicine. It's very aggravating to have to respond to their emotional demands when you're busy with everything else.

There are overwhelming periods when you just buckle down and do the best you can. Sometimes when you go home from those shifts you wonder what the hell you might have missed. You think, "Jesus, did I look at that X-ray carefully enough?" You start taking shortcuts, and thinking about those shortcuts can get you nervous.

We have three shifts, and the night shift—eleven to seven—is usually slower than the other two. But we're not staffed as heavily at night, so it doesn't take many patients to get overwhelmed. I work the night shift on Friday and Saturday nights. There's no other full-time professional head in this hospital who works the night shift or the weekends.

On Saturday night we get a lot of people who are victims of violence. During the week maybe ten percent of the patients have been hurt by somebody else, but on Saturday night it's usually close to half. Stab wounds, gunshots, we see everything. People with their heads blown apart, young ladies with a breast sliced off. There's a new thing now—some muggers can't wait for you to take your rings off, so they take a knife and cut off your finger. We've gotten very good at sewing up finger stumps.

Most of the time we don't get emotionally involved in it. We don't know the people, and we're busy just trying to get them stable. If I'm taking a look at your sore throat you probably think you've got my full attention, but at the same moment I've got ten other people on my mind. It gets to be draining at times. And frequently, after I've been home for an hour, I can't even remember what I saw that day.

We get a lot of people who've attempted suicide. It's pills mostly. If they shoot themselves, they're usually successful. But with pills, they're mostly asleep and we hardly have anything to do with them except pump them out and refer them to a shrink when they wake up. I'd be willing to bet that if we passed a law against resuscitating people from drug overdoses, the whole problem would disappear in six weeks. The only reason it exists is because we make such a big to-do about it, racing around in ambulances and getting everybody all upset. If they knew they weren't going to get resuscitated they'd think twice before they tried it. The Victorians were hung up on sex, and we're hung up on this idea of equality, the idea that every life is the same. If some poor slob wants to end his life, I say let him do it. Why should society intervene?

Working in the ER is like being a cop. When you deal with so many assholes, it really changes your perspective. I don't like people who break the covenants of our society, who mess up other people or who make impossible demands. I try to live my life in a pretty responsible way and I keep my nose clean.

I'm a single guy, but I was married for ten years. We had four kids right away, boom, boom, boom. We got married when we were both twenty-two. We were both in the first year of medical school. She dropped out, went back in again, dropped out, couldn't make up her mind. Finally, when we got divorced she went back and completed it. The divorce was caused in part by social pressures, me working too hard and her getting this women's-lib feeling that she needed her own career.

Maybe I made a mistake getting married in the first place. I was raised in a very traditional kind of household, and my wife was too, so there was a lot of family pressure for it to happen. But then I was working hard, and taking on all these things, and I needed a lot of personal room for growth that wasn't available in the marriage. I hardly knew who I was, and I didn't have time to find out. I came home so exhausted I'd just flop on the couch and fall asleep. I was getting fat, and I felt like I was dying inside. And my wife was so totally involved with the kids that she couldn't see what was happening.

For a while after things turned bad I thought maybe I should feel guilty about it. Maybe I didn't try hard enough, or work hard enough, to keep the marriage. But then I realized that there are some things over which you have no fucking influence at all. There are pressures that are way beyond our ability to comprehend— they're part of this particular moment in history. Divorce in today's world is something like that. A hundred years ago, Davy Crockett could take off for months at a time to experience personal growth. It was totally acceptable that he'd go into the wilderness and live as a pioneer without anyone going berserk. You just try leaving any modern woman for a couple of months while you get your head together.

After the divorce I went through a period of real intense social activity. A lot of different woman. I had to get that out of my system. But now I'm in a serious relationship that's lasted for two and a half years. She's a very pretty lady with a lot of interesting ideas. She's a former high school gym teacher who's doing a book on physical fitness. We live together, and actually I'm supporting her. She's thirty, ten years younger than me. She wants to get married, and if she didn't bug me so much about it I'd probably do it. But I made my name by knocking over giant bureaucracies, so when somebody meets me head on, I don't budge.

Except for the fact that we're not married, we have a very traditional arrangement. I play the role of the man, and I wouldn't be happy with anything else. Right now the males in this country are giving away their power, and they haven't gotten anything in return. I think that's crazy. You only give up power when someone takes it away. Once you abdicate it, it's awful hard to get it back! I'm not giving up anything, and I'm happy where I am. My ex was a lot more stable, but this woman now is a lot more fun. She likes sex as much as I do. And that's important, because I can do it twice a day, every day of the week, I don't care how tired I am when I get home. I'm always ready.

I like sports in general. I do weight lifting and karate and tennis. I run five miles every day. I go backpacking every summer. I'm in good shape except for a bad back. Last summer it got really bad and I was delirious with pain. I had to come through here as a patient. Right into the emergency room. They cared for me like I was

256

their kid brother, and they got a kick out of it. Why would I go somewhere else? This is the best damn emergency room in the state. These people are my best friends. They watched over me like no one else would. I had a viral infection in my spinal cord. They put me on some steroids and morphine and in a few days it began to abate.

In another part of the hospital maybe I wouldn't get that kind of treatment. Most of the other department heads don't like me. I live a much different life from your average rich physician. I dress like this all the time. I drive a pickup truck. I don't attend faggot parties. I don't use drugs. I don't go to charity dinners. I hardly attend committee meetings at Memorial. I have very few friends who are doctors. Most doctors are too rigid and materialistic, too wrapped up with being a doctor. I don't think of myself as Dr. Buckman. I'm just Jack Buckman to everybody I know. I go into a restaurant and I'm Jack Buckman. I don't say, "I'm Dr. Buckman here for my table." I'm not interested in the pomp and circumstance.

It bothers me that some of the physicians in our community seem to have lost the character of the Hippocratic oath. That's almost the religious part of medicine, where you're obligated to treat a sick patient no matter whether they pay or not. Our society has helped us abandon that viewpoint by having insurance and that kind of thing. So it becomes easy for you to reject a patient who has no funds and send them to County Hospital. There are lots of physicians on this staff who treat only wealthy people. They have high fees, the best clothes, the best offices, the best-looking nurses. All the important stuff, like taking care of the patients, paying attention to what you're doing, is subverted to that whole ethic.

I think my ex-wife could really get into that. She's in love with the idea of being a doctor. We lived together for ten years but she never understood my attitude to medicine. When she's done with her residency, she'll turn out like all the rest of 'em.

THE LATE BLOOMER

DR. LANNY BUCKMAN
Pediatric Resident

DR. MONICA WILKINSON, Chief Resident, Pediatrics

She's a good example of someone whose whole life was changed by the women's movement. If she lived ten years ago she would have ended up as a housewife, taking care of her kids. But as it is, she went back and got her M.D. and made a career for herself. It took a lot of guts. She could be like a role model for the modern woman.

BECKY KRIEGER, Nurse

I've known her since she was an intern. She always stood out from the rest because she's a lot older. I don't think she has any close friends at the hospital. It's like she always has her mind on something else, but she's still very good. Very capable. When she's on call at night, you know there's nothing to worry about. She'll get everything done that needs to be done and she does it right. And she doesn't play any power games like "kick the nurse." She won't take out her frustrations on the people around her. Her ex-husband is famous for being nasty to people. Lanny is just the opposite.

DR. JACK BUCKMAN, Director of Emergency Medicine

She's in her last year of residency and I think she's going to be a decent doctor. I get very positive reports from everybody who works with her. When we were married, she was always jealous that I was the doctor in the family. I was the one who made it. I was in the limelight, and she was just part of the woodwork. It's lucky she's got a man now who's willing to let her have the glory. He's kind of a nobody who smiles a lot and lets her call the shots. He's a nice guy, but I think she could have done better.

She's a smart lady and very single-minded. Right now, everything is centered around her career, and I think our kids got short-changed in the process. Nobody's going to tell me that you can go through medical school and internship and still give those kids what they were getting before. I've seen them change as she pulls further and further away.

I don't like the way she plays doctor with those kids. She loves to give them pills, almost like she's using them for guinea pigs. Right now we're having a big debate on the fluoride issue. I told her that all the city water supply already has a substantial amount of fluoride in it. But she persisted in giving the kids extra fluoride and as a result their teeth are stained. She is always doing things like that, doing procedures, making diagnoses, treating the kids like patients. She's not sure how to be a mother anymore so she goes back to playing doctor.

DR. CHARLOTTE KIRKHAM, Hematology Fellow

I always have to pinch myself to remember she's a doctor. She just looks like a typical mom from the suburbs, or one of those ladies in TV commercials who talks about floor wax. She's very pleasant but she's not someone I could ever get close to. She's not all that expressive about her feelings, and she's not all that bright. She got through medical school by working hard, and there's got to be a lot of tension under the surface. She started out later than everybody else and she's really killing herself to try to catch up.

————————

Arriving at seven in the evening for my interview with Lanny Buckman, I was greeted at the door by her live-in boyfriend, Bob, a pink-faced, good-natured hulk weighing somewhere in the vicinity of three hundred pounds. He led me to the cluttered family room at the back of the house, where he introduced the doctor and her four children. The two youngest, a pair of pigtailed little girls, sat on the floor and munched potato chips while watching That's Incredible! *on television. Their brother ran up and down the adjoining hall and attempted to teach a particularly slow-witted puppy to fetch. The lady of the house somehow maintained her calm in the midst of the turmoil as she sat on the sofa, helping her oldest daughter with her homework. Brushing aside a few strands of her stringy brown hair and smiling up at me with a square friendly face, Dr. Buckman requested five more minutes to work through a few additional math problems. When she had finished, we retreated to the master bedroom to begin the interview, but found ourselves constantly interrupted by one or another of her unruly brood. Finally, she got up and locked the door. The roar of her family and its televised entertainments could still be heard, but she cheerfully ignored the children when they came knocking at the door.*

I DON'T REALLY blame them for acting up, but sometimes I just have to shut it off. The kids are always excited at night because I haven't been home all day and there are a lot of things to talk about. Sometimes they complain that I'm away so much. Other times, you know, they're proud of me and what I do. The other day Nancy was asking me something about anatomy that she learned in her science class. And I could tell her how the lung worked, and how the heart worked, because I'd actually worked inside the human body. She said she thought I was lucky that I got to do those things when other mothers didn't get to do them.

Before I went back to medical school, I used to spend a tremendous amount of time with the kids. I really liked playing with them, doing creative things with them, just enjoying their company. But now my time is so limited that our relationships have changed. It's very different from what it was and it's very different from what I had when I was a kid.

My father is an electrical engineer and my mother is a housewife. She stayed at home, raised three children. When I was growing up I always wanted to be a nurse, and that lasted all the way to college. Then in my freshman year a counselor said, "You're good in science, so you should be in something like chemistry. You'd get bored with nursing." So I did a chemistry major, but I really didn't want a career in a laboratory. I wanted to work with people. That's when somebody suggested that I apply to medical school. There were very few women in medicine then, but I thought I would apply and see what happens.

I got in fairly easily and the very first day of classes I met Jack. He was the star of the whole class. I think from the moment he was born he felt he was going to be a doctor and he just knew he'd be a good one. I fell for him right away and we got married a year later. I took a year off from school to plan the wedding and get us set up in our apartment. I was going to go back after that, but then I got pregnant with my first child. Things were not as clear as they are now in terms of women doing things like medicine. There was a lot of prejudice among the people in the medical school; no really blatant hostility, but women were treated like pets, like it was nice to have us around but we really didn't belong there. So it was easy to just give it up and concentrate on my family.

The next eight years are kind of a blur. I had three more children and I was totally busy with that. Jack was very busy with school and with his residency program. He was planning to be a surgeon, and he seemed to feel good about that. Then one night in the last year of his residency he came home about three in the morning and woke me up. We went down to the kitchen, we had a cup of coffee, and he told me that he didn't want to be married anymore. He felt he had made a mistake. He had gotten married too young, and the children and I were holding him back from what he was destined to do. He wanted to be freer than he was.

At first I was angry. I felt like I had decided to quit medical school to have his children. He wanted me to stay at home, but after I did that, he suddenly saw me as just a boring housewife who wasn't good enough for him. The worst part of it was that part of me felt that he was right. I had sort of let myself go, I was dull, I didn't even like myself anymore. I couldn't even blame him for how he felt.

It was very hard for me to face the fact that we were breaking up. I was brought up to believe in monogamous marriage, and it was also difficult to adjust to the idea that Jack was seeing other women. I found out that he was cheating the last three years we were together. I more or less accepted it because I didn't think I had any choice.

It was more than a year from the time he told me he didn't want to be married till the time he finally left us. He had some personal problems at that time, and it was difficult for me to tell whether he was upset about our marriage or whether it might be something else. For one thing, his mother was dying of cancer. He really had a hard time confronting that illness of hers. Here he was, working with sick people all the time, but he could barely even go to see her while she was dying, and he felt guilty about it. Then he completed his surgical program but the first time he went for his surgical boards, they flunked him. Not because he didn't know enough, but because of his attitude. They said he was too arrogant, too cocky, and he was really crushed. At this point he wasn't sure what he was going to do with his life, so he went to a psychiatrist to try to sort it out. He also started working in the emergency room. For a while, it seemed like things were much better, but he was very erratic. He'd be very happy with us or he'd be in a rage, just furious. For no reason at all. It was just something going on with him. Eventually it got to the point where he realized he was so miserable that he had to do something, so he finally moved out. We still saw each other, but then maybe a month or two later, I decided that seeing him was just too traumatic for us. So it was a long, long process before we finally cut the tie.

Now we're on moderately friendly terms. I still like him, you know, and when I meet him in the hospital I enjoy talking to him. But he tends not to be very reliable, so I don't count on him for anything. Not even in terms of a commitment to have the children once a month. He's never been very involved with their lives.

When we first separated he totally removed himself and we couldn't count on him for anything. So I was faced with the reality of having to take care of them on my own. I had to go to work, get a job. And the prospects were either to start in a new field, like teaching, or go back to medicine, which I had already started.

The only part I wasn't ready for was the way medicine changes your whole personality. I'm a lot different now from when I first went back. In my junior year in medical school when I took my first clerkship in pediatrics I could barely stand to go on the wards and stick the kids, you know, to get blood from them. I had one little kid who was eighteen months old. He was too small to have blood taken from the veins in his arm, so I had to stick him in the heel, twice a day, every day, for six weeks. I loved this little kid, he was so cute, and I'd play with him in between and he'd be laughing and then I'd go stick him again! In the beginning he'd fight like crazy but as he got to know me he started to put his heel out for me. That really got to me. I would come home and feel just rotten. Eventually you get used to it, because you know you have to do it to help people, but there's a little bit of sensitivity and tenderness that's rubbed off.

It also carries over to your life outside. I'm much less patient than I used to be, especially if I've been on the wards for twenty-four hours. At the hospital you write an order and somebody does something for you. You do things efficiently. Then I come home and the kids start yelling at me. And my response is, "Leave me alone! Do it this way, that's the way it should be done. Don't question it!" I'm sure it's a carryover from the hospital, because when I'm on vacation or I have a weekend off, I go back to my old self. I'm much more tolerant, and I enjoy being with the kids and playing with them, and doing all the meaningless things that are fun to do. But most of the time, as a doctor, you can't afford to indulge yourself in nonproductive behavior. And you can't be weak.

I have to be at the hospital every morning by seven-thirty. That means I get up at five-thirty while everyone else is still asleep. I make lunches for the kids and get the house in order, so it won't be too disheveled when I come home. Then Bob gets up and he gets breakfast for the kids and gets them off to school. There's never enough time to do everything I need to do. There are just a thousand things I never get done. We started to redecorate like four months ago, and it's still only half done. I don't know when it's

263

going to get finished. We live our lives with things sort of half done. We sort of get used to it.

I've been sharing the house with Bob for two years now. We bought it together and we share all the expenses. We'll probably get married when I'm done with my residency.

So far, it's been a very nourishing relationship. We got together about a year after my marriage broke up. I knew Bob from our old neighborhood when we were both married. He has two kids from his first marriage, and we have them on weekends. It can be a lot of fun because all of the kids get along together.

We both go bananas at times, but he is an extremely happy person who will put up with almost anything. You know, he often ends up having to take care of my kids at night when I don't come home. And he has a busy career too. He was just made a partner in his accounting firm, and he's recognized as an outstanding person in his field. But he's unassuming about it. He doesn't have the same ego needs that Jack has.

It's partly personality, but it's also the atmosphere in that emergency room. Jack wanted us to give him adulation all the time because that was what he got from the people who worked with him. It's like they were his real family and we were just a substitute. That's nothing against them, you know, because some of them are very nice, very good people. Especially some of the technicians who have been with Jack for years. Joe Rivera is one name that comes to mind, because we had him for dinner several times. He's a nice guy and I think he's too smart to spend his whole life in that kind of job.

THE HANDYMAN

JOE RIVERA
Emergency Care Technician

DR. JACK BUCKMAN, Director of Emergency Medicine

Joe Rivera is damn good. He's been one of my best technicians since I started at Memorial. He knows enough about emergency medicine to run the whole department if he had to. He used to talk about going to medical school, but I think that's really more of a pipe dream. He'd have to go to college first. It's not realistic to start from scratch at the age of thirty, and he's too valuable right where he is. A couple of times he's caught doctors and nurses in the process of making big mistakes in patient care. He's not afraid to call them on it, and he knows I'm always going to back him up.

DR. DAVID ANZAK, Obstetrician-Gynecologist

I've seen Joe sit down with patients and spend a half hour explaining their condition. He not only knows the practical aspects of medicine but he also seems to understand the science that's behind it. Unfortunately, he sometimes acts like he knows more than the physicians who work with him.

When I first came to Memorial I spent a month in the emergency department. I didn't know anybody and Joe Rivera went out of his way to be friendly to me. He's a nice guy, but he's also kind of an oddball. He's a loner, basically. He is totally involved with his job—like this hospital is the only thing he's got going in his life.

———————

During the two hours that we talked, Joe Rivera went to the refrigerator at least six times and consumed three apples, a grapefruit, two cheese sandwiches, an entire box of Ritz crackers, and three cans of Diet Seven-Up. He apologized for his restlessness, explaining that he was scheduled to work the late shift that night and was worried that he had not gotten enough sleep earlier in the day to perform at peak effectiveness. A barrel-chested Mexican-American, Rivera wears a wispy mustache that seems out of place on his earnest face. When I asked him if he looked forward to spending the night on duty at the hospital, he snorted and shook his head.

You GOT TO be crazy to look forward to something like that! You got to be a little bit crazy to get into medicine to begin with. I got into it because of the service. I graduated high school in '69, right in the middle of Vietnam. I was drafted into the navy, and they put me into the Medical Corps. I went to corps school in San Diego and then they put me at the big hospital in Oakland. It turns out that was the receiving point for everybody from the war. I've seen sights that people in medicine would give their left arms to see! Like the burns—we used to get 'em from the flame throwers that shoot out and burn people. You just don't see those type of burns nowadays unless it's a big fire or something! We saw a lot of people who lost all their limbs. Or they've been hit in the stomach and

266

their whole stomach is blown away and they're kind of dripping into a plastic bag. Things like that are really interesting from a medical point of view, and you just don't see it unless it's wartime.

I handled it okay except for the beginning. When I was in corps school a marine came in, he'd been in a fight and he'd gotten cut across his head. His whole scalp was open and the blood was really coming down. It was the first time I'd seen that and I had to put my hand on it and hold it and that made me kind of queasy. But you couldn't faint, because if you fainted then he was going to die, so you stuck around. And you got used to it. It was different the next time a guy came in with a cut on his head. Nothing serious, just a little cut, but it was bleeding. I'd been up for twenty-four hours, and we hadn't eaten, we'd been busy. We ordered some pizza and it arrived at the same time as this jerk with the little cut on his head. I was tired, and I told him, "You can sit here and you can hold your head and let me eat the pizza first, or I'll sew you up right away, but I'm gonna eat the pizza at the same time." And he wanted me to do it right away, so I ate the pizza while I sewed him and everything turned out just fine.

When I got out of the service, I wanted to stay in the medical field. And just at that time Jack Buckman was building up the emergency department at Memorial and he was going for a lot of new blood. I got the job and I settled in right away. The main duties are support for the doctors, sort of finishing up. We do all the bandaging, all the castings, splinting. We go over the charts to make sure there's nothing they've missed. In the initial stage we'll see patients. We decide who has to be seen right away and who can wait. It's a big responsibility.

In the emergency room you see all kinds of people. One minute you're taking care of a prostitute, the next minute you're taking care of a corporate executive. You may take care of a person who got shot, and then the guy who shot him is on the other side of the room. You see the bad things in life . . . worse than wartime. You see the kids who get poisoned on Halloween. You see the wives who get beaten by their husbands. You see the little kids who get cut up by their parents. You see the beautiful actresses who come in at two in the morning with an overdose and there's nobody with 'em. They have no friends. And it's not a good part of life to see.

You also get the doctors and sometimes you get their kids. Overdoses, car wrecks, that kind of thing. Rich kids with fathers who work right here at this hospital. They've got everything going for them but they're unhappy. A lot of times they open up to you and you get to know them. They trust me and sometimes they come around just to talk.

If it's quiet, I can talk to them, but I like to work when it's busy. I don't like drug problems, psychological problems, that kind of thing. I like more of the trauma of the gunshots or the lacerations or the broken bones. If you're busy with a houseful of overdoses, nobody likes that. It's just messy. You have to put a tube into their stomach; they vomit on you, they vomit on the bed. You get this mess all over everything and you have to clean it up. I hate that. And I hate the rich people who come in. The ones with Gucci bags and Gucci shoes who treat you like you're a waiter. Their attitude is very spoiled, demanding; they want it their way.

I work forty hours a week and usually I take some overtime. The salary is about sixteen thousand and I don't think it's enough. They can't go higher because it's a political thing. The nurses get only a little bit more and they're not going to pay me more than them. The nurses make it bad for everyone else. They are not intelligent when it comes to business, they're not intelligent when it comes to life. They are predominantly females, they've taken the old-fashioned role. They let the doctors make all the money and pay 'em chump change for support systems, and we're stuck in the same boat.

The money's bad but the other parts are worse. We don't get credit for what we do. Let's say you're on a bed and you're bleeding and I notice your blood pressure is dropping. The doctor who's on may not be competent in this type of problem, but we've done it for years. So you go to the guy and you say, "Well, doctor, don't you think you ought to do this for 'em?" And then the doctor does it and the patient sees him and says, "Oh, doctor, thank you for what you did." If you're a tech or a nurse you can't go saying, "Hey, listen, buddy, it was *me* who did it, not him."

So you get left out, even though some of my work beats most of the doctors. One time I saved a woman all by myself. She had a tubal pregnancy and she almost died. It was late at night and it was busy and her doctor wasn't there. I had to start an IV on her, which is against the rules. In the service I started in IV, all right, but if they got me into court on this one, they could've come down on me. It was a gamble, but it was either take the chance and do it, or this woman was going to die. She was in shock. Her blood volume had to be brought up, so I started the IV and I did everything I could until her doctor got there and then we worked on her together. Then I had to go on to another patient and I forgot all about her. But three weeks later she called me up. She went to a lot of trouble to find my name. She said, "You saved my life. I know it. It wasn't the doctor. It was you." I heard that and I started crying right there.

I like having a sense of accomplishment. Things that I can do myself. I used to do plastic surgery, and I used to sew on a lot of patients. I'd fix up the sutures so there wouldn't be a scar. But then they came down on me. The nurses got jealous and they stopped it and I couldn't sew people anymore. No good reason. Just the rules. And I'm frustrated. I have all these skills and I can't use them.

I just don't enjoy working in medicine the way I used to. When I was in the service, I used to love it. I had a notion to be a doctor. But as I learned more about the field I lost the motivation. There are very, very few doctors who are dedicated the way they ought to be. You can't go into medicine anymore just to enjoy it. You have to go in as big business. The patients have changed too—they don't respect you. They pay you a lot of money so they figure they own a piece of you. Well, I'm not going to bust my ass to get through school to become a doctor and have a lot of people spit on me. I see the doctors, I see what happens to 'em. They're not happy. Their families are all screwed up. They work too hard and they get cold.

Maybe I was too idealistic when I started out. I've seen the good and the bad, and I don't want to stick with it anymore. I'm looking around in business and I'm going to take another kind of job. Dr. Buckman'll try to make me stay, but I've made up my mind.

Right now I live with my mother. I have to make a good living because I pay the bills. My father died when I was a baby and we always worked hard. I never had time to play. I want more of that now. I want to loosen up. I've got a girlfriend and I think we're going to get engaged. That's one reason I want a job in business. I want a future and I don't want to be stuck. I want to have kids, and

269

raise a family. And when they're growing up I'll tell them, "Don't even think about being a doctor." If they ask me why, I'll tell them why. Because you won't be able to spend time with your family. You'll always be competitive. You won't get the rewards you think you'll get. You'll look around and you'll go, "God! I'm making lots of money but I don't know how to enjoy myself! I don't know how to look on the bright side, because I'm stuck in the damn hospital all the time."

LOSING BATTLES

JOE RIVERA, Emergency Care Technician

There's one kind of case that always gets to me: child abuse. You never get used to it. I remember this one baby they brought in. There were big needles stuck into his body and they were all infected. He had cigarette burns all over his face. The mother and her boyfriend tortured him for weeks. They cut off one of his ears. A tiny little baby two years old, and on top of everything he was starving to death. His big sister brought him in to save his life, but he was dead when he got here. Nothing you can do except call the police. I took a break, right then. I wanted to cry but I felt too sick.

BOB ZACHARY, Morgue Room Supervisor

There's one part of my job that I really detest—abortions, especially the way they do them here. My God, it's like, if you don't want a boy, and you find out the fetus is a boy, you can abort. We get five or six abortions every day. They all come down to the morgue room. We get a gauze sack, filled with what looks like foamy blood clot. There's some tissue in it, but most of it's placental and you really can't tell what it is. We take a piece of placenta and a piece of fetus and have a slide made. And then the rest goes into a plastic snap-on jar, with formaldehyde in it, and it's saved for a certain period of time and then it's incinerated. It's treated like any other surgical specimen.

But a lot of times we get fetuses that are large enough for you to see it's a person. You get like a hand, a foot, a head, an eye. You just can't imagine what it looks like. Like this body that's very developed, at an early age, has been blown apart and there's just fragments, like limbs and bloody pulp.

It bothers me because it took my wife and me five years to have our first. I remember how desperately we wanted to have a baby. My sister went through the same thing, and a number of my friends. And then these people with their abortions. You see the names they send down to us. The same names, with maybe four, five, six abortions for the same woman. It's enough to make you sick.

DR. HARVEY FREDMAN, Professor of Gastroenterology

You can't take the personal side out of medicine no matter how long you've been doing it or how experienced you are. If I lose a patient, I still cry about it. Maybe not right there at the hospital, but later on, maybe when I'm at home and eating my dinner. I can tell myself I did my best, I kept the patient alive for longer than anybody else could have done. But rational arguments don't help. You had a connection with a human being, who was depending on you, and now that person is just wiped out. You have a basic human response. And if there's a doctor who doesn't feel it, I don't know if I'd trust him.

DR. MONICA WILKINSON, Chief Resident, Pediatrics

At times I blame myself for not thinking fast enough. One time I should have evacuated the thorax, cleared out the throat, a little more effectively. It was a kid who came in after swallowing a lot of water in a swimming pool, and I lost the patient. I blew it. I felt terrible, and for a while I couldn't sleep.

Then one day I was on the wards, but I couldn't concentrate because I kept thinking about the kid who drowned. I went out into the hall and I leaned against the wall and covered my eyes. One of

272

the older doctors came up and asked me what was wrong. I told him, and he said, "Every doctor knows that someday, somewhere, he is going to do something that will kill a patient. You have to accept it and then go on." Well, I knew he was right, and I started to look at the whole thing more philosophically. Things do proceed in the greater constellation of the universe, and losing one patient is not the end of the world. And if the same thing happened today, I don't think I'd take it so hard. Anyway, I wouldn't lose sleep over it.

DR. ARNOLD BRODY, Director of Medical Oncology

If you look at statistics, nobody does a worse job than me. My patients come to me with cancer. Sooner or later, they all die—almost all of them. In twenty years, I still haven't gotten used to it.

One episode that drove the reality home was a gift I received a few years after I started with oncology. Out of the blue, I get this nice big Christmas gift from one of the local mortuaries. I was never exactly pushing them, you know. I never had any intention of doing that. But just by sheer statistics, the signatures on the death certificates . . . I can hear them talking it over. "Hey, this guy Brody is all right. He sends us a lot of business. Let's send him a gift, man!"

I kept getting their gifts, and every year they had a kind of macabre quality. Like cutlery. I remember getting the knives in the mail and saying to my wife, "Now these assholes have sent me a do-it-yourself autopsy kit!"

Then the ultimate, the absolute gift came about two years ago. Instead of a great big box, I got a little envelope. Sure enough they had given me my own plot, for me and my family. You know, "We do a land office business with that guy Brody. Let's line him up with a nice plot, just for him."

DR. HARRISON O'NEILL, Gastroenterologist

There was an alcoholic patient that I admitted to the hospital with a ruptured appendix. He had no money and no insurance, and he was not a very attractive nice guy, so everybody else just wanted to get rid of him. I took him on as a favor to a lady I was seeing because he was her ex-husband. He needed surgery right away for his ruptured appendix, and I got a very fine surgeon to do it. Then the day after the operation this guy went into DTs and decided that he didn't like me. Part of the reason was he felt that I was trying to preach to him about his alcoholism. He was just furious, and he fired me from his case, and I felt like my ego was stepped on. He stayed on in the hospital, looking for another doctor, and the following night he died.

I had awfully mixed feelings. On the one hand, I felt fine—it served the bastard right! But I also felt a bit guilty—I had pushed him too hard regarding his alcoholism, otherwise he wouldn't have reacted to me as he did. And I also felt like a fool for wanting to say "I told you so" to a man who died. I didn't understand why I was so upset and insecure. Maybe I hadn't done the best job I could, maybe I made the wrong technical decisions. You never know. I kept arguing with him, arguing with myself, for about two months after it happened. The whole miserable feeling wouldn't leave me alone.

JEFF CARDEN, Critical Care Nurse

One time when I was working surgical ICU, they brought in a guy who had terminal cancer. They took him to the OR, opened him up to find out that he had pancreatic cancer, liver cancer, colon cancer. They snipped a few things out, put in a colostomy. That's where they cut a hole in the abdomen and bring the feces out through the hole instead of letting them go out the rectum. His pancreas involvement was really bad, because the juices were going out and digesting his insides. This poor guy was a mess, I mean a horrible mess. He was about sixty years old. He'd had a fairly decent life, I guess. So he started to get in trouble, respiratory distress, his lungs started filling up with a lot of fluid and the end was coming fast.

When I came back to the hospital the next night they had put this guy on a respirator. And I couldn't understand it. I mean, he was heading for the bottom, there was nothing they could do. They had already stuck this damn colostomy on him and he was oozing. He even lost the capacity to complain about his situation. Before, he had been pretty crazy. But with the respirator they stick a tube down your throat so you can't talk. So of course they had to tie him down to the bed because he kept pulling the tube out. And he died two weeks later a virtual prisoner.

I had to watch this whole thing, and I had to participate in it. And I couldn't stand it. I was supposed to draw blood gases on this poor guy. And it's a fairly painful process because you have to go with a needle way down in there, and if you miss, it slides around. So I went to the doctor and I said, "Doctor, why are we taking blood gases on this guy? He's tied down to the bed, he's dying. Why are we torturing him?" And the doctor got upset and berated me for fifteen minutes. How it wasn't my job, it was his job to make the decisions. And besides, he had a legal obligation. He said he didn't like it either, but what right did I have to remind him of it?

DR. MILTON TESSLER, Cardiologist

When I was a resident a patient came in, a black patient about twenty-five, with meningitis of some sort. We had to do a spinal tap. His family was all gathered outside, about twenty people in all. They were all poor and uneducated, but very religious people, and we had to persuade them to sign for a spinal tap. We assured them it was just a routine procedure, you know, and they didn't have to worry. So finally they agreed but they all started praying. As I went back to the OR some of them actually got down on their knees.

I went in and started the procedure. We put the needle in and started getting some fluid, when all of a sudden the guy sort of gasped. The next thing I knew he stopped breathing. So we called the nurses and got the crash cart in, and took an EKG. Initially, it was just a very slow heart rhythm and then no rhythm at all. We shocked him a number of times and tried to get him back. Then we started an intravenous, but we had trouble with it. Eventually we got it in, but we just couldn't get his heart back. It was a nightmare. The kind of thing that isn't supposed to happen. We did everything right but we just lost him. He died right there. We never found out what actually happened because his family wouldn't permit an autopsy.

And I was the one who had to go out to the waiting room and tell them he was dead. I spoke very quietly and all of these people were gathered around me in sort of a circle. They interrupted me before I got the words out and just started screaming. The whole hall was in a complete uproar. They were throwing themselves against the walls and rolling around on the floor and screaming out, "Lordy Jesus! Lordy Jesus!" The other resident and I got really scared. Some of the patient's brothers were really big guys and I thought they were going to kill us. We called security and two guards came back to ask the family to leave. It took half an hour to clear them all out. I got somewhat paranoid after that. Whenever I saw a group of black people in the hospital I thought it was his family, coming to get me. I guess it was an expression of my feelings of guilt and inadequacy.

DR. LANNY BUCKMAN, Pediatric Resident

You worry all the time about hurting somebody, making a mistake and doing the wrong thing. If you set them back, if you cause them pain, but they're still alive, then you blame yourself. But death is such a big thing, such a big change, you can't really believe you're in control of that. If that happens then you just say, "His number was up, there's nothing we could do." Whether that's true or not, I don't know. But it makes it possible to live with yourself in the morning.

BECKY KRIEGER, Nurse

Sometimes I think it would really help if I had more faith. I mean, it's almost a religious type of profession. I always joked when I went to nursing school that I might as well have gone into a convent, you know, as far as the hours and the company you keep and everything. Sometimes I can't accept what's happening and I'm pissed at Whoever causes all this stuff to go on. The other times, I keep saying to myself, "There must be a reason. There must be a reason." I get a lot of comfort at times, thinking of patients I've worked with, being in heaven or wherever they go, some place where they're not sick and they're not in pain.

As a kid I used to really enjoy going to church, and in college I was very involved in Catholic activities. Up here I haven't found a church that I really like, but I haven't tried that hard either. You know, I work every other Sunday. A lot of times I'll be walking to work and I'll see other people on their way to church. For a minute, I feel kind of guilty. But then I think to myself, hey, it's God's work, so it's okay.

THE BLEEDING
MARTYR

BECKY KRIEGER
Nurse

DR. ARNOLD BRODY, Director of Medical Oncology

Nurses used to be sweet little old ladies in white shoes who would hold somebody's head when they were vomiting, and look concerned, and flutter, and so forth. But recently the feminist movement has impacted in a big way. The gals know a lot more and they run intensive care units and they try to be very professional. But I'm glad that we still have a few individuals like Becky Krieger who combines the old and the new. She is tough and capable and technologically sophisticated, but she projects this Florence Nightingale image—a loving, tender, caring gal who will wade through all kinds of shit and yet nothing bothers her.

NANCY PROCTOR, Nurse

She's a good nurse and a good friend. Everybody knows about her dedication, but sometimes she's too dedicated, I think. She's got to develop some interests outside the hospital. Otherwise she's going to be a candidate for nurse's burnout. Last year I fixed her up with some of the single guys I know. She went out with them, but nothing happened. They all said the same thing: She's a great person but she's not a lot of fun.

Becky gives you a hundred and ten percent. She is very patient, very sensitive. I respect her as a nurse and I like her as a person. I even thought about dating her recently, but then something happened.

I was giving her a hard time about a patient of mine who was a vegetable. He was in the intensive care unit and Becky was the assistant head nurse responsible. I didn't like the idea that she had student nurses taking care of him. So I said to her, "Look, his family is paying five hundred dollars a day to keep him here. I expect better care than this."

Later in the day I saw her in the hall and she had tears in her eyes. I stopped her and said, "I hope that's not from me." She said, "Oh no, it's just been a bad day all around. Everything went wrong." But still I felt bad. I mean, there were four or five other people who were bugging her, then I came down on her too!

I called her that night to apologize, and she started crying again, over the phone. She said she was just exhausted, but I felt strange about the whole thing. After that, I never called her again.

_____

Despite the fact that she worked till ten P.M., Becky Krieger insisted that we schedule our interview one night after she came home from the hospital. She explained that she was so "wired" after work that she couldn't fall asleep and added cheerfully, "I'd rather talk to you than watch Johnny Carson."

I found her dressed in jeans and a bulky sweatshirt, a chunky, broad-shouldered young woman in her mid-twenties with a plain pleasant face, thick rimless glasses, and short blond hair. She poured me a cup of coffee and settled onto the couch. While I nursed my coffee, she sipped at a large cup of warmed milk, explaining that it helped to soothe her bleeding ulcer.

SOME PEOPLE GET headaches. Some people get diarrhea. I lucked out and got an ulcer! It started two years ago, and most of the people at work don't know about it. It's sort of embarrassing and I don't want people feeling sorry for me. I have to watch what I eat and I have to try to relax. The good part is that I had to be so careful with my food that I lost ten pounds, which I really needed to do. Sometimes I have pain, but it hasn't been so bad.

When I first got sick I thought about quitting my job. If I got away from nursing maybe I'd have an easier time. My mother was calling me up all the time with suggestions. She doesn't understand about nursing. And that's the trouble—there's nobody that understands. With ninety-nine percent of the population their first reaction is, "Oh, you empty bedpans." It's very frustrating, you know. I'm college-educated. I'm a very bright girl. And people think I empty bedpans! That's why a lot of nurses feel on the defensive about their job. Nobody comes over and says, "That's a valuable thing you do." It can be very demoralizing.

Since I got sick I let my frustration come out. I don't try to hold it in anymore. And if things get really bad, I usually cry. I cry at work. Maybe once a week, maybe more. It releases a lot of tension, and then I can go on and do something else. I think it's a strength, rather than a weakness, to be able to cry. But I try to keep it a private thing. I'm in a leadership position and it doesn't look real great if your assistant head nurse is walking around with red eyes or sniffling.

All kinds of things can go wrong. Maybe I get a call that two of the nurses on the next shift can't make it for some reason. That means I have to go to the nursing office and get some registry people or some floaters to fill in. But usually you can't get people on such short notice, so somebody's going to have to work overtime, to do a double shift. And usually that's going to be me.

Then let's say we have to get a transport together to go out and pick up a sick patient somewhere. This means arranging for a critical-care nurse, which isn't always easy. Maybe that same night we have a couple of emergency admissions. And we don't have the beds, it's a full house, but the resident is saying, "I don't care if you don't have the beds, I don't care if you don't have the nurses, that's no reason to refuse admissions." Then I've got to move some patients around, I've got to make something give, because you can't put two people in the same bed! All the time I'm doing this, I'm away from my patients. Maybe some of them are real sick and I get to the point where I feel like I'm being a bad nurse for the patients I have, and I'm being a bad leader for the nurses on the floor. I'm not doing justice to any of the jobs I'm supposed to be doing.

The patients are the best part of this job—the relationships you develop with certain people and certain families. It's nothing I'm going to be able to stick in my jewelry box or my photo album and look at twenty-five years from now. But I know I made a difference at a pretty intense time in somebody's life. Of course that can also be frustrating, because you're there with them in this crisis in a big way, but when it's over, it's over. The relationship just stops, and sometimes you're left hanging there.

When I was working in pediatrics, we had a little girl who had biliary atresia, which is usually a fatal-type thing. She was two years old and she'd been in and out of the hospital her whole life. The family was there all the time, and they were very nice people. Chinese people who ran a grocery store. A kind of a social relationship developed, because I was one of their main resource people. But when the kid died, I didn't even have a chance to say goodbye to the parents. It felt unfinished, but there was nothing I could do. When a kid dies, a whole family dies for you. A whole group of people.

If you are a normal person you lose a handful of people in your lifetime. Your grandparents, your mom and dad, that's about it. My dad died when I was in high school, and it was hard to take. But that's nothing compared to what it feels like when you start having lots of other people go, people that you get fairly involved with. The first year I was working here, there was one woman I got very involved with. She was twenty-six, just a little older than me, and she was dying of cervical cancer. It became like life and death to me whether I took care of that woman or not. I wanted to be with her all the time. When she died, I was almost nonfunctional.

Since then I don't let myself get so involved. It hurts too much, and starts to affect your work. You can't always be the one in tears.

The family's falling apart, and you've got to hold it together for them. Sometimes you're the one who has to give them the news of a death.

And once we had a baby with severe brain damage—and that was even worse. The mother had gone home before we knew what was wrong and we kept the baby for observation. It was a Mexican family that didn't speak any English. Their doctor was away on vacation, so I was the one who had to call and tell them the bad news in my college Spanish. You know, "Señora, your baby's head is formed wrong. He will never talk. He may never walk. Maybe someday he'll learn to get a bottle to his mouth." That was far worse than if I'd had to say he'd died.

For some reason, most of the bad stuff happens at night. It's almost a mystical kind of thing. People have done studies about it, and even with people who have a long, lingering illness, when they finally die it's much more likely to happen at night. I'm aware of that, but the evening hours are still my favorite time at the hospital. I used to work mornings, but that's very, very busy. You're going to the operating room, you're going off for tests and procedures. You've got to get all the bed baths done, you've got to get all the sheets changed, you've got to get breakfast out. Then before you know it you've got to get lunch. And the doctors are coming through on their rounds and there's a feeling of hustle and bustle. Then afternoon comes and it starts to slow down. But for me, I'm just coming on and there's all the problems to worry about. It isn't till the evening that it really starts to get quiet. A lot of people, the nonmedical people, are going home. It's more a winding-down time, you know. You put people to bed. You have time with them. The families are usually there in the evening. You get to spend some quality time.

I remember one afternoon when everything was going wrong, everybody had a complaint. Then Laurie, a student nurse, pulled me aside, and we went and sat out on the stairwell, had a cigarette and watched a sunset, and things seemed to fall back into place. The memory of that time still has a calming effect on me.

I always get to break for dinner, and that's a very important time for me because I can get away from the wards. You can sit down for forty-five minutes and take deep breaths.

There's usually one table in the cafeteria where we all sit together, a whole group of nurses. We make a concerted effort to stay off the subject of work. We'll talk about social life, who's going out with who, that kind of thing. It's funny, but none of the doctors will ever sit and eat with us. Not even the interns and the residents who are our good friends. You'll see a guy walk by, maybe even someone you're going out with, but he still won't sit down. Not if he's a doctor. It's an unwritten rule. You can eat together at a fancy restaurant but not at the hospital cafeteria!

I don't go out that much. There are a couple of guys who I see off and on, but there's nothing serious, nothing regular. I have a lot of male friends, but I don't think I've ever been in love. Maybe I'm afraid to be in love with them. After my father died I had a stepfather for a while and it was a very, very bad scene. He was alcoholic and crazy. He left my mother when I was in college, but she never got a divorce because she's a very strict Roman Catholic. Recently she's been working as a teller in a bank. She's very proud of me because I have a college degree and I'm supporting myself, but she wants me to get married and start having babies.

Part of the problem is that I like spending time by myself. After all the people at work, it can be really pleasant. I like this apartment, and about ninety percent of the time, I guess, I just come straight home after work. I like to watch TV while I fix myself a snack. The shows are so stupid that it kind of relaxes you. I also like to read. I read good books along with trash, but mostly trash. I just bought a novel about doctors, but God, that's all you need is to read more hospital stuff on your days off!

It's hard to make a separation between what you do at the hospital and the rest of your life. There's part of the hospital that gets into everything else you do. Lots of times I dream about things that I didn't do, mistakes that I think I've made, even if I haven't made them. When I first started working the evening shift I used to work the nursery. I would wake up in the middle of the night and I'd jump out of bed, thinking it was time to feed so-and-so. And I would dream that there were babies in my living room waiting to be fed. I'd have to talk myself through it, saying, "No, you are at home. There's no one in your living room. There are other nurses at the hospital who are taking care of the patients. You can go back to sleep now."

Some of my friends have been telling me I've got to pull back or I'll get burned out. A lot of nurses quit their jobs after two or three years. Most people in the first year are so gung ho and so enthusiastic that they're ready to give everything. But if you give everything, there's nothing left to take home. You get very involved in these work situations that are very high-powered, very intense and very dramatic. Your personal relationships aren't ever going to be as exciting as what goes on at work. If you do try to get that same kind of excitement, your personal life is going to be very bizarre. An example of that would be Dr. Peskin, who's a psychiatrist who works with terminal cancer patients. He really has to strain to make an outside life that's going to compete with the same range of feelings he gets in the hospital. I always get the feeling he is very, very strange.

THE OUTSIDER

DR. REUBEN PESKIN
Director, Hospice Project

DR. BEN BRODY, Psychiatric Resident

Reuben is an outstanding psychiatrist and I really admire him.
He's not that well known, because he's still a young guy, but the
residents who work with him think he's the best. He's very creative
and very sensitive and he's got a human quality that you don't see
in a lot of doctors or a lot of psychiatrists. He lets his patients know
what he's feeling and what's going on with him, and he's also very
up-front about being gay. He's not swishy but he's not embarrassed, either.

DR. HARRISON O'NEILL, Gastroenterologist

He called me a couple of weeks ago and he wanted to have a
talk. I hardly knew who he was, but he came over to the office.
He was looking for referrals. He runs the hospice program at
Memorial but he's also got a private practice. I got the idea he
was hurting for patients. He came to me because we do a lot of
referrals to psychiatrists. A lot of gastrointestinal problems are
psychologically related. I said, "Fine, I'll see what I can do for
you." But he wouldn't leave. There was something else. He

wanted me to know that he's gay so I could tell all my gay patients to go to him. Strange idea. You can't say to a patient, "Hey, I know this nice gay psychiatrist and you ought to see him. He's one of your own kind." Up to now, I haven't sent him anybody.

DR. JACK BUCKMAN, Director of Emergency Medicine

I don't like faggots, and Reuben Peskin, in a lot of ways, is a typical faggot. But he's also smart and he knows how to be tough. He's not afraid of going up against the bureaucracy to get what he wants. I give him a lot of credit for this hospice project. It's something new, and he had to fight like hell to get it.

———————

Dr. Reuben Peskin rents a spacious flat on the top floor of a gaudily painted Victorian house. On the night of the interview, his front window offered a fairytale view of city lights which, along with the big-band music on the stereo, conveyed the atmosphere of a late-night TV talk show. Peskin wore a black cashmere sweater that emphasized his pale skin and sparse red hair. A pair of tinted glasses in bright-red frames added a somewhat forlorn touch of merriment to his otherwise gaunt and somber appearance. As he switched off the stereo and sat down, an obviously pampered Siamese cat leaped onto his lap. Peskin reached forward and lifted a dictionary from the coffee table. He turned to a page that had been marked in advance.

I KNEW YOU were going to ask about the hospice project, so I decided to do my homework! "Hospice" is a very old word. As it says in the dictionary, "A shelter or lodging for travelers, often maintained by a monastic order." The most famous one was the Hospice of St. Bernard in Switzerland, where they had the big dogs out with little kegs of rum to rescue people from the snow. What we do today is to help a different kind of traveler; we help people on a journey to death.

To some people, that sounds depressing, but the hospice is not a depressing place. We make people comfortable. We bring them Comfort, Company, and Care, and that's with capital C's. Why should that be depressing? If one isn't phobic about death, one can alter the individual tragedy by reducing the suffering and pain. In other parts of the hospital, the doctors still use inadequate amounts of pain medication. They want the patient to stand it as long as possible, like it's a test of strength. It's crazy. But here we put the needs of the patient first, along with the psychological needs of the family.

We have a ten-bed inpatient unit, and we have a home-care program for people who want to die at home. We also serve as consultants elsewhere in the hospital, dealing with psychological issues of death and dying, pain control, and control of other symptoms.

There are a number of other hospice programs in the Bay Area, and there are more than twenty in California. For Memorial, this is a pilot project. I drew up the initial proposal a long time ago when I was working in the psychiatric ward. I'd been working there for four years, but I didn't enjoy dealing with psychotics and very disturbed people. What appealed to me in the hospice idea was the potential for real relationships with people who are physically ill, but whose psychological problems fit more in the realm of the normal. There's more intimacy with this kind of patient than with someone in the psychiatric ward who thinks he's Jesus Christ. The whole hospice idea looked very appealing and humane, and so far it's the best thing that ever happened to me.

The only problem is that in order to get the project going I had to accept a very small salary. Officially, it's only a half-time position, but I spend about fifty hours a week on hospice work. I also have a private practice where I see patients in an office. Right now I have nine hours but I'd like a lot more. Nobody there is terminally ill. They're all healthy neurotics! The majority are gay. It's not because I want it that way, but given the referral sources that are available to me, that's how it works out.

A lot of the private patients come to me to be "cured" of their homosexuality. If that's what they want, I'll explore it with them, but after a while I might say, "Well, it's going to be very difficult for you." If in fact the only reason they want to be heterosexual is because their parents want it, but all their erotic arousal and all their internal fantasies are homosexual, you owe it to them to say, "We can try this, but I don't think it's going to work. Another choice might be to accept yourself as you are and see what kind of meaningful life you could have as a homosexual. Maybe that's not such a terrible thing, you know."

It's a lot easier for people to accept themselves if they're living here than if they're located in other parts of the country. San Francisco is a Mecca for gay people, and for gay physicians, too. There's an organization of gay doctors with over two hundred members. We have monthly meetings. Every specialty is represented—anesthesiologists, dermatologists, endocrinologists, you name it, but more psychiatrists than anything else.

In every specialty, I think, gay physicians have a tendency to be more sympathetic to the patients. That's not just gay pride talking. I think it's logical—our troubles make us more sympathetic to other people's troubles. Homosexuality is a struggle, even in San Francisco, and it helps you to understand human tragedy and struggle and all the pain people go through.

There's another pattern that I've noticed with those of us who work with terminally ill patients. A highly disproportionate number are people who lost a parent or another close relative when they were young. That experience makes you more concerned with that kind of suffering, more tender. And it also gives you more of an acceptance of death as a part of life so you can go on working in that situation year after year.

My own mother died when I was thirteen. It's part of my whole sad, sordid story! It was the week after my bar mitzvah. We had a huge, catered affair at a temple in Boston and she had been working very hard on it. I was the oldest child and I was a momma's boy so she wanted everything to be just right. The day afterwards, she went to the hospital and she never came back. She was diabetic and she had complications and she died. She was only thirty-six years old. That's younger than I am now.

My father carried his grief around inside of him and worked harder than ever. He was an insurance salesman and he was already very frustrated about his career. He remarried too quickly, I think, and he chose a woman who was absolutely wrong, for him and for us. My mother was a great beauty and she was delicate and frail and very refined. My stepmother was fat and loud and coarse. She was a chain smoker, and one night she was smoking in bed and she set the house on fire. My sister was lucky to get out of her room alive.

A month after that my father had a heart attack. He was shoveling snow one afternoon and he collapsed. He was hospitalized for four months, and when he was released he got the news that he had been fired from his job. We were almost out of savings and we were getting desperate. At that point my father decided to try his luck in the golden land of opportunity, California.

We moved to San Diego and we were all miserable. I started high school and by the middle of tenth grade my stepmother left us and went back to Massachusetts. I was glad to see her go, but my father couldn't get along without a woman. He begged me to call her and ask her to come back. I didn't want to, but I always was a good boy. If my father said, "Cut off your toe," I think I would have cut off my toe. So I made the call for him and got her to come back. For a while, things were better—my father got a job as assistant manager of a clothing store and I was doing well in high school. By senior year I had finally come into my own. I was co-editor of the yearbook, I was president of the chess club. I didn't feel like "one of the boys," but people liked me and I was accepted.

Then I graduated and went away to Berkeley. My mother had always wanted me to go into medicine, and there was no question that was what I was going to do. I was on scholarship because my father was out of work again. He was really struggling, and when I came home for Christmas vacation my sophomore year, he made a big point that he wanted to talk to me. The day before I went back to school we took a drive all the way out to Point Loma. He drove and didn't say a word. We stood at the lighthouse and looked at San Diego Bay and the ships and the city and he still didn't say anything, then or on the way home. The next day I flew back to school.

My father killed himself that week. He shot himself in the head.

My sister found him when she came home from school. The police called me two hours later and I drove down from Berkeley right away. I found that my father's suicide had been well planned. He left letters that told me exactly what to do about Social Security, about the car, about my sister.

It was a difficult time, and I was depressed. I'm well aware of the statistics which show that children of suicide victims are much more likely to do the same thing. If I kill myself someday, then somebody will relate me to those statistics. But I can't say there's a real connection. I'd kill myself out of my own desperation. I'm not suicidal currently, but I've felt that way at times. The bottom line is that I don't love life so much, even when I'm not depressed. Even when things are good there are so many gaps, so many holes. But I don't think I would ever do that to my sister. I mean, that sounds peculiar, right? But in a way what keeps me alive is my commitment to my sister, along with a few of the friendships I've had along the way.

The most important friend in my college years was my roommate, Nick. Looking back, my feelings for him were obviously more than I realized at the time. The intensity between us! He's married and he has twin sons and he named one Reuben. I think I was in love with him and I think he was in love with me, but we never expressed it. Nick was spirited, attractive, very quick. Also premed. And popular with the girls.

I was also going out with girls at the time, but I was never that successful with them. They always liked me, but they wouldn't go out with me if they had something better to do. It was sort of the part that Ronald Reagan used to play in his movies, the second lead. Except he got to marry Ann Sheridan at the end of the picture and I never found Ann Sheridan! I always thought if I met the right Jewish girl, then these other feelings would go away. But at this same time, in college, I was starting to buy men's magazines, physique magazines, and I would hide them under the bed and look at them before I went to sleep. So I knew, and yet it was like the kid that doesn't want to masturbate. I'd try to fight it, as if I could get rid of it, as if it was some kind of malignancy.

Then my roommate Nick got into medical school at Stanford and I didn't—I was going to the University of Washington. I thought the separation was going to kill me, especially since the relationship seemed so much more important to me than it was to him. That first year I wrote to him twice a week and he always wrote back. After that he got engaged and we just drifted apart.

Meanwhile, I loved medical school. The first two years I was an average student, but the second two years, the clinical years, I came into my own. I was good. I also had a lot of friends, and it was a wonderful time for me in a sense. I continued to go out with

289

girls, but I couldn't bring myself to have sex with them. I couldn't force myself to do it. One time a friend of mine took me with him to a prostitute, but I was more interested in the friend than the prostitute!

Then in my fourth year I was working on the wards with a resident, a guy named James Webberman. I knew, intuitively, that this guy was gay. I was drawn to it like a magnet. But I wasn't an attractive fellow and it took all my courage to ask him to go to lunch. When I arrived at his apartment to pick him up he answered the door in his underwear. We sat across the room from one another, but I didn't know what to do. I had no sexual experience with men and only unsuccessful experiences with women. Finally he got dressed and we went out to lunch.

Over the rest of that year we stayed in touch. The most that ever happened was that we made out one night on the way from a movie. He said to me, "Peskin, sometimes I think you really are a faggot." It made me feel terrible. I think he was still struggling with his own sexuality. It was like the blind leading the blind. If the guy had been a little more aggressive he could have really brought me out, but unfortunately that didn't happen.

Then I finished at Washington. I came back to the Bay Area for my residency. I always had the idea that I wanted to do psychiatry. Even as a kid back in the eighth grade I was the advice giver, the listener, the confidant for everyone else. I was the Dear Abby of the eighth grade. It's been that way ever since, so psychiatry seemed like a very obvious step.

But when I started my residency, something disturbing happened. We were all sitting in the cafeteria with the director of the program. He was somebody who I really respected. Somehow the conversation came around to homosexuals, and he said, "People like that don't belong in psychiatry. If I could keep them out of the profession, I would." I kept quiet, but I was very upset. You know, if I had been doing an ophthalmology residency and some ophthalmologist made a nasty comment about homosexuals, it wouldn't have mattered. But this was a fully trained psychiatrist, an important man in the field, and I thought, maybe he's right, maybe I am sick. I decided at that point that I might as well face it.

About a week later I went into San Francisco and walked around near Union Square. I picked up a guy, a hustler, and we went to a hotel. That was the first time for me. It cost thirty dollars, and he stayed all night. A real queen, but sweet. I didn't tell him it was my first time, but I think he understood how naive and innocent I was.

The next day I was completely depressed and I spent the whole weekend thinking about suicide. I had almost a full year of psychiatric training behind me, but I didn't understand what the hell was happening to me. I couldn't do my work and I went to see my supervisor, the guy who made the comments about homosexuals. I didn't tell him anything about the sexual thing, but I told him I was suicidal and he said, "I think you'd better see somebody."

I picked this nice middle-aged attending psychiatrist, the epitome of a Jewish father. Extremely bright. During the first session I talked about my father's death, my sister, the problems with my stepmother. And it wasn't till the last two minutes that I finally opened up and said, "You know, I am homosexual." I was twenty-seven years old and that was the first I'd ever said that to anybody.

I saw this therapist for the next two years, but we had a problem. He tried to be very accepting of the fact that I was gay, but there was a mixed message which was "It's okay to be anything you want, but why don't we focus on your problems with women?" But I have no erotic arousal for women whatsoever. My problem was accepting my reality, not trying to change my reality to something else.

So I switched therapists. I've been with this second therapist for ten years now and he's been very good for me. He's from France originally and he's only a few years older than me. I started with him twice a week, then graduated up to four times a week for a long time. Full analysis. Then when I went to work at the hospice I cut down to three times a week. There's no "professional courtesy" when it comes to analysis. I've paid for it all myself, but it's worth more than the money. Sometimes I think about quitting; or I worry that I'm really too dependent on my analyst. But it's useful for me, so I continue. It's also an enormous education, and it helps me to deal with my own patients.

After I finished my residency I had to make a career decision. I could concentrate on private practice or I could stay at the hospital and help train new residents. By that time it was well known that I was gay, and that became a factor for me. I wanted people to see that someone who was gay could get beyond that and focus on other people's problems. I wanted to prove that the supervisor was wrong, that homosexuals could do an excellent job in psychiatry with every kind of patient.

So I stayed at Memorial, but one consequence of that decision is that I'm always short of money. I try to send something to my sister every month, because she's a perpetual student and she's in graduate school. I never spend a lot on myself, but there's never enough to go around. I'd like to be rich and I'd like to be free of money anxiety. Not because I want a Rolls-Royce but just so I can stop worrying about it. I'm working really hard at the hospice but I hope that my practice starts to catch on. I'm thirty-eight, and goddam, I'm a physician! I never thought I'd have to struggle for money.

Through all these years there's been an occasional date and an occasional affair, but nothing that's really satisfying. I always say, "I can have anybody I please, but I just don't please anybody." There's a lot of gay social life in San Francisco, but most of it is cruising and I don't enjoy that. I'm more conservative, more of a nest builder.

Just this spring there was a psychiatric meeting in Los Angeles and I drove down with a friend of mine. He's married and there's nothing sexual there but we had this great conversation. Sometimes I think a good conversation is better than a good orgasm. Then we attended our meetings and afterward I went to some of the bars in Hollywood. I was still dressed up from the meeting and looked very respectable. Right away I noticed one young man who I found very attractive. He looked back and finally he came over and chatted for quite a while. Then we walked out together and I saw he had a motorcycle. Immediately, my reaction was, can I be interested in some twenty-year-old kid with a punk haircut and a motorcycle? But he said, "Maybe you'd like to go for a ride in the hills." So I got on and we rode up and looked at the view and then we went back to his apartment. We didn't make love, but we had tea and we talked till dawn. It was the beginning, and I fell in love with him. We had a wonderful ten-day affair. My friends were even more excited than I was—"Reuben finally met someone!" I was willing to do whatever he wanted, but he was afraid of making a commitment. It's over now because he's young, and the gay thing is still a real issue with him. He's beautiful but he's not very smart.

Sometimes I think, "Wouldn't it have been nice to be born blond and beautiful and empty-headed?" In a theoretical sense, I'd rather be heterosexual. I'm actually very straight. That's the irony.

Gay people have this reputation but I'm not loose at all. Yesterday afternoon a patient, a gay man, was talking about an orgy. This guy makes a lot of money in an important business, and he was telling me about his party over the weekend, with cocaine, amyl nitrate, Quaaludes, and dozens of bodies.

That doesn't appeal to me. I have a little marijuana in the freezer that I bought four years ago. I've tried cocaine on two occasions but I think it's much ado about nothing. And listening to this patient talk about his life I kept thinking, "Gee, I'm so straight!" And it's not just in comparison to other people who are gay. I think even by the standards of the straight world, I'm very old-fashioned.

I feel like Job sometimes. I'm an expert at suffering. I've got to guard against self-pity because if I invest a lot of energy in feeling sorry for myself then I won't be as effective for the patients I want to help. The only reason I feel sorry for myself right now is that I desperately want a relationship. If I had one that lasted for a year or more, I think I'd feel satisfied even if it broke up. Just to have that experience. There are several different kinds of significant relationships. The most significant are parents, child, and then spouse or lover. Right? I lost my parents young, I'm never going to have children, and I still haven't had that love relationship. That's a big empty area in my life. Nobody has more friends than I do, but friendships, no matter how wonderful, are limited to a second level.

But I'm not interested in pickups. What I really want is a stable, monogamous relationship. I'm as old-fashioned as that. That's my dream, but I don't know how to make it come true.

Basically life is disappointing. My analyst would say that's my depressive side talking, but I think it really is a disappointment. I mean, what people do to each other! The way they hurt each other for no reason at all. My sister recently decided she is deeply troubled about my homosexuality. She's embarrassed in front of her friends. She doesn't want me to come visit her, she wants me to change. But what's important except trying to get a little happiness out of life? I have to struggle, she has to struggle, we all have to struggle, but she won't take the time to understand.

The one place you think everybody would understand is the hospital, but even here people can be so destructive. There's this one

293

nurse, Jeff Carden, who works with some of the hospice patients. He's very intelligent and very kind so I wanted to get to know him better. Most of the male nurses are gay and I assumed he was too so I asked him to join me for lunch. But it turns out he's straight and he's an ex-marine and he was very offended. He was very nasty to me and he made me feel terrible.

THE ONE THAT GOT AWAY

JEFF CARDEN
Critical Care Nurse

PEGGY HAGERTY, Head Nurse, Delivery Room

Jeff Carden is one of the most interesting people I've ever met. He used to work nights, and they would float him down to us when we were short-handed. He's a very attractive man, a big blond guy who looks like a surfer, but he also happens to be an Orthodox Jew. Very religious. He'll say a prayer before he drinks a cup of coffee! As a nurse, he is really fantastic. He knows everything about everything. He argues with the interns about the residents and he usually knows more than they do. He doesn't take any crap from anybody. There's a feeling of integrity about him, a real dedication and strength.

DR. CARL GORMAN, Neurosurgeon

He always struck me as an oddball. Any guy who goes into nursing has got to be strange. But this one is off the scale. He is very conceited and difficult. If you give him an order, he'll start arguing to do it his way. He refuses to show respect.

BECKY KRIEGER, Nurse

He's not very popular with the other nurses. Maybe it's because he's a very macho guy who doesn't like working with women. He's not a team player. The other male nurses go out of their way to be friendly and nice but Jeff keeps to himself. He's very serious and he sticks to his job, but I don't really see what he gets out of nursing.

———————

Jeff Carden lives in a small rented house in the Berkeley "Flats"— the crowded working-class district between the university and the bay. On the afternoon of our interview I found him in the front yard, pruning the rose bushes. As he pulled off his gardening gloves, he greeted me with a bonecrushing handshake and a radiant smile. He was built like a fullback, with short powerful legs and a huge torso. Long blond hair slanted across his forehead, and a thick beard covered most of his face.

As we went into the house, Carden took down two shot glasses and poured bourbon for both of us. "You've got to help me celebrate," he said. "Here, L'Chaim!" The occasion for this merriment was his decision to get out of nursing; he had quit his job just three days before.

KNOWING THAT I don't have to go back, that's the main thing. I've got two weeks to figure out what I'm going to do next, that's what I'm giving myself. We just found out that Sarah is pregnant. I want to save some money before the baby comes, and you can't make money as a nurse.

Even if they paid me more, I don't think I'd go back. I've been thinking that I don't want to be a healer. I want to start worrying about myself for a while. It's a big change, but I've had so many changes in my life that one more doesn't matter.

I was raised in Montana on a cattle ranch, way back in the hills. My interests were hunting, fishing, branding cattle, breaking horses, working in the fields, fixing equipment. Trying to make it day to day. My grandparents were Baptists but my parents never went to church. We had to work every day, Sundays included. We had fifteen hundred acres and about three hundred and fifty head of cattle. We were doing well until a hard winter wiped us out. All our cattle froze to death. From then on, it was staying one step in front of the bank.

On a day-to-day basis we were our own veterinarians. I remember one time I was down trying to catch a horse and I ran her into a fence and the barbed wire cut a nasty, horrible gash in the horse's shoulder. We took her back to the house and my mother sewed her up right there. She did a good job, too—used silk thread from a parachute we had picked up.

I thought it would be great to be a veterinarian, but I had no idea how to go about it. I didn't know anyone who went to college, let alone veterinary school. I figured I'd probably go into the service, then come home and take over the ranch.

The nearest school was fifteen miles away—fifteen miles over gravel road. I enjoyed the science classes, but when something came by that I didn't like—spelling and English, that sort of thing—I let it go. The rest of the time, I was heavily into sports. I went to a high school with only thirty-six students, and half of those were girls, so it wasn't difficult to make the teams. I was the same size that I am now, but stronger because I worked on the ranch all summer. I was the star of the football team, quarterback and linebacker.

Right after high school I was in love with a girl named Robin. She was no great beauty but she liked me—that was the main thing. We were going to be married, but first I had to go into the service. I didn't want to wait around and get drafted, so I joined the Marine Corps. I went away to boot camp and right away Robin ran off with another guy who worked in a garage. I knew him; he was from the next town. As soon as I left, he moved in. When I came back on leave I looked him up. I was just out of marine boot camp and I was in pretty good shape and I beat the shit out of him. The last time I was up in Montana I checked on the situation, and the two of them had five children and another one on the way. So I guess he wasn't beyond repair.

The Marine Corps was four years. It was sort of like facing a Montana winter—you just have to accept it. I was a teletype operator, and then I got into cryptography and I really liked that. It's encoding and decoding secret messages. We were stationed in Okinawa, and I was lucky because I just missed Vietnam. I got out of the corps in 1965 and I really had no place to go. My father sold the ranch while I was in the service. Took the money from that and bought a tacky little house in Boise. I never forgave him for that one. I hated Boise, so I ended up in Oregon. Grew a beard, let my hair grow long. I started getting stoned one day when I picked up a hitch-hiker. What a gorgeous lady! Long brown hair down to her waist. She whips out a joint and says, "You want to turn on?" It could have been a movie. So I was seeing her for a while and going to a lot of parties.

I was working on a rock crusher at the time, but then I got fired and drifted down to Eugene, where the university is. I went to work in a coffeehouse as a singer. I wasn't very good. I'm tone-deaf, as a matter of fact, but I picked up the guitar when I was in the corps and I learned a bunch of folk songs. I could fake it. At least I looked like a folksinger. So I had to sing every night in return for room and board. Lasted six months, then I came back to California and landed in Sacramento. This guy I knew from the Marine Corps was just starting a lawn-sprinkler business. Neither one of us had any experience in that sort of thing before, but I can do anything. We had some lean times but we had good times too. Then after that I bounced around. Worked in a car shop and then ran a tire shop. A couple of years here and there. Finally, I decided I wanted to go to school. I was twenty-eight. So I sold everything I had and went down to the junior college and started school. I signed up for the GI bill and that helped me out.

I loved school. Really, that was my element. I enjoyed learning and I also enjoyed being around a lot of pretty women. I got straight A's and I didn't have to work that hard to do it.

By the time I was thirty I was ready for Davis. That's the University of California campus outside of Sacramento. Specializes in the sciences. My plan right then was to go on to medical school.

And that's when I first began to be aware of Jewish people. Davis has a large Jewish population, especially in premed classes, and the Jewish people I met I really liked. I thought they had real sparkling minds. I figured it must be more than coincidence that

298

over ninety percent of my friends were Jewish, and so I tried to pin down those qualities that I liked. I ran into a rabbi up there who started answering my questions about Judaism. A Reform rabbi at the Hillel foundation.

I never had much of a religious background, but I got involved right away. Started going to dinners Friday night at the Hillel foundation. Worked on different things, building *succahs,* setting up the Purim party, that sort of thing. I made friends there.

It says in the Talmud that somebody who converts to Judaism has really been a Jew all along. He had it inside him from the beginning, he just needed time to let it come out. That's how it was with me. It felt right. So I converted in my senior year at Davis. I had my bar mitzvah that same year at the age of thirty-two.

The only problem was that I wasn't circumcised. My rabbi, the Reform rabbi, said I didn't have to worry about it. But after I converted it still bothered me. I couldn't feel Jewish unless I was circumcised, so I went to a surgeon to get the job done. For an adult, it's serious. I was in the hospital two days, and I thought I was going to die. Every time I'd go to sleep I'd get a hard-on—that's standard procedure for me—and I'd rip my stitches. It got infected. The whole thing was black and blue! For a month I was in horrible pain. In the Torah, Abraham does himself when he's ninety years old. Then he gets better in three days. He must have been a better man than me, I'll tell you that!

Getting involved with Judaism was the good part of that year. The bad part was finding out about medical school. My grades were pretty good but everybody told me I was too old. The medical schools weren't even going to look at me. It really knocked the props out from under me. Then somebody told me about a program for physicians' assistants, which is really a paramedical position. I went down to the nursing school in Sacramento looking for information, and they told me I wasn't qualified for that one either. They wanted nursing experience, or medic experience in the service, some sort of experience. I had none. I was ready to give up and was walking out the door when the nursing director stopped me. "Why don't you apply to study nursing? That's something you can do." It sounded all right to me, so I made the application and I got in.

In my class at nursing school there were forty-five women and two men. The other guy quit after the first month, and I wish I'd gone with him. I don't have the character to be a nurse. I'm a pretty independent sort of fellow and I like to be respected and I don't like being in a subservient position. Nursing requires a certain kind of mind. I have a problem-solving-type mind, but in nursing you don't ask questions. I never enjoyed it, but I did what I had to do.

I went into critical care nursing. I thought that would be better. I worked the intensive care units—cardiac, neurological, surgical— all the ICUs. It beats working on the wards because you don't have so many patients and sometimes you even get to make decisions.

When I started at Memorial, they put me on a unit known as the Vegetable Patch—5C, on the south wing. They have ten people in there, all brain deaths, and they have them on machines keeping them alive. I worked out of the registry and they sent me there a lot because they just couldn't get their own staff to work there. It was too horrible.

For a nurse, it's the worst job there is. Suctioning stuff out of their lungs, changing dressings, turning them a lot. They have tubes that go down into their stomachs and take care of the bowels and stuff. They have bedpans, but we can also do it by another method. We have a thing called a chuck. It's kind of like Pampers, only it's much wider and it lies flat on the bed. We have suppositories which you just pop in and it causes contractions of the bowels and you evacuate them.

I used to worry about their level of reception. There are studies that show that people in deep comas do have some hearing. When people come out of the comas, they can sometimes recall things they heard. I would always try to establish the level of consciousness—see if the patients would blink or move in response to sight or sound. In the Vegetable Patch, we never had one who would respond at all. And nobody ever came out of it.

And you go in and take care of them every day. You have to wash out their mouths or else bacteria will start growing in there. We use brushes, swabs. Sometimes the mouth is closed really tight and you have to open it up and put a box in there to keep it open while you work. And you have to keep moving them, keep turning them. They say every two hours, but I like to turn my patients every hour. You have ten patients like that, it's a pretty full day.

It's not my nature to get depressed, but I got real tired. It disturbed my whole life. I had a lot of anxiety and a lot of tension. I would have daydreams about killing my patients. Just to put them out of their misery. Mercy killings, that sort of thing. There was part of me that really wanted to do it. And it's horrible to have to fight with that.

After a while I wasn't my happy-go-lucky self anymore. My sex life slowed down because I didn't have the urge. You can't go directly from the Vegetable Patch and get involved in a night of love. And there were other changes going on at the same time. Mainly, I was becoming more religious.

When I moved down to the Bay Area a friend told me to check out the synagogue in Berkeley. I didn't know it was Orthodox. At that time I thought that Orthodox was a lot of people in black coats and beards. But I went to the synagogue one Friday night and I liked it. About a hundred people, all very friendly. There were a lot of faculty people from the university, a very intellectual crowd. I began to show up every week and I made a lot of friends. I always knew I liked Jewish people, but I never understood before that the rules and rituals produced their special qualities. Their grandparents and their great-grandparents lived apart and followed the discipline of the Torah. But today, most Jewish people don't know about those rules. They act like everybody else and their grandchildren will end up like everybody else. But I don't want my children to be punks. I want them to take over some of what I pass on. That's the basic idea of the Jewish tradition.

I didn't jump in all at once and take up the whole thing. I took it slow, step by step. But I found out that I liked these things. I liked keeping kosher, I liked keeping the sabbath. Doing without modern conveniences for one day a week is a centering thing. It pulls you out of the rat race. Every step was an experiment. But I found myself feeling good if I did these things, and guilty if I didn't.

Right in there is when I met my wife. We were in a Sizzlers restaurant, so I know it was before I started keeping kosher! I saw this pretty lady and I sat down next to her. We started a conversation and we just kept on talking. I didn't get her last name and we didn't exchange phone numbers, but I had a feeling I'd run into her again. Then a few days later she called me at Memorial; she just asked for "a nurse named Jeff." It's a big hospital but we only have a few male nurses, so she found me. I was flattered that she would call and I pulled out a little pad and I wrote down her number. Just that minute I had a code blue down the hall. You know, that's for somebody who's dying. I ran over and pumped on the guy's chest. I had this guy as a patient a few days before and he really impressed me as a remarkable fellow. When I leaned on his chest I broke all his ribs and it was the first time that I felt those ribs break under my hand. It was pretty gross, but you sometimes can't avoid it in cardiac resuscitation. Later I thought about how some time in the future they're going to be excavating graves from this time period and they're going to think that when a person reached a certain stage of debilitation that there was some sort of ritualistic sacrificing of them where we all jumped on their chests and broke their ribs. Anyway I was pounding away but he was too far gone. He was about eight-three or eighty-four, an old Jewish guy from Poland. When I talked with him a couple of days before, he seemed accepting of his situation. He was almost cheerful about it, and he got a real kick out of the fact that I was Jewish. He kept telling me I should settle down, I should get a wife and have a family and make a good Jewish home. He died that same night that Sarah called, so it sticks in my mind.

After that I started going out with her. She was surprised I was Jewish, and I'm not sure she was happy about it! She comes from a Reform Jewish home but all her other boyfriends were goyim. When her parents found out how religious I was they started to get worried. Maybe they would have an easier time with a gentile son-in-law! But Sarah started to get more involved in Judaism and everybody got used to it and now it's pretty comfortable all around.

We got married two years ago and that was a good move for me. The only problem was that I still hated my job. I felt more and more out of place. There are only a dozen male nurses in all of Memorial and all the rest of them are homosexual. They all assume I'm one of them. I get passes all the time. Once I was coming out of the men's room as another nurse was going in. I felt a little pinch on my rear end, and I turned around to see this sweet smiling face. I didn't smile back. I told him if he liked his fingers he'd better keep his hands to himself.

But the main problem is the supervisors. I can see the stages they went through. First they think you're a homosexual, then they find out you've been in the Marine Corps and they think you've got this big macho thing going. When they find out you're an Orthodox Jew, they know for damn sure that you hate all women, and they really start laying for you. They assume that we put our women in boxes and won't let them work or anything like that. I tell them my wife works as a teacher but it doesn't make any difference. They still have this prejudice and you can't talk them out of it.

They would always give me the worst patients. And mostly it turned out to be little old Jewish women. They can be a real pain in the ass, but I could allay their fears and make them think that somebody cares. If I did well with a patient who was driving everybody else up the wall, that only made it worse for me. They tried even more to set me up.

I used to think I was paranoid, but I know now that they were out to get me. The wrong medications would be put in my box—different dosages, or the wrong medicine altogether. It could hurt the patient and it would get me in trouble.

Then there was a big issue about my meals. I would go down to the cafeteria and eat the food that Sarah packed for me. Then I would come up to my office in the nursing area where there were no patients around, and I'd put on my yarmulke and I'd sit down and I'd *bench*, say the Grace After Meals. Softly, to myself. They blew up. They said it was not proper to do that in a nursing area. They filed a complaint, and they ordered me to stop.

I started hating it more and more. In order to survive in this hospital you've got to fight and stab backs, gather information, documentation, cover your ass so much. And I don't want the responsibility anymore for other people's lives. People pay a price when they carry that burden. They become so calloused that they become insensitive and are no longer people. Just machines. And very unpleasant. Or else they just don't care and they become sloppy technicians and murderers. Also unpleasant. I have not seen anyone in nursing who hasn't been adversely affected by it. The whole glory of medicine, of doctors and nurses and working in a hospital . . . it's just something I don't respond to anymore. It stinks. I want out.

I don't know exactly what I'm going to do. Maybe I'll go into construction for a while; maybe I'll start up a painting business. I want to be active, and I don't mind getting dirty. You can always clean up afterwards and that makes you feel good. But I'm also going to keep my nursing license up to date. Something might come up, in terms of industrial nursing, something like that. Or some sort of a part-time thing.

We're also talking about going to Israel and maybe we'll have our baby there. I've always wanted to check it out as a place to live, thinking maybe I could get back to the land. Where else could I go on enjoying my cosmopolitan, intellectual Jewish friends and still go off and be a farmer? If that doesn't work maybe I'll head back to Montana. Take a whole bunch of Jewish people and start ranching cattle together. An Orthodox kibbutz in Montana, that's just what they need.

But whatever it's going to be, I feel good about it. I'm glad to be done with Memorial. There are some things about me that I like the way they are, some qualities that I want to keep. I had to get out before I lost them, because if you stay long enough you're going to start breaking down.

CRACKING

JEFF CARDEN, Critical Care Nurse

When you work off the registry you start to hear stories—people in different hospitals who can't handle it anymore. There was this one story all over the papers about a male nurse down in Los Angeles. They called him the Angel of Death because he started knocking off his patients and he got about twenty of them before they caught him. He was a hundred percent nut case, and his supervisors thought he was an excellent nurse.

DR. JACK BUCKMAN, Director of Emergency Medicine

I had a doctor on my staff last year who had a psychotic break. The police picked him up at his house. He was throwing things and screaming and breaking all the windows. When the cops came he said he'd shoot them if they tried to get in the house. But the poor bastard didn't even have a gun!

This is a guy I worked with every day. He had a run of personal problems, but no worse than anybody else. Things just came together at one instant in time. His fiftieth birthday, breaking up with a girlfriend, some heavy gambling debts. The night he freaked out he worked in the ER till ten, and he seemed fine to me. Then he went home, had a few drinks and used some Quaaludes, and that pushed him right around the bend.

He wound up in the hospital for three weeks and I went to see him as much as I could. But when he got out, I had to tell him I was going to let him go. He was a very close friend of mine, and it was a heavy-duty number.

DR. DAVID ANZAK, Obstetrician-Gynecologist

Some people just can't take the pressure. I remember one fellow in particular, a very bright Jewish guy who was an intern when I was. Tall, extroverted, he played the violin very well. In the course of the year he became more and more effusively extroverted until people were getting a little irritated at him. I remember one day he called me at around five in the morning, and said, "Hi, David, how're you doing?" As if it was the most natural thing in the world to call somebody at five in the morning! I kind of put him off, and the next thing I heard was he was in a psychiatric hospital. The story was that he had killed his cat. He cut off his cat's head and nailed it to the wall and wrote some words underneath in blood. The landlady found out about it and called the police and he wound up in the hospital.

DR. BEN BRODY, Psychiatric Resident

In the time I've been working the psychiatric ward we've had several physicians who came in as patients. The worst case was an older guy, a neurologist. He had become addicted to Demerol. It's a narcotic pain-killing drug that is very commonly abused by doctors who have a drug problem. This neurologist was working too hard, like most of us, and he had a bad case of insomnia. He started with the Demerol to put himself to sleep, but his body built up resistance to the point where he'd wake up in the middle of the night and he'd have to give himself an injection. This went on for three years before he realized he was addicted. He made the diagnosis himself and he didn't mess around. He said, "Look, I'm addicted, and I need help.'' We helped him, and he went through withdrawal in a couple of months and then he was finished with Demerol.

The problem is that when a drug addict gives up his drug, that leaves a big empty space and sometimes it's not easy to live with. He was still working too hard in his practice and he wasn't taking care of himself. Then one day he locked himself in his office. He had patients waiting but he refused to come out. The receptionists waited until the end of the day, and they called his wife. She finally got him to come out and then she brought him back to us.

He was here for about a month with acute depression. He wouldn't get out of bed, wouldn't go to the bathroom, wouldn't do anything. We worked with him and started giving him big doses of antidepressant medication. That's one part where I'm not sure we handled it right. With somebody who's been a drug addict, you've got to be extra-careful that you don't replace one dependence with another. He's still on the medication and he's been out almost a year. He's practicing medicine again and he seems to be doing fine. But I worry about him, and who knows what's going to happen.

DR. ALLEN BARSAMIAN, Staff Psychiatrist

Physicians have a greater incidence of alcoholism, and they also have a higher incidence of getting hooked on medications like Talwin and Demerol and other injectable opiates because of their greater access to them. Here at Memorial I knew an orthopedist who passed out in the middle of doing knee surgery. When they took a look at him they saw needle marks all over his body. He's been addicted to Talwin for nine years and nobody knew. He was irritable and eccentric but he kept practicing all that time and he did an adequate job.

I recently read a paper by a psychiatrist who studied physicians who are severely psychotic, completely bananas, but they keep right on treating patients. The only thing that stops them, in most cases, is if they commit suicide. It's well known that psychiatrists have the worst suicide rate, but for all doctors, it's way above average. I think it has something to do with the familiarity with death. As a physician you see it all the time and you get used to it. You lose the awe of death that other people have. In a moment of decision I think that can be a factor.

307

DR. STEVEN EBERSOLL, Radiologist

I know a very successful radiologist who killed himself. Everybody thought he was just a together guy. Very talented, very well-known guy, but I know he was having trouble at home. He left his wife and kids and he was playing around for a while. But then he got engaged to someone half his age. It's the old story—she decided he was too old and she dumped him. That's when it happened; he put a gun in his mouth and pulled the trigger.

I know so many stories like that. It makes you wonder what's going on. It's like a war, or a plague, when you've got buddies who are dropping all around you.

BOB ZACHARY, Morgue Room Supervisor

I've been doing autopsies for ten years, but when they brought Dr. Lassiter down I didn't want to touch him. He's the one who killed himself upstairs in the hospital. He locked himself in his office and shot air into his veins. I never knew him well but I knew who he was. I thought about getting one of the technicians to handle it, but it was my job, okay, so I went ahead. Five minutes into it, I stopped worrying.

IGOR OF THE COOLER

BOB ZACHARY
Morgue Room Supervisor

DR. MONICA WILKINSON, Chief Resident, Pediatrics

When you hear about somebody who runs the morgue you think of some ghoul with a humpback and a long beard and Frankenstein over in the corner. But the one time I had to go down there I met this good-looking guy with a big smile and a big hello. I was feeling down because I had just lost a patient and that's the time you really appreciate a guy like that.

DR. ARNOLD BRODY, Director of Medical Oncology

The morgue is a separate operation under the pathology department. Most people stay away from it, but I don't have that luxury. It's the nature of my practice that I have to go down there fairly often when they do autopsies on my patients. Bob Zachary runs that procedure, and he often makes presentations at the pathology conferences that take place afterwards. I've been very impressed by his thoroughness and competence. That whole operation is clean, efficient and—God help us!—almost cheerful.

Matthew Zachary, age four, sat upon his father's knee and prattled amiably for several minutes about the white rabbit his nursery school teacher had brought to class that morning. His father listened patiently and seriously, then kissed the child and sent him off to bed.

Bob Zachary took obvious pride in his precocious son, as he did in every detail of his suburban tract home. He gave me a tour of the house, and seemed particularly pleased when I commented on the striking color photographs of redwoods and waterfalls that decorated the walls of every room. A tanned, athletic, easygoing Californian, Zachary explained that camping and photography were his two favorite hobbies. Back in the living room, I asked if he had ever used his photographic skills to capture images of his work environment.

ARE YOU KIDDING? I don't need pictures of that place. I've been there for eight years and I know it blind. It's a big room, okay, well lit and white. There's a concrete floor and a lot of room to work and then just the boxes on both sides. We have trays for the bodies, the kind that roll out, just like the movies, like *Quincy*. Then there's a glass partition in one corner going all the way up to the ceiling. On the other side of the partition there's a section that was originally designed as a viewing area, where the family could come and look at the body. We don't get a lot of viewing nowadays, so we spray-painted over the glass and put a desk in there and that's where I have my office. If familes want to view the body, they come right into the morgue and we put it on a hospital gurney and put a sheet over it and fix it up real nice. It's more personal than looking through the glass.

When people come in they usually expect that it's going to be cold, because the morgue is known as the cooler. But the only part that's refrigerated is the boxes. We keep them about thirty-seven degrees. The rest of the room is normal temperature, just like the rest of the hospital.

We're on the bottom floor, the lowest level, below the street. It seems like autopsy rooms and morgue rooms are always on the lowest level. That's where the freight access is, and the loading dock, so it's easy for the morticians to get the bodies when we're done with them. We don't have to wheel them the whole length of the hospital to the front entrance. There's no special elevator for bringing the bodies down, but we've got a cart with a special white shroud that goes almost down to the floor. The transporters are supposed to keep it private when they go down in an elevator and not let anyone else on. But people end up riding down with the bodies all the time and I don't think there's any doubt in anyone's mind what's under there.

My main job is to supervise the autopsies. I'm primarily involved with training the residents in pathology. Most of them don't like doing autopsies or being near autopsies, so I really take over, because I like doing it. We've been averaging about three hundred a year, so you figure five or six a week. There are eleven hundred deaths a year, so we do autopsies on around twenty-five percent. What happens is that one of the attending physicians will ask the family for authorization for an autopsy. There's a form, okay? If the family grants permission, it gives us access to every part of the body and removal of any part for scientific purposes. But sometimes they put restrictions on—"no brain" or "heart only"—and that makes it harder. We have to work around that and follow the instructions.

After we get the signed form, the resident who's on duty will call us together and we start the autopsy. I have two techs who work with me and they will go in, get the body, unwrap it, and put it out on the autopsy table. They get all the fixatives ready, all the stock jars, all the paperwork. Then I come over and check what's going on and make sure we don't make any mistakes. Check the name. You'd be surprised how many people forget to look at the name on the body. We had a case like that where we were doing a newborn baby. The resident was in the middle of cutting it open when I came over and checked the authorization. The baby we were supposed to be doing had died in open-heart surgery, but this baby had no surgical incision. It was also the wrong sex! The resident got really worried and I thought he was going to cry. But I checked the records on the baby we were doing and fortunately we had a disposal permit. We do disposals for families—we cremate the infants. So we cremated the baby we did by mistake and then went ahead and did the autopsy on the right one. So nobody knew and nobody got upset.

When we do an autopsy, we make a big Y incision with a scalpel from each shoulder to the middle of the chest and then down to the pubic bone. The skin flaps are opened up down to the sides and up to the neck above the larynx. Then we take these branch cutters to cut the ribs. Some places use a bone saw, but we like the branch cutters. We clip all the ribs from the diaphragm right up to the clavicle. Then the chestplate comes off, and we put it aside on the autopsy table. Then we open up the pericardial sac and draw blood for blood cultures.

From then on, the autopsy dissection can be done in three ways. Organs can be removed individually, or they can be removed in certain blocks, or you can take them out all together. We like to do it in blocks. First we'll tie off the carotid artery, and we leave the little string attached so the embalmers can find it. That's so they can embalm the face and head. Then we take out the whole chest block—the heart, lungs, trachea, bronchi. The resident will start dissecting the chest organs while we're removing the ones in the abdomen. When we're through, the whole body will be completely emptied out, from the shoulders down to the pubic bone. It's just like an empty shell. When we're working, the face is supposed to be covered, but usually we don't bother with that. Most people who have been doing autopsies for a while find it hard to think of the patient as a living individual. We just concentrate on the work and do what we have to do.

And after the body's emptied out, okay, we go up to the head. We open it up and go for the brain. We use a bone saw and make cuts from just behind the ears and then all the way across. We lift off the entire skull and expose the brain. There are thick membranes you have to cut through. Then you cut the carotid arteries, the optic nerves, and the cervical cord. You reach down with a scalpel as far as you can and the brain more or less rolls into your hand. You lift it out and you weigh it. Then we put the brain in a white opaque bucket, called the brain bucket.

The whole thing, the whole autopsy, can get done, with assis-

312

tance, in less than an hour. Or if the resident is really slow, it'll take four or five. It all depends on who's doing it and what we find.

It's amazing sometimes the surprises that you get from doing an autopsy. Okay, let's say a woman has ovarian cancer, like this one we got last week. They do surgery on her, but she's got tumor all over her abdominal cavity and it's the kind of cancer that seethes and spreads. So they treat her with chemotherapy and hope. Then six months later she dies. Cause of death: "Metastatic ovarian carcinoma." But we did an autopsy, and there was no cancer down there—they cured her but she died anyway. So what did she die of? Did she die of her treatment? Did they deplete her bone marrow so much she couldn't fight off disease? Did she have a heart attack? The fact is that she actually died of pneumonia, which came as a big surprise.

Most of medicine is like that—it's just a guessing game until they get an autopsy and they find out what really happened. The doctors who really care about what they're doing always come down to our autopsy conferences, because they can learn a lot about what they did wrong, what they did right. All the organs are laid out on separate trays on a steel cart with a towel over them. They're fixed in formalin, which is a fixative like formaldehyde, and it makes everything kind of brown. But it's all there, okay, and they can see anything they want to see.

When they're done, one of the technicians gets the body ready for removal. He puts the chestplate on and sews it up, even though inside it's empty. He puts the bone back on the skull and puts maybe two or three stitches up there. Then the body's washed and rewrapped in its plastic shroud and put into the cooler box until the morticians come around. Once they get hold of it and get it ready for the funeral, nobody knows the difference. All the incisions are covered by clothes. Sometimes they'll use a wig up on the skull, and even with the brain out, they can still embalm the face. Nobody would ever know. There's no mutilation with what we do. We really pay attention to that.

Once we had a physician who watched our autopsy on his wife. We tried to pretend he wasn't there, but we were the most uncomfortable we've ever been. He was asking questions about what we were doing, and every once in a while he'd interject something about their personal life. When we were taking out the stomach he

313

was saying how lobster always used to be her favorite food! It made everybody stiffen up. I don't think I'd ever allow it again.

The worst part of the job is cleaning out the intestine. It's opened over a sink that has a disposal unit for the feces. It's like working in a toilet. If someone's been sick for a long time the smell is even worse.

There's one case that really bothered me. It was a man who had a brain tumor that spread all the way to his scalp. It was maybe two and a half inches thick, lots of tumor mass, and it was breaking down and ulcerating. When we lifted the scalp, it kept tearing and oozing, and the smell, and the sound, and the sight really got to me. I got kind of nauseous but I held it in.

Something like that is really the exception, because most of the time the atmosphere is okay. We have a radio on when we're working, or else a cassette player. Usually it's a jazz station or soft rock. One resident liked opera, but we told her no more.

There are funny incidents that come up now and then. I remember one man who died and he had a prosthetic penis. It was a balloon that he had inserted into his penis, like a hydraulic, and he had this sack underneath his skin in the abdomen, and whenever he wanted an erection he pressed and pumped it up. We saved the whole thing and we still have it in one of our jars. Sometimes we show it to the secretaries who visit from upstairs.

I have a pet black widow spider on my desk at work. He lives in a glass jar. I figure he fits into our department, because sometimes we'll do things that are pretty wild. Last year for Christmas we got out an intestine and put it on a pan, okay? About twenty-five feet of intestine, really ugly and bloody, and we tied some green and red ribbon around one end. Then I took a picture of it, and we printed it up. That was our little Christmas card. It said, "Seasons greetings from your friends in the cooler." We sent it to other people in the hospital and they were a little bit surprised.

We also have an incinerator in the back of the morgue, and sometimes we make jokes about that. We use it for burning autopsy tissue. We don't put anything back in the body as other places do. When we're done with the organs, we dispose of them. The incinerator will burn twenty-five pounds an hour of wet tissue. That's a lot. There's a blower and two burners and it really gets hot. You have to watch it, and put the specimens in one by one, and then turn it off when you're done.

The only part that bothers me is when we have to burn a newborn baby or a fetus from one of the abortions. Maybe that's my Catholic background showing through. My family was very religious and we went to church every Sunday. My dad has a construction business and he's a big supporter of Catholic education. He doesn't feel so great about his son working in a morgue, even though autopsies are okay with the church. There's no objection because the human life is already over and the soul has already gone wherever it's going to go.

I went to the best parochial schools in San Francisco, but when I left home to go to college I sort of went wild. At Sonoma State I joined a fraternity and I had a ball. I should have done a lot more work but I was too busy drinking beer. I applied to dental school but I didn't get in. Vietnam was starting up at that time, so I enlisted in the army's Medical Corps so I wouldn't have to go over and get killed. I was assigned to a hospital unit in Yokohama, Japan, and it was an interesting three years.

When I came home, I had no idea what I wanted to do. My father wanted me to go into his business, but I wasn't any good at it. Then I heard about a program to train as a physician's assistant. I was eligible because of my experience in the service, and I went into the pathology program because that's where they had an opening. When I finished, I got a job right away at a hospital in San Jose and then I switched to Memorial in '73.

I met my wife that same year at a party at a friend's house. She's from Iowa originally and she was working at a department store in San Francisco. I was twenty-eight years old, footloose and fancy free, but when I saw Carole, I knew right away. We got married a year later and bought ourselves a little house.

It took her a while to get used to the idea I was doing autopsies. At first she didn't want to sleep with me because of the whole idea of the morgue and working on all those bodies. There's also a smell that you get when you're doing this work. Your hair will pick it up and you have to shower. I come home with blood spots on my shoes and on my pants and the smell of an autopsy, and my wife doesn't even want to talk about my work.

But it's a good job and she knows it. I make twenty-eight thousand dollars a year and I'm due for another raise. I work forty hours a week. I'm there at seven-thirty every morning and I usually leave at four, unless something comes up and I'm cutting surgical specimens and I have to stay until they're done.

I usually get out as fast as I can, because I don't like being in the morgue at night. It's not a good feeling, especially if you're alone. One night I had to stay really late and it was very quiet, and I was sitting in my office and I thought I could hear noises from the morgue, from the body trays. I got out of there right away and left my work till the next day.

There are some spooky things and you can't get away from it. Some of the technicians are always afraid that when they open a tray, a body is going to sit up. They've heard stories, and it does happen. It's sort of instant rigor mortis, and even though the body is dead it sort of jerks up when you open the drawer.

And then we're always worried we'll have a body down there who's not dead. It's happened in other places; you can read it in the papers. A person is pronounced dead and they're not dead. You're getting ready to do an autopsy and the body moves. I don't really understand how it happens.

We had one like that about five years ago, and I still don't like to talk about it. We were working on an old lady, just getting started with the autopsy. We made the Y incision when we noticed the blood coming out at a more rapid rate. She was really bleeding, like she was still alive. The resident and I just looked at each other. I thought, "Oh my God, please don't make her alive!" We were afraid to listen to her chest because the blood was still coming out. It was so quiet in there I thought we could hear her breathing. Then after ten minutes the bleeding stopped and we listened for her heart. We didn't hear anything, and we went on to finish the autopsy. I was scared the whole time. When we finally had all the organs out, I made a comment—"Well, she's dead now." The resident just nodded his head and made me promise not to tell anybody.

Most of the time I'm not ashamed of what I do, but I never want my children to come down to my office. We have two kids now—Matthew, who you met, and the baby, Christy, who's eighteen months. Matthew already started asking what I do when I go to work and I just tell him I work in a hospital. I don't think it's good for kids to think about the idea of a morgue.

If anything happened to any of us, to me, or Carole, or the kids, I wouldn't want anybody to do an autopsy. It's just a feeling I have. I don't want to think of my family on an autopsy table. When I think about my cases, they're just cases, okay? Their personality is gone, they're just empty shells. But the people in my family are *people*.

We had to work hard to have those kids. We went to a fertility clinic for four years before Carole finally got pregnant. Then the second time with Christy it was a lot easier. We're getting good at it, and we want to have some more. I was in the delivery room both times, and it felt great. But of course, while I was congratulating my wife, I looked over the placenta. Thank God, everything looked okay!

THE RETURN OF
HARVEY FREDMAN

A butterfly can be impaled upon a pin and exhibited permanently in a display case; living human beings, however, maintain the frustrating habit of changing direction and squirming away from all attempts at definitive classification. Harvey Fredman offers a case in point. Several months after I had completed the interviews for this book, he placed an urgent long-distance call to my home in Southern California. He wanted me to fly to the Bay Area as soon as possible to interview him a second time. Unless I allowed him to bring me up to date with the "amazing changes" in his life, he threatened to revoke his authorization for my use of the original interview.

I flew to San Francisco the following Sunday and met Dr. Fredman in his office at Memorial. The effusive warmth of his greeting, the jagged smile and careless laugh, along with a strange, manic light in his eyes, all suggested a state of almost feverish excitement. It was a cold day of intermittent downpours and distant thunder, and as we sat down together a gust of wind blew a veil of water against his sixth-story window. Fredman reacted with delight. "Just look at that, the way the rain runs down! So beautiful against the glass!" He made the observation with such heartfelt and childlike joy that I began to fear for his sanity. Perhaps here was yet another physician who had pushed himself over the edge into a nervous breakdown. It even seemed possible that his bliss-ful state had been caused by involvement with an otherworldly religious cult, or by one of the exotic systems of "personality reori-entation" that flourish in California. Fredman cut short these speculations when he smiled across his desk and ordered me to turn on the tape recorder. Questions were unnecessary, he told me. I need only sit back, relax, and listen.

WHEN I WAS interviewed last time I talked about my experience in psychoanalysis for the past two years and the way I was begin-ning to change in subtle ways and some ways that were not so sub-tle. For the first time, I was starting to trust people, and I found that I could let people take over for me at work. I recognized that I had always denied myself pleasure, perhaps in reaction to my parents and their denial in their own lives. And I also saw that I felt intense anxiety and fear around young women who were attractive and normal—as opposed to a woman like my ex-wife. Then, through whatever process of evolution one goes through in analysis, I felt that fear had left me. Right after I talked to you, I actually had a premonition that good things were going to happen to me.

And through the fall, for the first time in my life, I was able to date a really beautiful woman. It wasn't very successful, but it was a beginning and I felt good about that. We went out three or four times and then we stopped. It was Charlotte Kirkham, who I had known for years. I was very surprised she went out with me, be-cause we never really got along when we worked together. But I still found myself attracted to her and I asked her to have dinner with me one night. We had some good conversations while we were dating but I couldn't get her to relate to me on a man-woman level. One night she said, "I've always been curious about you and I just wanted to find out what made you tick." It was just a casual comment, but it bothered me because it felt like a put-down. We clearly weren't making any progress, so I more or less decided to stop seeing her.

And about that same time I was becoming aware of another young woman, a new resident named Sharon Klein. She had come out from New York to do a year at Memorial as part of her training in pediatrics. I was immediately attracted to her, in a physical sense. She is very short, about five feet tall, with long brown hair and very blue eyes. She isn't flashy, the way Charlotte is flashy, but she is always ladylike and nicely dressed and she has a way about her that's soft and gentle and also a little bit seductive.

One night when she was on call as the senior resident, I had a very sick patient, a five-year-old with rectal bleeding. His parents brought him in with chronic diarrhea, and one of the other residents did a rectal biopsy, and the patient had hemorrhaged. He was losing a lot of blood, and I came in after midnight to help the house staff decide how to handle the problem. I called the resident who had done the procedure and told him I thought he did an inferior job and he should come in right away to help us rectify the situation. But he didn't feel there was any reason for him to come in—he was supposed to be off for the night and I was there to handle it. I was ready to blow up, but Sharon came over and got me to calm down. Suddenly, I was on my best behavior. Instead of really going off like I sometimes do, I just stayed calm and cool all night and helped her along. I enjoyed watching her the whole time, because this was somebody who was feminine and very sweet but still a super-competent physician.

After that I wanted to ask her out, but I wasn't sure I could do it. She was a resident and she was twenty-nine and I was one of the people who was responsible for her training. So I just stood aside and watched her and saw the way she was sensitive to the needs of her patients. She was unbelievably compassionate, especially with the children who were dying. I saw in her something that I see in myself—a great need, a great ability to give. I kept thinking about seeing her socially, but I still felt hurt by what happened with Charlotte. I told myself that even though somebody related to me and respected me as a doctor and a teacher, that didn't mean they could relate to me as a man.

That's when Charlotte came into it again. I met her in the hall one day and she was acting very friendly. She asked me if I knew that someone from the house staff had a big crush on me. I thought she might be teasing me, so I didn't say anything, but then she said, "It's the new resident, Sharon Klein."

320

I still thought Charlotte might be playing a game, but that same day, by a stroke of fate, another doctor came to my office and invited me to a party. He said, "If you want to bring someone, bring someone." I thought about Sharon right away, and I kept on thinking about her all week, but it just seemed that I could never get her alone.

Finally that Saturday, the day of the party, I sat in my office for almost an hour, going over the pros and cons. I didn't want any gossip, and if it didn't work out I'd have to face Sharon on Monday morning. I'd already been rejected so often that I didn't want to face it again. Then I just said, "This is ridiculous. I'll try it and see what happens." It was already one o'clock on Saturday afternoon and I was sure she would have plans already. But I stopped her on her way out of the hospital and asked her if she wanted to go to the party. She said yes, and it made me feel very good.

When I picked her up at eight o'clock, she was wearing a light-blue dress and pretty blue shoes. She looked like a little girl and very sexy, all at the same time. We went to the party, and it was better than I expected. There were a lot of interesting people there, a lot of nonmedical people, and I had a wonderful time watching her and listening to her talk. She has a life to her, an intensity, whatever it is she is doing. And I also liked seeing that she was a little bit conservative, because she had only one glass of white wine, which she didn't even finish, while everybody else was getting fairly drunk.

At eleven-thirty I took her home. I remember driving in the car and wanting to hold her. For some reason, I felt no anxiety with her at all. I just wanted to determine the right approach to take, because I'd never before met anyone like her. We sat in the car in front of her apartment and talked for a while. She told me she was a little bit surprised that she had such a good time with me at the party. She had heard so many stories about me from other people at the hospital she didn't know what to expect! She heard how I used to sleep in my office and how I had a terrible temper and forced the house staff to go on rounds at two in the morning. One of the other residents told her that I had tunnel vision and the only thing I cared about was my work. But at the party she saw that I could talk about things outside of medicine, that I was interested in what other people had to say. She said she was glad to see that, because she always thought I was a good person and she had a strong instinctive feeling that she wanted to be my friend. Well, when she said that, I asked her to go out with me the next week, and then I gave her a nice, friendly goodnight kiss. I didn't want to push her too fast.

The next week's schedule was miserable, because she was on call or I was on call and there was always something in the way. That Friday night I was supposed to go to Houston to present a paper at a medical meeting and I'd be gone for a week. But I just had to go out with her again before I left! So I did something that I would criticize someone else for doing. I came up to her on Friday morning when she was on call, and I said, "I know you're supposed to be in the hospital, but I want to take you out for lunch. There's a nice place about a block away and if there's an emergency you can be back in three minutes." She didn't think she should do it, but I told her, "Look, I'm the overall director of this floor, and I'm saying it will be okay."

So we sat down in this little German restaurant and we talked. I found out all about her family, which is a very impressive medical family. Her father is a urologist in Philadelphia, her brother is a fourth-year student at Yale Medical School, and her sister is an intensive care unit nurse who is married to an internist. They are all brilliant people, but Sharon is the most brilliant of all! She graduated first in her class at Radcliffe and then she was number three at Columbia Medical School. For a man's ego that can be very hard to deal with, and if I were her age and still in the middle of my training, I don't think I would date someone who's so bright and competitive. But I'm twelve years older, I've already made my career and my reputation, so I'm not afraid of her.

While we were eating she told me that one of the reasons that she came out here was to recover from a love affair. She had been living with one of her fellow students off and on for two years. But it just wasn't right, it wasn't going anywhere, so they broke up. She decided she needed a year away from that environment to see how things would be. She confided in me, and then before she went back to the hospital and I had to pack to go to Houston, we made plans to get together for a third date!

That next time was a very special occasion. About five years ago I took care of a man who owns one of the best Italian restaurants in San Francisco. He was very sick, but we managed to pull him out and he always felt grateful for what I did. So every year he makes a special dinner for me at the restaurant.

This year I took Sharon as my guest, and it was magnificent. My friend at the restaurant brought a bottle of his most expensive champagne and sat down with us. There was a violinist there and he came over to our table and played romantic music. I had such an alive and good and happy feeling throughout my whole body! I knew then that I wanted to marry her. We went back to her apartment, and we sat on the couch, hugging each other, caressing each other. I said, "Sharon, maybe you're not ready for this, but I've got to tell you how I feel. I am very much in love with you. I know it's right and I know it's going to work." Before she could answer, I said, "There are three things that I want. First, I want you to have your career, because you're brilliant and it would be a crime to take you away from medicine. Number two, I want you to be my wife, because I love you, and I know there's so much that I have to offer. And number three, I want you to be the mother of my children."

It took her a while to catch her breath. Then she said, "You're the first man who has put my well-being first. No one has ever offered me a relationship where I was going to be equal. But I don't know if I'm ready for this yet. You have to give me a chance to think this through." And of course I was going to give her a chance. I didn't want to jeopardize anything. I didn't want to be too aggressive. I just gave her a kiss and said goodnight and told her to take her time before she gave me an answer.

The next Monday morning I saw her on rounds. I was with my boss, so I just gave her a little smile. She told me later that when I smiled at her that day, she started to make up her mind. It's uncanny what a difference little things can make to people!

That Saturday night we planned to go out to dinner and then to a movie. I had decided to get off work early, get some flowers, and go home, take a shower, and get dressed. I was going to make sure the apartment was in great shape, because I was going to make my move with her that night.

But that afternoon and evening there were five emergencies and the first thing I knew it was seven o'clock, and I had told Sharon I would pick her up at six-thirty. So I called her up, and she was very understanding. I tried to hurry, but it took me another hour before I could finish with the patients and the interns. Finally I got out of there and I was driving over to pick her up when I realized I hadn't been home and I hadn't had a shower all day and I needed a shave. But I decided life isn't perfect, so she might as well see me on a bad day. I came into her apartment a little wound up. She kissed me hello and said, "Why don't you sit down on the couch and relax?" I did, and she gave me a glass of Tab. She held my hand and listened to my day, which to me was great.

We went out for dinner, and afterwards we came back to my place, and I said, "Sharon, I was going to seduce you tonight, I wanted things to be perfect, but you're not having flowers and the bed's not fixed up and the apartment's a little bit of a mess." And I said, "If our love was going to be consummated tonight, I wanted things to be perfect. But I guess it's part of medicine that it doesn't work out that way." Well, that just struck a chord with her. We did make love, and it was perfect anyway without the paraphernalia.

Since then I've been on cloud nine. We're going to be married three months from now. We would have done it sooner, except her mother wanted time to plan a wedding. Her parents are members of a large temple in Philadelphia and that's where the wedding is going to be. Then we're going to come back here for a big celebration with our friends right here in the hospital. It'll also be a going-away party, because we're both leaving Memorial.

Sharon has to go back to New York to complete her residency program at Columbia. She made a commitment, and I'm going with her. I told her that I'd always let her career come first, and I'm living up to it. I'm taking a sabbatical year, and I'll be a visiting professor at Columbia. As soon as we got engaged, I called them and asked if they had a position available. Right away they got very excited that they could list Harvey Fredman for a whole year on the faculty.

We are both looking forward to the wedding and to moving to New York. When we get there, Sharon will be in this intense kind of program whereas I'll be more relaxed, without all the pressures that I have around here. I've told her, "I've been alone for twenty years and I can take pretty good care of myself. There's no reason I can't help take care of somebody else. I can push buttons on the washing machine and I'm not fussy about what I eat. I'm not looking to you to be a maid. I'm looking to you for love and moral support and to share your life with me. And if you're going to be busy next year with your training, I don't mind taking most of the responsibility at home."

I told my parents about my engagement and I expected them to be really happy, but my father said, "Uh-oh, you're marrying another doctor. You married a doctor before and look what happened." Leave it to him to say something like that! A lot of people are worried these days about the strain of two careers, but I know we can handle it. I've never been so sure of anything in my life. We share common goals and common ideals. We are both concerned about medicine, about the patients, and we both want to have a family. We don't want a small family either—we want three kids at least. I just hope that we're lucky enough that she'll get pregnant right away.

Since we announced the engagement last week, everyone at Memorial has been just wonderful. Her friends on house staff bought Sharon a gold bracelet. Then one day I came up to my office and found a giant bunch of flowers with a note, "From all of your friends in honor of the world's greatest lover." Everybody comes up and wishes me congratulations; they tease me a little, but I don't mind at all. I didn't know that people cared as much as they did. It gives me a good feeling about this whole hospital and all the years I've spent here. Whatever the stresses and strains and the little hostilities, there's still a family feeling with everybody who works here.

But just three days ago one of the residents came up to Sharon and said, "Well, I guess the honeymoon must be over!" Why? Because on Tuesday I blasted a bunch of doctors who work for me for being late and being inconsiderate of the patients. So they all said, "Oh well, Harvey's up to his old tricks again." I said to Sharon, "What do they expect me to do? To tolerate incompetence just because I'm in love with you? That's absolutely ridiculous!"

Then on Friday we had a very sick patient, an older gentleman who came in from Reno, Nevada, because in GI we're supposed to be one of the best in the world. I spent part of Thursday night with the house staff going over his care, but when I came around on Friday afternoon, they hadn't done any of the things we had discussed. The poor guy was dying, so I gave hell to the resident. I said, "If this was your father, you would be pissed off at the doctors for not taking care of him!" I really read them the riot act and then I walked out. I met Sharon for dinner and then I went to her apartment. We were intimate, and then afterwards I looked at my watch. It was eleven-thirty and I needed to go back to the hospital to check on this patient. But I was a little hesitant because I know how women are in that situation. We were comfortable, we were lying in bed together, and here I was getting ready to go out in the middle of the night. So I said, "If you don't want me to go, I'll stay here. But I'm very concerned about this one patient, because unless everything goes absolutely right, he's probably going to die." She looked at me for a minute and I didn't know if she was going to smile or cry. But then she smiled and said, "Go ahead, and I'll be waiting when you come back." I said, "Are you sure you're not mad at me?" And she said, "Harvey, I wouldn't want you any other way."

A CELEBRATION

In mid-June the newlyweds, Dr. and Dr. Fredman, returned from their wedding in Philadelphia for additional festivities at Memorial Medical Center. A number of their friends had arranged a combination wedding celebration and going-away party in their honor. The organizers might have chosen a more elegant setting than the hospital cafeteria, but they could not have found one more appropriate to the occasion. As Nancy Proctor observed on the night of the party: "It's a good thing we're having it right here at Memorial. Otherwise old Harvey might not want to come."

Someone had strung up a few strips of blue and white bunting in a rather feeble attempt to lend a festive air to the institutional environment; more effective was a hand-lettered banner that proclaimed, "GOOD LUCK HARVEY AND SHARON." Beneath this sign a buffet table offered a variety of salads, fruit, cold cuts, and pastries, while waiters at either end poured champagne into rows of plastic goblets.

Becky Krieger, one of the prime movers in planning the celebration, came over and expressed her satisfaction at the way the evening had begun. "Isn't it wonderful!" she said. "It's a tribute to Harvey that so many people turned out." She wore a floor-length burgundy gown and had a fresh gardenia in her short blond hair. As she scanned the more than two hundred guests who had already arrived she seemed unconcerned that no one else had dressed as formally as she had. At the far end of the cafeteria a five-man rock band began playing a medley of Rolling Stones favorites. Becky told me that the musicians were all surgical residents and they called their group The Butchers. Unfortunately only a half-dozen couples took advantage of the opportunity of dancing to the group's somewhat ragged performance. By far the most accomplished of the dancers was Georgianna Harlan, her ripe figure undulating in time with the music. As I came over she recognized me, smiled, and intensified her efforts—which visibly pleased the small crowd of young male physicians who had gathered in her vicinity.

At nine o'clock the arrival of the guests of honor provoked applause and whistles from their guests. Harvey Fredman wore a euphoric smile and waved both arms over his head like a victorious politician on election night while his bride looked soft and radiant in a simple pink dress. A line of well-wishers formed immediately to congratulate the happy pair. Harvey Fredman unwittingly delayed its progress by spending too long with every individual who filed past him; he treated each of these interchanges as the occasion for an emotional farewell. Standing to one side with Becky, I commented on the generally youthful composition of the crowd, which included many nurses and members of the house staff but relatively few of the older attending physicians. "That's because they're snobs," she explained. "They wouldn't come because it's not a snazzy affair in some big hotel."

Despite her pessimistic assessment, a few of Dr. Fredman's senior colleagues did eventually make an appearance. Dr. Arnold Brody came in briefly and solemnly greeted the newlyweds before departing. Jack Buckman proved similarly unwilling to waste his time on social niceties. Ignoring the receiving line, he shouldered his way up to Fredman, pounded him on the back, kissed the bride, and marched off.

While helping myself to a cup of coffee I met Stanley Ruckert at the food table. I watched him fill a paper plate with a wide selection of pastries; he had arrived late because of responsibilities on the wards, and this snack would take the place of dinner. Having completed his internship, Ruckert had begun a residency in internal medicine and found himself busier than ever. In the course of our conversation, I asked him if his wife, Dr. Kathy Merkin, had made

328

it to the party. He shrugged his shoulders and said without emotion that they had separated three months before. He still had no clear idea of what had gone wrong between them, but he guessed that their decision to undertake internships in the same year had contributed significantly to their problems. In any event, he hoped that they might someday reunite under more favorable circumstances. "Who knows?" he mused as he finished a napoleon. "Maybe when we're all done with residency we'll go into practice together."

For most people, the party represented a welcome chance to chat with old friends or to get to know new ones. Dr. Burton Webber and his wife, Fran, stood in one corner of the room making genial small talk with Dr. Milton Tessler. I expressed surprise at finding them together, given the Webbers' distaste for Dr. Tessler's anti-establishment views, but Burton Webber responded to this observation with a sly laugh. Holding a champagne glass in one hand, he threw his other arm over Tessler's shoulder. "It's all part of my master plan!" he hissed in a conspiratorial stage whisper. "I'm going to take care of this troublemaker by co-opting him into the County Medical Association!"

By ten o'clock the crowd had started to thin and the table reserved for receiving wedding gifts had accumulated a mountain of gaily wrapped parcels. I caught David Anzak in the act of adding his present to the pile, and he was eager to give me an update on his long struggle with Garland Lockwood. In view of the controversy that continued to rage around his head, Lockwood had voluntarily departed the scene, finding a place for himself at a small community hospital in Marin County. Anzak shook his head. "There's really no way to stop a guy like that. He can go on moving from one place to another and he can keep on killing people. At least we got him out of Memorial, and I think I have a right to feel good about that."

Jeff Carden had also withdrawn from the world of this particular institution, and I missed his presence at the party. He had dropped me a note a few weeks before in which he reported he never regretted his decision to leave Memorial but after three months working as a house painter and handyman, he found it impossible to stay away from nursing. After a determined search, Carden got a job in another local hospital as associate director of a newly organized rehabilitation and exercise program for cardiac care patients.

329

He looked forward to making a genuine contribution in a far more upbeat setting than Memorial's Vegetable Patch.

Stepping out for a breath of air before saying my goodbyes, I walked onto the patio adjoining the cafeteria and was struck by the unmistakable odor of marijuana. I found a small group huddled in a dark corner under a eucalyptus tree and managed to pick out a familiar voice and laugh: Charlotte Kirkham sat on a small patch of lawn sharing a joint with two orderlies. She seemed somewhat embarrassed and immediately got up and abandoned her companions. "Occasions like this really bring me down," she confessed, and as we walked together across the patio I tried to understand. Was she lamenting the fact that she had yet to find a permanent relationship of her own? Was she upset that Harvey, who had dated her first, had found such obvious happiness with someone else? As if reading my mind, she offered her own explanation. "It's got nothing to do with Harvey or Sharon. It's just the hospital, the whole thing. At times like this you just look around and see how pointless it all is. There's nothing magic about it. And why should I want to stay in this kind of trap when I don't even like the people?"

I had to cut short my conversation with her because I had committed myself to leave the party with Allen Barsamian. We had discovered earlier in the evening that we held reservations on the same late-night flight to Los Angeles. I was returning home, and Barsamian, having made what he considered to be an obligatory showing at the Fredman party, was headed south for a psychiatric conference in Beverly Hills. We naturally agreed to travel together, and on the way to the airport, I innocently asked what was new in his life. He answered with a lengthy and vivid description of a series of traumatic experiences over the last six months.

This latest round of personal disasters began when he was asked to deliver a paper to a small professional meeting in San Francisco. As the moderator introduced him, he suddenly experienced an unprecedented "anxiety attack." He couldn't catch his breath, and stood at the podium for several minutes unable to bring forth a single word. "It caused quite a stir in the psychiatric community. Everybody kept coming up to me and saying, 'Are you all right?' After a while I started worrying about myself."

He began suffering similar attacks in the course of his normal schedule. He might be meeting with a private patient or presiding over a meeting of house staff at Memorial when, without warning, he would feel short of breath, dizzy, and incapable of performing even the most minimal function. "I had this unbelievably strong, irrational desire to just go home, get into bed, and pull the covers over my head. And I didn't know what to do with it."

Barsamian immediately sought help and began seeing a therapist every day. "I knew deep down what the problem was. It was all the emotional battering from the last few years. The death of my first wife, and the remarriage to Janie, and suddenly three stepsons, and then my wife is pregnant at the age of forty-three! Thank goodness she gave birth to a beautiful baby girl! I should have been happy, but I felt terrible, and I knew what was happening. It was all these other things from the past, where I never allowed myself to react with enough emotion. I tried to swallow them, to keep them down, and then they just got the better of me."

One month after this first anxiety attack, Barsamian entered a clinical depression. "I questioned my competence. I questioned my sanity. I questioned what right I had to give other people advice and to hold myself up as some kind of all-knowing healer, when inside I was feeling so lousy about everything." Nevertheless, he managed to drag himself through all his professional obligations and he took pride in the fact that none of his patients and few of his colleagues suspected that something was wrong. "But for the first time in my life, I felt I wasn't in control. I felt as if anything could happen. That I could kill myself. And I was terrified." Knowing what he did about the occupational hazards of the medical profession, he asked his wife to watch him carefully and to avoid, as much as possible, leaving him alone for more than a few minutes at a time.

When we arrived at the San Francisco Airport Barsamian interrupted his narrative so we could concentrate on catching our flight. I remained in suspense, until we had taken off. As the plane settled into the familiar flight plan over the ocean, Barsamian resumed his story. He described a dramatic recovery from his depression, giving major credit to the Jungian analyst he had been seeing for the last three months. They now met twice each week, and worked almost exclusively with Barsamian's dreams. They looked for symbols and archetypes that could help to expose his deepest concerns.

In the midst of this process of self-exploration, he discovered a profound significance in the life of his newborn child. The baby grew and thrived, despite her father's problems. Barsamian saw that she did beautifully, no matter how much anxiety he felt about it; the world continued, regardless of what he chose to do. He recognized that life was basically indestructible, and this gave him courage to continue his work. "Maybe," he said, "the added sense of vulnerability actually helped me. I stopped thinking I had to be superhuman. I stopped thinking I had to be the center of every situation. I really feel that I'm a better psychiatrist than I was before."

Barsamian concluded his account at midnight and fell abruptly silent. He turned his face to the window as I became conscious of the dark cabin, and the drowsy rumble of the plane. After a few moments of quiet, an announcement by one of the flight attendants jolted us into full attention: "Ladies and gentlemen, if there is a doctor on board, would he please come to the rear of the cabin immediately." Barsamian leaned forward, looked around uneasily, and waited for someone else to stand up. When the stewardess repeated her announcement, he rose without a word and slouched toward the back of the plane. Only a few minutes earlier he had been talking of his own problems, describing his pervasive sense of unworthiness, his fears of madness and suicide. Now all eyes followed him as he walked down the aisle; he was already a hero. Never before had the magical power of the medical profession seemed so tangible to me. While the rest of us fidgeted in our seats, the doctor moved to center stage to take charge of the crisis.

When he returned ten minutes later the glances of the other passengers focused on him even more intently than they had before. The people in the row behind us pushed forward in an attempt to overhear his explanation of what had happened. "It was nothing, really," Barsamian said, as he climbed back into his seat. "An old man with a heart condition got dizzy and fell when he was coming out of the bathroom. I took his pulse and told them to get the oxygen ready, but he seemed all right to me. I'm sure he'll be fine. That's what he needed, I guess—someone with the title 'doctor' to tell him he's okay."

As Barsamian fastened his seat belt and turned toward the window, I realized that this pear-shaped intellectual had suddenly become the largest figure on the plane. Physicians, with all their faults, must always seem greater than the rest of us. Their work is the world's most important work and even their routine and trivial tasks are matters of critical consequence. They are daily martyrs to our cause: If they sacrifice their personal lives and suffer in the process it is because we demand it. At our own moments of panic and hurt, we need them as we need no other strangers. We may distrust these doctors and despise their human flaws, but we will continue to love them in spite of ourselves.

ACKNOWLEDGMENTS

It is only at the conclusion of a project that one can fully appreciate those who have made it possible from the beginning.

Nurse Leslie Kessler, for instance, provided me with my introduction to hospital life, along with the insight and encouragement that enabled me to undertake the writing of this book. Mr. Sol Genuth, a brilliant writer with a busy career of his own, took time off to help with research on the state of the medical profession in America. Charles Kaufman devoted many hours to reading this manuscript in various stages of development, and his enthusiastic moral support made a major contribution to its completion.

Fred Hills, my friend and editor at Simon and Schuster, demonstrated his commitment to this project over the course of two years. In the beginning, he fought for the right to publish it, and at the end he played the role of an uncredited co-author in bringing it to its final form. Meanwhile, my agent Richard Pine and my attorney Gregg Gittler provided the professional support that allowed the work to proceed.

Several outstanding physicians assisted me with professional and technical evaluations of the interview material. Among them were Drs. David Morrow, Sanford Small, Auri Spigelman, Peter Kraus, and others who preferred not to be identified by name.

Which brings us to the sensitive task of acknowledging all the generous help I received from personnel at "Memorial Medical Center." I would like to list them all, but to do so would defeat my efforts to guarantee the privacy of those people described in the book. Given the sensitive nature of their profession and the candor of the stories they told, it is not surprising that so many of the doctors who are profiled in these pages expressed concern that neither they as individuals nor the institution with which they are associated should be readily identifiable. In deference to their wishes, the best I can do here is to offer a general word of appreciation to the sixty-three people who endured the rigors of the interview process, including those thirty-five whose interviews have not been included in the final version of this book. Along with many other employees of "Memorial Medical Center," they went out of their way to share information, ideas and feelings, while providing me with a virtual home away from home during long months of difficult research.

Though I am sensitive to the risk of making this list seem interminable, two more people—both of whom happen to share my last name—deserve specific thanks.

Harry Medved—brother, kindred spirit, and erstwhile co-author on several other projects—furnished timely assistance during the final preparation of this manuscript. His editorial suggestions were perceptive and practical, while his cheerful company during the small hours of the morning worked far more effectively than coffee.

And finally there is my wife, Nancy Medved, who among other things—

—transcribed every interview

—edited and typed every page

—pursued background research on all relevant topics

—and put up with an irascible author while sharing his often frustrating effort to move a great unwieldy mass of human material toward some coherent form. Whatever valuable elements are to be found in the preceding pages reflect her love and creativity, for which I offer thanks yet one more time.

368

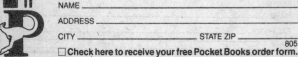

Private Lives of Very Public People